THE PRESIDENT
AS WORLD LEADER

THE PRESIDENT
AS WORLD LEADER

BARBARA KELLERMAN

RYAN J. BARILLEAUX

St. Martin's Press   New York

For Ernest F. Kellerman,
whose veneration of Franklin Roosevelt and
his comrade in leadership, Winston Churchill,
was the source.

BLK

and

For Gerard, Madeleine, Christine, and Paul

RJB

Senior editor: Don Reisman
Managing editor: Patricia Mansfield
Editorial assistant: Rob Skiena
Production supervisor: Katherine Battiste
Cover: Tom McKeveny

For information, write:
St. Martin's Press, Inc.
175 Fifth Avenue
New York, NY 10010

ISBN: 0-312-03603-5

Acknowledgments

We were ably assisted by several friends and colleagues. Marilyn Barilleaux, Steven DeLue, George Edwards, Kenneth Greenwald, William Jackson, Herbert Levine, and Frank Sherman gave advice and counsel, and Michael Zousmer provided invaluable research assistance. Our work was also improved by the suggestions and comments of those who read the manuscript: Cecil V. Crabb, Jr., Louisiana State University; Roy Licklider, Rutgers University; Bruce Miroff, State University of New York at Albany; Richard M. Pious, Barnard College; John M. Rothgeb, Jr., Miami University; Steven A. Shull, University of New Orleans; Priscilla L. Southwell, University of Oregon; Jay Speakman, Rutgers University; and Roy Thoman, West Texas State University. In particular, we thank Don Reisman who was an unusually thorough and thoughtful editor. Our book benefited greatly from his firm editorial hand. The contributions of each and all are sincerely appreciated.

Preface

As described in Kellerman's book, *The Political Presidency: Practice of Leadership*, four of the six most recent presidents—John Kennedy, Richard Nixon, Gerald Ford, and Jimmy Carter—failed to exercise leadership on behalf of the domestic priority that each had deemed most important.[1] What, we wondered, were the implications of this finding for American foreign policy? If American presidents had so much trouble leading at home, in a contained environment with which they were ostensibly familiar, how could they ever exercise leadership abroad? Could it be that different skills come into play in domestic and foreign affairs, that the same president might be successful as a leader in one domain but not in the other? If so, why? And if not, does that compel us to conclude that Americans frequently elect presidents who are simply incompetent as leaders both at home and abroad?

Once again the issue is not whether our presidents are wise, clever, or just. Rather, the focus is on their ability to get others to follow where they lead. *The President as World Leader* explores how effectively five recent executives shaped the American foreign policy process with regard to at least one major initiative and affected attitudes and events relating to this initiative beyond America's borders. We know that in the American political system the president is ultimately responsible for formulating, articulating, and implementing foreign policy. We also know that simply by virtue of the fact that the chief executive holds the highest office in one of the most powerful countries in the world, his global influence is thought to be extensive. But we have never really done comparative studies of how presidents accomplish, or fail to accomplish, their foreign policy tasks. Nor have we compared their effectiveness as agents of change at the international level.

In "The Two Presidencies," written two decades ago, Aaron Wildavsky explored the differences between the president's role in domestic and foreign politics. "The President's normal problem with domestic policy is to get congressional support for the program he prefers," Wildavsky wrote. "In foreign affairs, in contrast, he can almost always get support for policies that he believes will protect the nation. . . ."[2] Wildavsky's essay presaged the findings in *The Political Presidency*, which confirm that in order for presidents to exert leadership in the domestic arena, they must demonstrate political skills that go well beyond those it takes to get elected. What remains to be seen, however, is whether in fact presidents "can almost always get support" for the programs they really want in defense and foreign policy. What also remains to be determined is the extent to which leadership in American foreign policy is synonymous with leadership in world politics. For there is no reason to assume automatically that presidents who are able to influence domestic political elites will be able as well to influence political elites in other countries. In fact, these second "influence relationships" tend to be of a quite different nature. For example, when the president tries to get another national leader to follow his lead, what we have is not a leader-follower relationship in any conventional sense. Instead, a leader-leader relationship is forged, in which both parties are ostensibly equals, with few, if any, cultural or historical ties to bind them.

Moreover, times have changed since Wildavsky developed his "two presidencies" argument. At home, the post–World War II consensus on foreign policy has given way to post-Vietnam dissension.[3] And the international environment has changed in ways that reduce rather than enhance opportunities for leadership on a global scale. Among the recent changes that have taken place are: the stunning decline of communism worldwide, particularly in Eastern Europe and the Soviet Union; the waning of the cold war; an increase in the number of sovereign states; growth in the relative military strength of the major powers; proliferation of nuclear weapons; the increasing independence and militancy of Third World countries; and the declining position of the U.S. in the global economy.

Presidential leadership in world politics, then, is a two-step process. Step one consists of shaping and articulating foreign policy; step two consists of implementing that policy and then managing the consequences. Put another way, in order to be a leader in world politics the president must first exercise leadership at home. And then he must exercise leadership abroad.

To shed light on how these very different leadership tasks can be met, this book focuses on three key elements: the leader, the followers, and the situation. We address such questions as:

- What is the president's role? What is the scope of his authority? What is his personality like? What leadership skills does he have? And what are his sources of power?
- Who are the followers? What is the nature of their relationship to the president? What motivates them to go along with his attempts at direction? Or, alternatively, why do they ignore or even resist him?
- What are the domestic and international contexts within which the leadership process is taking place? What is the long-range history pertaining to this particular issue? And what are the tasks and demands immediately at hand?

Part I of this book responds to the above questions by exploring the contextual and personal aspects of leadership. The focus is on the domestic and global environments within which the president must lead if he is to make his mark on world politics; on those whom he would have as followers; and on the president himself. Chapter 1 is thus devoted to a broad-based discussion of the international environment. It argues that while America's position is still very powerful relative to that of most other nations, it has both political and economic competitors with whom it must inevitably reckon. Chapter 2 is an overview of American foreign policy since the beginning of the Republic. It provides some of the history with which contemporary presidents must contend if they are to lead effectively in foreign affairs. Chapter 3 looks directly at the president's role in the making of American foreign policy. What becomes clear, above all, is that despite the president's role as chief initiator and architect of foreign policy, there remain considerable constitutional and legal constraints on the executive's freedom to act. Chapter 4 addresses the personal and psychological dimensions of presidential leadership and then places these in the context of the international environment. It explores how a president can marshal forces on his own behalf in relationship to key players at home and abroad.

Part II of the book narrows the focus. Here the material presented in Part I becomes background for case studies of presidential leadership in world politics over the last quarter century. Presidents Kennedy, Johnson, Nixon, Carter, and Reagan are scrutinized in terms of how well they led the nation and the world with regard to a foreign policy goal in which they were heavily invested.* In particular, we ask whether the president's goal was clearly articulated and communicated; how energetically he used his authority and exercised power and influence; which tactics of power, authority, and influence he employed; what motivated domestic and foreign constituencies to accept, or reject, his attempt to lead; which sources of power, authority, and influence were most effective; and whether implementation was in fact accomplished.

We selected the cases according to three criteria: First, we asked what the president himself, at the outset of his White House tenure, claimed was most important. In at least one administration—Kennedy's—the foreign policy initiative he insisted was most important—the Alliance for Progress—was, arguably, not. But of the fact that Kennedy, like the other presidents, staked his reputation on the Alliance, invested major resources in ushering it through the policy-making process, and came back to it time and again, there is no doubt.

A second criterion for selection was that the case had to be an example of *directive leadership*—that is, of leadership that gave evidence of the president as an initiator rather than merely as a responder to events imposed on him from outside.

Finally, the case had to be an example of how leadership in foreign policy is exercised under *routine,* or noncrisis, conditions. Routine conditions may be defined as those in which problems abound but no single one is perceived as presenting an imminent threat to the national welfare. Under such circumstances there is generally no domestic consensus on which of the many pressing foreign policy issues should take priority, or even on how to address fundamental and enduring concerns such as how to reduce the threat of nuclear war. In short, each case study is an example of how presidents led, or tried to, in domestic environments in which there was no clear or widely agreed-on foreign policy agenda.

The case studies (chapters 5–9) are divided into four sections. The first provides a context for the particular case by describing the leadership tactics and strategies with which the president was generally associated and by demonstrating how his *Weltanschauung,* or view of the world, shaped his foreign policy agenda.

The second section moves on to the facts of the case at hand. It chronicles

*Probably due to the unusual circumstances under which Gerald Ford became president (which dictated an overriding emphasis on resecuring a sense of normalcy at home), as well as his short tenure, it is impossible to identify a major foreign policy initiative during his administration. He is not, therefore, a subject of this book.

what happened on the domestic front with regard to what was, during the early years of his administration, the president's most important foreign policy initiative. In particular, it reveals how the executive tried to mobilize the support of key groups and individuals—within the administration as well as outside it—on behalf of what was deemed a top priority.

The third section of each case study contains an analysis of the president's leadership at the international level. As we will see, American presidents, for all their power and influence relative to other national leaders, find directive leadership in world politics to be difficult at best. Power is usually costly to assert, influence is typically in short supply, and formal authority is nonexistent.

The final section of each case study consists of an analysis and assessment of the president's capacities as world leader. Was he ultimately an agent of change? If so, to what can we attribute his effectiveness? Conversely, if the goal remained elusive, to what should we attribute the president's failure?

The book closes with a chapter that comments on the effectiveness of particular presidents as foreign policy leaders, compares them and the changing environments within which they conducted foreign affairs, and offers a few conclusions about the American president as world leader in the late twentieth century. An epilogue on George Bush constitutes the last word.

No single case study of leadership in foreign affairs should be considered a judgment on overall presidential competence. Different cases suggest different conclusions, and every president has a broad range of issues to which he in one way or another responds. In particular, chief executives generally have more than one foreign policy initiative in which they are invested. The case studies in this book, then, are descriptive rather than definitive. Together with the material in Part I, they shed light on how the constellation of leader, followers, and situation interact to promote—or resist—political change at the international level. They also allow us to make at least preliminary comparisons, for while the differences among presidents and the situations they encountered necessarily outweighed the similarities, the leadership task itself suggests certain commonalities: How accurately were circumstances assessed? How well drawn was the agenda for change? And how successfully were followers engaged?

Our canvas is large, for we are talking about leadership in foreign policy and international relations and about political actors at home and abroad. Given the rapidly changing nature of world politics, the lessons learned on how one person can make a big difference—or fail to—should be of practical as well as theoretical consequence.

NOTES

1. Barbara Kellerman, *The Political Presidency: Practice of Leadership* (New York: Oxford University Press, 1984).

2. Aaron Wildavsky, "The Two Presidencies," *Trans-Action* 4 no. 2 (December 1966).

3. For an elaboration of this theme, see, for example, I. M. Destler, Leslie H. Gelb, and Anthony Lake, *Our Own Worst Enemy: The Unmaking of American Foreign Policy* (New York: Simon & Schuster, 1984).

Contents

The transaction of business with foreign nations is executive altogether.
—THOMAS JEFFERSON

Part I

THE BIG PICTURE: Presidential Leadership in World Politics

1

The International Environment

When the First Congress of the United States met in 1789, it brought to life the government created in the Constitution. Among its first concerns were the title, salary, and protocol for the president.[1] While Americans did not want a king, they believed that their Republic's leader would be respected at home and abroad only if he were vested with the familiar trappings of authority. Thus the president was given a large salary ($25,000), a grand house was ordered for his residence, and certain rules of etiquette were established to separate him from other citizens—although the House of Representatives ultimately rejected a Senate proposal to address the chief executive as "His Highness the President of the United States."[2]

The founders' attention to the dignity of the executive highlights the fact that the president has always been much more than the key figure in national politics. He has been a leader of international prominence as well. Even in those early days of the Republic, the president was a player in the realm of international politics—a peer of kings. The "two presidencies" thus has its roots in the very nature of the office itself. Inevitably, the chief executive was then as he is now: the United States' most important link to the world outside.

This outside world has undergone considerable change since America's founding period, but its essential elements have remained the same. Let us then proceed to examine the international environment and America's place in it in the late twentieth century.

THE STRUCTURE AND DYNAMICS OF THE INTERNATIONAL ENVIRONMENT

Today's international political order has its roots in the diplomatic settlement concluded among the European powers after the defeat of Napoleon. The Congress of Vienna (1815), which arranged the settlement, provided that no single government would rule world affairs. Neither the old Holy Roman Empire nor Napoleon's French empire would be replaced by other regimes that would seek world dominance. International politics, which at the time meant European politics, would be conducted among national states bound together only by voluntary arrangements and a code of diplomatic behavior.[3]

But the patterns and habits of world politics in the nineteenth century were transformed in the twentieth. Two world wars and the tensions of the

U.S.-Soviet "cold war" inevitably left their mark.[4] The "superpowers" divided the world into spheres of influence and struggled for dominance among developing nations. During this period, American foreign policy was directed toward the containment of Soviet influence around the globe as Moscow supported revolutionary and anti-American movements in Asia, Africa, and Latin America. The United States used force to intervene in Korea, Vietnam, Cuba, and the Dominican Republic in attempts to halt the spread of communism. However, since both sides possessed enormously powerful weapons and feared the consequences of a nuclear war, direct conflict between the superpowers was avoided.

Eventually, changing circumstances eased U.S.-Soviet tensions. The growth of nuclear arsenals alarmed not only Soviet and American policymakers but the rest of the world as well. Moreover, each of the superpowers saw a need for greater cooperation: the United States hoped that the Soviet Union could assist it in resolving the Vietnam conflict and reduce the risk of war in the Middle East; for its part, Moscow desired trade with Western nations to provide food and shore up its weakening economy. Each side remained wary of the other, most especially during Ronald Reagan's first term, but by the late 1980s the superpowers had come to see even greater benefits from warmer relations. Soviet leaders faced growing popular demands for consumer goods and a higher standard of living, which could be purchased only by reducing Moscow's heavy commitment to defense spending. At the same time, American officials were under pressure to reduce the nation's large budget deficit, which also required trimming military expenditures.

During the last decade in particular, international relations have been in transition from the bipolar politics of the cold war to a situation of complexity and fragmented power. The allies of the superpowers have felt increasingly free to develop their own independent foreign policies toward the rest of the world. In the early 1980s, for example, West Germany and several other European nations encouraged construction of a Soviet natural gas pipeline to the West, despite American objections. Political and economic power has also become more diffuse. Japan is the most outstanding example of a country that, through its economic prowess, has come to play a major political role as well. A "Third World" of developing nations, most former colonies of the European powers, has grown in number and importance. And the United States, once confident in its role as the capital of the noncommunist world, searched for a new definition of its role in a rapidly changing environment.

Despite these changes, however, the essential structure of the international environment remains the same. The most fundamental characteristic of world politics is *anarchy,* that is, the absence of an overarching government to establish and maintain order. World politics resembles what eighteenth-century thinkers such as Hobbes and Locke called the "state of nature." It is not a state of chaos, but one in which certain conditions prevail: relations between individual states are regulated by force and/or voluntary cooperation; conflict is frequently used to settle disputes; and whatever "rules" exist (whether diplomatic protocol or international law) are essentially customary in nature and enforceable only to the extent of the willingness of the parties involved to obey those rules.[5]

International anarchy does not mean that world politics is a constant "war of all against all." But it does mean that there is no appeal to a central authority that can ensure justice, peace, and order. Each unit in the environment must therefore rely on self-help and/or on the voluntary (and often self-interested) help of others.

Two types of units participate in international affairs: The first, states, are by far the most important actors in world politics. The second, nonstate actors—groups or organizations that play a role in world politics but do not share the characteristics of states—at times compete with them for influence over the direction of world affairs. These groups range from the United Nations (UN) and the Red Cross to the Palestine Liberation Organization (PLO) and International Telephone and Telegraph (ITT).

Modern states share certain characteristics: First, they have a territorial basis,[6] exercising administrative control over specific territories and all that is included within their boundaries. These boundaries may have been imposed without regard to ethnic, religious, or even geographical divisions, as in Nigeria and many other African states that were once European colonies. At the same time, borders often do parallel natural and social boundaries, as in Spain or Japan. In any case, the modern concept of the state, in contrast to ancient and medieval notions of tribal communities, is of an entity that possesses a kind of "shell" in the form of fixed borders.

Second, states possess sovereignty and political independence. Theoretically, they are free from control by other units of the international environment and exercise absolute authority over their own internal affairs. In reality, many states do not actually possess sovereignty and independence: they are "penetrated" in a variety of ways.[7] For example, many small states rely on large ones for economic, political, and military support. Cuba depends heavily on the Soviet Union for economic survival and its protection against possible military action by the United States. Similarly, the Philippines and Israel are examples of states that depend on American economic and military aid.

Political independence is further compromised by the fact that in the late twentieth century most states in the international environment are economically interdependent. This situation results from the fact that even large, powerful states lack sufficient resources to meet all of their needs. The United States, for example, must import chrome, magnesium, and an array of minerals that are vital to the manufacture of weapons, computer hardware, and other advanced technology.

Finally, the modern state is also a national state. That is, it is the focus of group identity for its population. *Nationalism* refers to the development of strong emotional ties by individuals to the ethnic group and/or to the state to which they belong. In some states, such as the U.S. and most European countries, the *nation* and the *state* are essentially the same thing. However, in other states, such as those countries artificially created from former colonial territories, deliberate attempts have been made to develop a sense of national identity around the central government.[8] Pakistan, for example, was formed by uniting three rival Muslim groups who were once under British rule. Since its creation in 1947, it has struggled to develop its people's identity with the national state rather than with their own ethnic groups. The country's difficulty in affecting such a change was highlighted by the creation of the new state of Bangladesh out of the territory of East Pakistan.

The fact that some state borders do not correspond to ethnic, religious, or cultural divisions is frequently a source of political unrest. For instance, the division of Ireland into the Republic of Ireland (Eire) and British-controlled Northern Ireland is a source of continuing conflict. The Catholic population of the North identifies with the Irish Republic, while their Protestant neighbors identify with Great Britain. Some groups may be included in a larger state even though they want to be independent and control their own destinies. Nigeria includes in its population a group called the Ibo, who have long sought to form their own state independent of the existing central government. During the civil war of 1967–1970, the Ibo unsuccessfully tried to win independence, proclaiming their area of eastern Nigeria the Republic of Biafra.

Despite the broad power and influence of states in the international environment, they do not satisfy all the needs of the world's peoples. But there is no world government that can serve purposes beyond those of existing states. The fact of international anarchy thus motivates governments and other groups to create organizations that can do what states cannot or will not do. Three types of nonstate units are important:

First, there are a number of territorial nonstate units.[9] These are groups that focus their activities within a state but develop ties and linkages to other governments, political groups, or international organizations. The Palestine Liberation Organization, for example, was formed to press for the creation of an independent Palestinian state in all or part of the current state of Israel. Although the PLO bases its operations in Jordan, it has its own "foreign policy," maintains diplomatic relations with several countries and other nonstate units, and possesses permanent official observer status at the United Nations.

Another kind of nonstate unit is the international nongovernmental organization. These organizations are characterized by activities in more than one state, objectives that do not relate to interests in any particular territory, and component units that are essentially nonpolitical in nature.[10] There are about forty-two hundred such organizations in the world today. One of the oldest is the Roman Catholic church, which maintains its headquarters in the Vatican but has operations in nearly every part of the world.

Two newer kinds of nongovernmental organizations are international charities and multinational corporations. The International Red Cross is foremost among world charitable organizations, acting as a neutral body for the transmission of messages across the lines of conflict, disaster relief, and aid to prisoners of war.

Multinational corporations conduct business in more than one state and provide testimony to the increasing interdependence of the world economy. They represent a large share of world economic power, with forty-one of these businesses ranking in the top one hundred global entities (corporations and countries) in terms of annual product.[11] While these enterprises have facilitated the dispersion of technology around the globe and brought jobs to a number of Third World nations, they have also come under attack for exploiting less-developed host countries. Because of their economic power and international reach, corporations such as Gulf Oil, Exxon, IBM, and General Electric can remain aloof from the control of the states where they operate and even influence political developments. ITT, for example, has been linked to the 1973 military coup that overthrew Chilean president Salvador Allende.

The third type of nonstate unit is the intergovernmental organization (IGO). These institutions frequently play an important role in world politics as well as in the domestic politics of member states. The largest IGO is the United Nations, which has existed since the end of World War II as an organization for intergovernmental cooperation and communication.

At times, the UN has been an effective instrument for reducing conflict in world politics. For example, in 1956 Egypt seized control of the Suez Canal, despite a treaty guaranteeing its international ownership. In response, Britain, France, and Israel invaded Egypt and reclaimed control of the waterway—thereby threatening a major war. The United States and the Soviet Union, ignoring other differences between them, joined to use the UN to sponsor a peaceful end to the conflict. A United Nations Emergency Force, made up of soldiers from several nations, replaced the invading armies and secured free passage of ships in the canal for a decade.[12]

Similarly, in the early 1960s, the United Nations helped to bring about the creation of the Congo Republic and the resolution of a crisis in that region. The former Belgian colony had been granted independence in 1960, but three rival centers of power soon developed: one, a conservative faction allied with France; the second, a Marxist group; and the third, a moderate group with ties to Belgium. Central to this struggle was the role of Patrice Lumumba, the radical leader. His ascendancy in Congolese politics raised the prospect of Soviet influence extending to Africa, which would have certainly stimulated an American response. After protracted negotiations, the dispatch of a UN peacekeeping force to the Congo prevented a civil war and precluded the spread of the cold war into central Africa.

Over the course of the past thirty years, UN peacekeeping operations have also been used in the Middle East, albeit with mixed success. UN missions in the Sinai Peninsula helped set the stage for the return of that territory from Israel to Egypt in 1979 and have assisted in moderating some of the conflict in war-torn Lebanon.[13] Obviously, however, an overall settlement in the region has so far eluded the UN, as it has Britain, the United States, and individuals such as Jimmy Carter and Henry Kissinger.

The UN is the subject of both scorn and praise. On the one hand, it is frequently attacked by the United States and its allies for general ineffectiveness, mismanagement of funds contributed by member states, and the often anti-American or anticapitalist tone of its resolutions. Critics of the organization see it as a waste of time and money. But the United States and other members continue to support the UN, both because of its promise as an international forum and because of its record of intermittent success in helping to resolve certain international problems.[14]

Another type of intergovernmental organization is the military alliance, which commits a number of states (usually in a particular region) to a policy of collective defense. Currently, there are approximately three hundred IGOs. Two of the most significant are the North Atlantic Treaty Organization (NATO) and the Warsaw Pact. Both were formed after World War II as cold war tensions divided the United States (West bloc) and the Soviet Union (East bloc). NATO joins the United States, Belgium, Canada, Denmark, France, Great Britain, Greece, Iceland, Italy, Luxembourg, the Netherlands, Norway, Portugal, Spain, Turkey, and West Germany in a defensive arrangement to protect the security of its member states. The Warsaw Pact similarly joins Bulgaria, Czechoslovakia, the German Democratic Republic (East Germany), Hungary, Poland, and Romania under the aegis of the Soviet Union. Together, these alliances have solidified the political split between East and West that has dominated international politics since the late 1940s. Their future in a world in which Soviet-American tensions have eased remains to be seen.

Economic alliances also shape intergovernmental relations. Two of the most significant such arrangements are the Organization of Petroleum Exporting Countries (OPEC) and the European Community (EC) or "Common Market," as it is popularly known. OPEC includes Algeria, Ecuador, Gabon, Indonesia, Iran, Iraq, Kuwait, Libya, Nigeria, Qatar, Saudi Arabia, the United Arab Emirates (UAE), and Venezuela. Member states are committed to common policies on oil prices, sales to nonmembers, and production quotas. In 1973, OPEC reacted to Western support for Israel in the October War by simultaneously raising the price of oil and enacting an embargo on its sale to the United States and a number of European countries. The embargo was later dropped, but the price of oil remained high. For the next decade, OPEC was one of the most forceful actors in international politics.

In 1983, internal disagreements within the cartel overwhelmed the organization. Poorer members, such as Venezuela and Indonesia, wanted to exceed production quotas or reduce their price in order to gain a larger market share. The wealthier Arab states, including Saudi Arabia and the UAE, resisted change. Moreover, the bitter Iran-Iraq war made agreement between these members virtually impossible. Ultimately, the cartel's internal discord, combined with concerted efforts in the United States and Europe to reduce dependence on OPEC oil, led to a decline in OPEC's influence. But OPEC still functions and its customers continue to worry about its potential for influencing international economic affairs in the future.

The European Community was created to produce a common market—hence its nickname—for the states of Western Europe (although Britain, now a member, initially opposed its creation and resisted joining until 1973). The EC has a unified tariff on imports to member countries; moreover, it bargains as a single unit in many international trade negotiations. The economies of EC member states are becoming increasingly integrated into a general European economy. In 1992, further barriers among the nations of Western Europe will fall: most tariffs between EC members will be reduced or eliminated; uniform EC product standards will be enforced; goods, workers, and even professional credentials will flow freely across borders; and a greater equality of taxation will be implemented. Once these reforms take hold, the EC will have reached the point of becoming one of the world's dominant economic powers.

Sometimes state and nonstate units act in concert. But because their choices are governed by a continually shifting dynamic of cooperation and conflict, and because they are responsible for their own security and prosperity, more often than not they act alone. They develop and pursue their own self-interested foreign policies based on their internal situations and on the nature of the international environment at the time. In other words, the units engaged in world politics proceed on the assumption that in order to survive and prosper, they must fend for themselves.[15]

To be sure, cooperation among state and nonstate units is not uncommon. But to repeat: It is strictly voluntary. In world affairs there is no single authority and there are no police. Thus, while there is a body of international law and the United Nations sponsors an International Court of Justice (also known as the World Court), nations around the world find they can ignore international legal codes and institutions when their national interest dictates. Indeed, the United States, like many other countries, has rejected the decisions of the World Court when they opposed American interests.[16]

The interests of individual units, then, drive world politics. These interests may motivate international actors to use force or to cooperate to get what they want. When a state or nonstate unit wants help from another unit, it must rely on the voluntary (and often self-interested) assistance of its benefactor. This is not to say that actors in the international environment never work to advance a larger good. For example, in recent years the United States, Catholic Relief Services, Oxfam, the Red Cross, and other states and charities have provided relief to the victims of famine in Africa. This sort of humanitarian activity is fairly common. But so is the pursuit of war, peace, or economic advantage according to the interests of the parties involved.

Clearly, the various entities active in world politics do not possess equal power with which to pursue their interests. The anarchic nature of the international environment emphasizes inequality and the consequences that flow from it. Japan and Mexico are equal in principle, but in reality the first is an economic superpower while the second lives in danger of financial collapse. With regard to military power, there are two levels: the superpowers and everyone else. The United States and the Soviet Union have military resources far in excess of those possessed by any other state. While both have large armies, navies, and stocks of conventional weapons, what really distinguishes them are their large and complex nuclear arsenals. Each has tremendous destructive power directed primarily at the other; each is also capable of extending its reach to anywhere on earth. Other nations fall into one of three categories: they are formally allied with the superpowers (NATO and the Warsaw Pact); they are informally dependent on them for defense (Israel, South Korea, and the Philippines with the U.S.; Finland and India with the Soviet Union); or they are militarily incidental to world politics (for example, Uruguay, the Ivory Coast, Sweden, or Nepal). Purely in terms of military power, then, the world remains bipolar.

In political and economic terms, however, the world has changed in the last two decades: now it is multipolar. In other words, the military dominance of the United States and the Soviet Union does not extend to political and economic realms of activity. The superpowers' allies have room to seek economic and political relationships that cross the conventional East-West divide. One example is the purchase of Soviet natural gas by West European nations. Another is the political and cultural relationship that has emerged between the two Germanies over the past twenty years as these states have attempted to deal with problems of broken families, emigration, and the issue of German reunification. Moreover, other states have considerable leeway to act as well. Major players such as Japan, China, and India can chart relatively independent political and economic courses. Finally, it should be noted that the distribution of economic resources does not necessarily follow from the distribution of military resources. Whereas the Soviet Union is one of the world's two foremost military powers, in economic terms it is an underdeveloped country. In contrast, Japan, South Korea, Taiwan, Singapore, and Saudi Arabia are all minor states from a military perspective; but they are major actors in the international economy.

These inequalities and differences make contemporary world politics considerably more complex than it was only a short time ago during the cold war.[17] They also strain the superpower alliance structure. Neither the United States nor the Soviet Union is comfortable with military allies who seek so often to test their economic and political independence. Nor are they fully at ease with the economic power of smaller states, such as Japan and South Korea, that challenge their influence in world markets.

The complexity of world economics also means that issues of development and dependency loom large in international affairs.[18] Because not all states have achieved the same level of development, many of the world's poorer nations are to some extent dependent on the superpowers or other advanced industrial countries for help. Although interdependence is a characteristic of the world economy, developing nations of the Southern Hemisphere charge that they are disadvantaged in their economic relations with the richer industrial states of the North. One issue is Third World debt. Brazil, Mexico, Turkey, and most other developing states owe a total of over $1 trillion to banks and governments of industrial nations. Since even servicing this obligation is a drain on their economies, debtor states have been pressuring international creditors to reschedule or even forgive loans. In the meantime, the magnitude of this debt means that these countries face severe budget constraints and must seek further international assistance to support their economies. Another issue is terms of trade. The poorer nations of the South are often both the source of agricultural commodities (e.g., coffee, rice, cocoa, tobacco, and tea) and raw materials (e.g., petroleum, copper, rubber, tin, and iron ore) for the industry and technology of the North and the market for finished products produced by the United States, Japan, France, and other developed countries. Southern nations maintain that prices for their exports vary erratically and have undergone a long-term decline, while prices for the finished goods they purchase from the North continually increase. Because of these problems, developing nations have called for a New International Economic Order to restructure the relationship between North and South. While expressing concern for the plight of developing nations, industrial states have resisted attempts to alter existing arrangements. Growing North-South tensions further complicate the international environment.

THE CURRENT STATE OF THE
INTERNATIONAL ENVIRONMENT

As the preceding discussion suggests, the international environment is in flux. The simple bipolar world of the cold war of the 1940s, 1950s, and 1960s is gone, but what exactly will replace it is not yet clear. We can, however, identify several key characteristics of contemporary world affairs—even beyond those of movement and change:

First, nuclear weapons and U.S.-Soviet relations still dominate world politics.[19] For all the changes taking place in international relations, this situation remains stable. Because each superpower is vulnerable to destruction by the other, the search for greater national security—whether through technology (as in President Reagan's Strategic Defense Initiative or the Soviet antimissile defense system) or arms-control agreements (such as SALT I, the Intermediate Nuclear Forces Treaty, or reductions in conventional forces in Europe)—remains a key aspect of bilateral relations. The United States and the Soviet Union have put time and effort into both kinds of initiatives, seeking negotiated settlements while at the same time searching for unilateral means of achieving security. Of course, cold war tensions have given way to relations between the superpowers that are considerably more relaxed. But the two superpowers remain adversaries, and the power of arms remains critical. Moreover, the relative equality of the United States and Soviet nuclear arsenals means that the drive to avoid nuclear war continues to affect the behavior of many states and nonstate actors.

Major changes, however, are taking place within the Soviet Union and, to a lesser extent, in China. Responding to economic problems in particular and to their relative poverty when compared to market economies, these communist powers have embarked on programs of internal reform. In each nation, pressure for change has come from within the ruling elite and from elements within the population, such as students and intellectuals. While reforms in the two states are not the same, they do share certain characteristics: a substantial reduction of central economic planning and the introduction of a limited market economy; integration into the global economy; moves away from the Leninist and Maoist ideologies that have governed these societies; and some measure of political change.[20] In the Soviet Union, political reform has moved faster than economic change; President Gorbachev has had an easier time promoting his allies in the ruling Politburo and restructuring the Soviet constitution than in introducing market mechanisms. In China, the reverse is true. While economic reforms have been implemented, repression of the student democracy movement in 1989 demonstrated that political liberalization will not come soon.

From the American perspective, the most significant developments are those taking place in the Soviet Union. Under the leadership of Mikhail Gorbachev, the Soviets have initiated new market-sensitive pricing of some goods, allowed the expansion of private enterprise, installed more competitive elections, increased the role of an elected legislature and the state president in their system of government, and begun to alter the role of the Communist party in politics. Moreover, Soviet foreign policy is on a new course. After ten years of war, Gorbachev withdrew Soviet forces from Afghanistan; he visited China in 1989, thereby ending over thirty years of hostility between the communist giants; he made a number of ambitious proposals regarding arms reductions that have captured the attention and imagination of many in the West, particularly in Europe; and he has sanctioned or at least tolerated the decline of communism in East Europe. Bulgaria, Czechoslovakia, East Germany, Hungary, Poland, Romania, and Yugoslavia turned away from one-party rule in the late 1980s with astonishing alacrity.

The extent and future course of these changes are not yet clear, for no one knows whether Gorbachev will succeed in achieving all his attempted reforms or even whether he will remain committed to them. *Glasnost* (openness) and *perestroika* (restructuring) have unleashed popular pressure for more rapid reforms, including calls for autonomy and even independence in the Soviet republics of Lithuania and Azerbaijan, for multiparty elections, and for an end to the Communist party's monopoly on political power. Conservatives in Moscow, or even Gorbachev himself, may repress dissent and reverse these reforms if they believe that such measures are needed to hold the Soviet Union together. Indeed, as former undersecretary of state William Bundy has written: ". . . the Soviet Union of today and tomorrow is in flux to the point where its own rulers almost certainly do not know what sort of shape they will be in a decade from now."[21]

The second key characteristic of contemporary world affairs is the influence of economics. One important reason for this situation is in fact the bipolar nature of world military power. For example, the countries of Asia, protected by the American nuclear deterrent and conventional forces, have enjoyed the luxury of concentrating a large share of their national resources on economic development. Japan is a case in point. Barred by its American-imposed constitution from maintaining a large military force, Japan has been able to channel its assets and energies into becoming one of the world's dominant economic powers. It is now the world's largest investor and greatest donor of aid to poorer nations. Moreover, the Tokyo Stock Exchange now rivals in importance the exchanges of New York and London. All of this has been accomplished with defense forces that have only local significance.

Because economic matters are no longer subordinate to military issues, states in both the East and West are inevitably concerned with the economic dimensions of security. Indeed, Gorbachev's initiatives to change the Soviet economic and political systems can be traced to the failure of the Soviet economy. Meanwhile, Americans now worry if they can compete successfully with their Japanese, Korean, and even European trading partners.

The economy of the United States has not matched the might of its military forces. Because of inflation, a low savings rate, twin deficits in trade and the federal budget, and stiff competition from other industrial nations, the American economy has declined in recent years. The United States is now the world's largest debtor nation, and its markets are increasingly vulnerable to foreign competition. Whereas in 1947 the American economy accounted for 50 percent of the world gross national product, today it accounts for only slightly more than 20 percent.[22]

A third aspect of the contemporary international environment to merit particular attention is the profusion of actors in world politics. There are now 174 states in the world. Approximately half of these were created in the last half century, as the European empires built in the nineteenth century broke apart after World War II. These new states, which are found primarily in Africa, Asia, and Latin America, contain roughly three-quarters of the world's population.[23] In spite of what is in some cases their considerable poverty, these nations are determined to maintain their political independence from the superpowers.

The salience of these states to American foreign policy fluctuates. For example, for a time in the mid-1980s there was widespread attention to the famine in Ethiopia. Then, almost as suddenly as the issue arose, it vanished from front pages and television screens. Problems in Libya, Nicaragua, the Philippines, Haiti, Paraguay, and any of a number of countries appear and disappear from our collective consciousness with unsettling speed.

Furthermore, there has been a proliferation of nonstate units as actors in international politics. While states clearly remain dominant, terrorist groups (e.g., the pro-Iranian groups operating in Lebanon), multinational corporations (e.g., International Telephone and Telegraph), and other international organizations (e.g., the World Council of Churches and Amnesty International) all vie for influence over world affairs. For example, nonstate actors such as OPEC and the Arab League are as important to shaping the course of events in that region as are national states such as Israel and Egypt. Similarly, NATO and the EC influence European politics as much as Britain, France, and West Gemany. Exactly what effect these nonstate actors will have on regional politics remains to be determined.

The final characteristic of contemporary world affairs is the proliferation of issues to which international actors are addressing themselves. The following examples illustrate this point:

- *Development issues.* The Third World generally, but the "poorest of the poor" in Africa particularly, continues to keep economic development at the center of international politics. This includes problems of debt repayment, foreign aid, resource development, and trade relations with other states.
- *Health and environmental issues.* A number of concerns in this area have received attention in recent years, including the worldwide AIDS epidemic, scarce resources, population growth, air and water pollution, acid rain, depletion of the earth's ozone layer, and the "greenhouse" effect.
- *Economic issues.* There now exist world financial, securities, monetary, and commodity markets that affect the economies of all nations. The value of the American dollar, the Japanese yen, and other major currencies is determined by a global market that responds immediately to political and economic events such as war, shifts in the stock market, or trade agreements. Trading on the New York Stock Exchange is affected by what happens overnight at the Tokyo and London exchanges and, in turn, affects those markets. Japanese banks and American firms such as Citicorp and Bankamerica operate around the world, shifting wealth and credit across national boundaries. Third World debt is a key element of international finance, since a $1 trillion obligation is a problem as much for creditors as it is for debtors. Amid these problems, the shape of world economic power is changing as Japan, the EC, South Korea, and Singapore gain ascendancy. In response to these challenges to American economic dominance, pressure mounts

for the United States to adopt protectionist policies that will shield domestic industries from international competition.

- *Nationalism.* The interdependence of states' economies has not diminished the power of nationalism to influence world affairs. The Soviet Union has encountered problems arising from nationalism among its military clients such as Poland, Hungary, and Czechoslovokia as well as from among its own citizens in Armenia, Lithuania, Georgia, and other Soviet republics. Nationalism also fuels conflict in Northern Ireland (between Protestants and Catholics), Nigeria (between the Ibo and the majority Yoruba), Ethiopia and Somalia (over the province of Eritrea), Sri Lanka (from the Tamil minority), Cyprus (between the Greek majority and the Turkish minority), Yugoslavia (from conflict among several ethnic groups), Spain (from Basque and Catalan separatists), France (from Bretons and Basques), Canada (from Quebec nationalists), and throughout the Middle East.

- *The emergence of China in superpower politics.* As it expands its nuclear arsenal, China develops the potential to become the third superpower. In light of the 1989 Sino-Soviet rapprochement, such a development means that the delicate triangular politics begun by President Nixon's 1972 visit to China could alter the essentially bipolar world military order. Of course, internal affairs will also greatly affect the international behavior of both communist giants. Each wants good relations with Washington and with each other. But a desire for cordiality does not mean that superpower peace is inevitable. The Soviet Union and China remain rivals, but they might become more friendly and form a coalition against the United States.[24] On the other hand, a superpower China might face the same problem now confronted by the Soviet Union: possessing military might that is not backed by corresponding economic power. With the rise of Japan, the EC, and South Korea in the international economy, the result of China's ascendance as a nuclear power may be to complicate the global military balance but have little affect on the international economy. In other words, China could change the shape of the international arena, but as part of a larger shift in world politics.

- *The changing role of Europe and the growing importance of other regions.* No longer dominant in military might, Europe is adapting to its new role as an economic competitor in world affairs. In the fast-moving world economy, the continent faces competition from states on the "Pacific Rim"—Japan, South Korea, New Zealand, and Australia—for influence in world markets. In the political realm, even EC integration cannot alter the fact that Europe is now one region among many (albeit one of the most important regions). Even the very notion of "Europe" is rapidly changing. Since the end of World War II, the East-West split has meant that the region has effectively ended on NATO's eastern boundary, with Warsaw Pact nations firmly in the Soviet orbit. Since the revolutionary events of 1989, however, there has been a growing sense in both West and East that Central and Eastern European nations will soon forge new political, economic, and cultural links with the community of continental states. The United States, so long concerned with NATO, finds itself reducing its presence on the continent while turning with greater attention to problems in Latin America, the Middle East, Asia, and Africa.

THE UNITED STATES IN THE
INTERNATIONAL ENVIRONMENT

The preceding discussion has suggested the role of the United States in world politics, albeit indirectly. Chapters 2 through 4 will examine American foreign policy more closely, as well as the president's role in shaping and implementing it. But we can set the stage for that discussion by placing the United States in the context of the international environment. We begin by recalling the United States' status as both a military superpower and a dominant economic power in the world.

America continues to play the role it assumed after World War II: the defender of the noncommunist world.[25] Although it does not dominate the Western Alliance as it once did, the United States is still the central actor in NATO. Moreover, the nation remains the protector of the Western Hemisphere, although states such as Cuba and Nicaragua reject this role and even America's friends want freedom to pursue their own foreign policies. Further, the United States has pledged itself to the defense of Israel, Japan, South Korea, and the Philippines. Finally, America has taken a leading role in guaranteeing the freedom of commercial shipping (i.e., oil tankers) in the Persian Gulf.

At the same time, the quest for Western security has led the United States to initiate or participate in efforts to promote international peace. This includes support for intergovernmental organizations such as the United Nations, although in recent years U.S. diplomats have criticized the UN for an anti-American bias. The nation is also party to a series of international treaties and conventions intended to lessen the risks of nuclear war, including the Partial Test-Ban Treaty (which prohibits atomic explosions in the atmosphere), two strategic arms limitation treaties (SALT I and the unratified but observed SALT II agreement), and the "hot-line" agreement (providing for direct communication between the White House and the Kremlin).

In economic matters, the nation's position has changed. As Richard Rose has noted: "The United States is a rich country, but it is no longer the only rich country in the world."[26] Moreover, America is now the world's largest debtor nation, with a total debt in excess of $2 trillion. For the past decade, we have consistently incurred large budget deficits, which reached a high of almost $200 billion in 1983 and dropped to approximately $150 billion per year by the late 1980s. This overspending has been financed by borrowing from investors both home and abroad, with foreign creditors holding more than 13 percent of the national debt. The United States remains wealthy, but it no longer dominates the world economy as it once did.

Foremost among America's competitors is Japan. Indeed, the international economy is now a marked *bigemony*[27]—an economic environment in which the United States and Japan are the two leading nations.[28] Over the last decade in particular, the two countries have become economically interdependent. Japan relies on the United States for defense and as a market for

40 percent of its exports. In return, the United States depends on Japanese investment to help finance the large budget deficits the nation has run since 1981. Other links, from Honda auto plants in the United States to the use of Japanese electronic components in American-made products, bind the two economies.[29]

America's shifting economic status has motivated its leaders to seek a greater economic security. On some occasions, the result is a greater willingness to open U.S. markets in exchange for the opening of foreign markets, as in the free-trade agreement between the United States and Canada. On other occasions, the quest for econonmic security has increased pressure in Congress for legislation to protect national industries against competition from foreign goods.[30]

Because of these developments, the United States can now be considered one of those states whose sovereignty and independence has been "penetrated." The nation retains a special and powerful role in the international environment, but it is no longer the unchallenged leader in all areas of world affairs.[31]

This mix of constancy and change places the United States in a somewhat ambiguous position. A variety of states still depend on America for military and/or economic reasons. Furthermore, the nation has its own interests to protect. But these circumstances do not clarify—for the American president or for anyone else—the kind of world leadership that other international actors expect the United States to provide. As former secretary of state Henry Kissinger has written: "The most profound challenge to American foreign policy is to develop some concept of order in a world which is bipolar militarily and multipolar politically."[32] One could also add the phrase ". . . and bigemonic economically."

Many countries, both developed and developing, want the United States to demonstrate some leadership in shaping world events. However, for a variety of reasons they fear too much American influence. Similarly, America's allies depend on it for conventional and nuclear defense. But they are sensitive about being obliged to support American positions on nonnuclear issues. Finally, while the United States is a principal trading partner of all major industrial nations, these countries trade with others and have their own interests to protect—including good political and economic relations with Moscow.[33]

For the president of the United States, these ambiguities are facts of life. Moreover, the president has a dual role in global affairs: he is the chief architect of American foreign policy, and he is a world figure as well. The two roles are not necessarily the same. While both grow out of the presidential office, the president's *formal* authority stops at the American border. Thus, his success as a world leader depends in large part on his skill as a player of global politics. To be sure, merely by virtue of being president of the United States, an American head of state exercises influence abroad. But it is his personal qualities as a leader and diplomat that will ultimately determine his impact on world affairs.

If the president is to be a world leader, he must understand the context in which the United States is necessarily embedded. It is with this fact in mind that our discussion began with the international environment.

Notes

1. Forrest McDonald, *The Presidency of George Washington* (Lawrence, KS: Univ. Press of Kansas, 1974), pp. 28–29.

2. Ibid.

3. See Rene Albrecht-Carrie, *The Concert of Europe* (New York: Columbia Univ. Press 1968); Henry A. Kissinger, *A World Restored* (Boston: Little, Brown 1957); and Edward V. Gulick, *Europe's Classical Balance of Power* (Ithaca, N.Y.: Cornell Univ. Press, 1955). For a survey of thought on the functioning of international politics, see F. Parkinson, *The Philosophy of International Relations* (Beverly Hills, Calif., Sage: 1977), chapter 3; James E. Dougherty and Robert L. Pfaltzgraff, Jr., *Contending Theories of International Relations* (New York, Harper & Row: 1971); K. J. Holsti, *The Dividing Discipline* (Boston: Little, Brown, 1985); and Hans J. Morgenthau, *Politics among Nations*, 5th ed. (New York: Free Press 1972). For a survey of the development of international politics, with particular emphasis on the nineteenth and twentieth centuries, see Hedley Bull and Adam Watson, eds., *The Expansion of International Society* (Oxford: Oxford Univ. Press, 1984).

4. On the cold war, a good place to begin is William Safire, *Safire's Political Dictionary* (New York: Random House, 1978), pp. 127–29. Although tensions between the United States and Soviet Union have eased considerably since the 1950s and 1960s, the term "cold war" is still occasionally applied to that relationship (such as speculation about whether the cold war is "over" or has "begun again"). On the nature and development of the cold war, see L. E. Davis, *The Cold War Begins* (Princeton: Princeton Univ. Press, 1974); J. C. Donovan, *The Cold Warriors* (Lexington, Mass.: Lexington Books, 1974); John Lewis Gaddis, *Russia, the Soviet Union, and the United States* (New York: McGraw-Hill, 1978); idem, *Strategies of Containment* (New York: Oxford Univ. Press, 1982); Louis J. Halle, *The Cold War as History* (New York: Harper and Row, 1967); Paul Y. Hammond, *Cold War and Détente* (New York: Harcourt, Brace, and World, 1975); Thomas G. Patterson, *The Origins of the Cold War* (Lexington, Mass.: Lexington Books, 1971); and Amos Yoder, *The Conduct of American Foreign Policy Since World War II* (New York: Pergamon Press, 1986).

5. On anarchy, see Hedley Bull, *The Anarchical Society* (New York: Columbia Univ. Press, 1977); Oran R. Young, "Anarchy and Social Choice: Reflections on the International Polity," *World Politics* 30 (January 1978): pp. 241–63; Kenneth N. Waltz, *Man, the State, and War* (New York: Columbia U. Press, 1959), pp. 159–70; and John Spanier, *Games Nations Play*, 6th ed. (Washington: Congressional Quarterly Press, 1987), pp. 606–11. On international law, see J. L. Brierly, *The Law of Nations*, 6th ed. (New York: Oxford Univ. Press, 1963); Morton A. Kaplan and Nicholas DeB. Katzenbach, *The Political Foundations of International Law* (New York: John Wiley & Sons, 1961); Francis Boyle, *World Politics and International Law* (Durman, N.C.: Duke Univ. Press, 1985); and Antonio Cassese, *International Law in a Divided World* (Oxford: Clarendon Press, 1986).

6. Spanier, p. 58; John Herz, "The Rise and Demise of the Territorial Nation-State," *World Politics* 9 (July 1957): pp. 473–93; and K. J. Holsti, *International Politics: A Framework for Analysis*, 4th ed. (Englewood Cliffs: Prentice-Hall, 1983), p. 65. See also Ivo D. Duchacek, *The Territorial Dimension of Politics* (Boulder, Colo.: Westview Press, 1986).

7. See Spanier, pp. 55–58; Holsti, *International*, pp. 65–67; Alan James, *Sovereign Statehood: The Basis of International Society* (London: Allen & Unwin, 1986); and Andrew M. Scott, *The Revolution in Statecraft* (Durham, N.C.: Duke Univ. Press, 1982), especially chapter 1. On interdependence, see James M. Rosenau, *The Study of Global Interdependence* (London: F. Pinter, 1980); and Ray Maghroori and Bennett Ramberg, eds., *Globalism versus Realism: International Relations' Third Great Debate* (Boulder, Colo.: Westview Press, 1982).

8. Holsti, *International*, p. 67; Spanier, pp. 58–60; Bertrand Badie and Pierre Birnbaum, *The Sociology of the State* (Chicago: Univ. of Chicago Press, 1983); Ernest Gellner, *Nations and Nationalism* (Ithaca, N.Y.: Cornell Univ. Press, 1983); and Yale H. Ferguson and Richard W. Mansbach, *The Elusive Quest: Theory and International Politics* (Columbia, S.C.: Univ. of South Carolina Press, 1988), pp. 127–29, 209.

9. Fred W. Riggs, "The Nation-State and Other Actors," in *International Politics and Foreign Policy,* rev., ed. James N. Rosenau (New York: Free Press, 1969), pp. 90–93; Spanier, pp. 80–81; Werner J. Feld, *Nongovernmental Forces and World Politics* (New York: 1972); Robert O. Keohane and Joseph S. Nye, *Power and Interdependence* (Boston: Little, Brown, 1977); and Pei-heng Chiang, *Non-Governmental Organizations at the United Nations* (New York: Praeger, 1981).

10. Samuel R. Huntington, "Transnational Organizations in World Politics," *World Politics* 25 (April 1973): pp. 333–68; Spanier, pp. 79–80; and Philip Taylor, *Nonstate Actors in International Politics* (Boulder, Colo.: Westview Press, 1982).

11. On multinational corporations in world politics, see Robert O. Keohane and Van Dorne Ooms, "The Multinational Enterprise and the World Political Economy," *International Organization* 26 (Winter 1972): pp. 84–120; and Richard J. Barnet and Ronald Muller, *Global Reach: The Power of the Multinational Corporation* (New York: Simon and Schuster, 1975). Of the top fifty entities in the world in terms of product, forty-one are multinational corporations.

12. On the Suez crisis, see Walter S. Jones, *The Logic of International Relations,* 5th ed. (Boston: Little, Brown, 1985), pp. 544–45; Halle, pp. 338–42; Gabrielle Rosner, *The United Nations Emergency Force* (New York: Columbia Univ. Press, 1963); and *United Nations Emergency Force: Summary Study of the Experience Derived from the Establishment and Operation of the Force,* UN Doc. A/3943, 9 October 1958. For a history of UN peacekeeping through the 1960s, see Larry L. Fabian, *Soldiers without Enemies* (Washington: Brookings Institution, 1971).

13. On the Congo affair, see Georges Abi-Saab, *The United Nations Operation in the Congo 1960–1964* (New York: Oxford Univ. Press, 1978). For an American perspective, see Roger Hilsman, *To Move a Nation: The Politics of Foreign Policy in the Administration of John F. Kennedy* (New York: Doubleday, 1967), pp. 233–71. For a brief summary of this example, see Peter Calvocoressi, *World Politics Since 1945,* 5th ed. (New York: Longman, 1987), p. 96. On the Middle East, see Jones, pp. 546–50. See also Bjorn Skogmo, *International Peacekeeping in Lebanon, 1978–1988* (Boulder, Colo.: Westview Press, 1989); and Ramesh Thakur, *International Peacekeeping in Lebanon: United Nations Authority and Multinational Force* (Boulder, Colo.: Westview Press, 1987).

14. A useful introduction to this debate is Ernest van den Haag and John P. Conrad, *The U.N.: In or Out?* (New York: Plenum Press, 1987). The literature on the UN is extensive, but a good recent survey is Peter R. Baehr and Leon Gordenker, *The United Nations: Reality and Ideal* (New York: Praeger, 1984). See also Evan Luard, *A History of the United Nations: The Years of Western Domination,* vol. 1 (New York: St. Martin's Press, 1982); and John F. Murphy, *The United Nations and the Control of International Violence* (Totowa, N.J.: Rowman & Allanheld, 1983). For an American perspective, see Toby Trister Gati, ed., *The US, the UN, and Management of Global Change* (New York: New York Univ. Press, 1983); Jeane J. Kirkpatrick, *The Reagan Phenomenon and Other Speeches in Foreign Policy* (Washington: American Enterprise Institute, 1983); and Daniel Patrick Moynihan, *A Dangerous Place* (Boston: Little, Brown 1980). The UN also publishes an extensive list of materials and documents.

15. See Roger D. Masters, "World Politics as a Primitive Political System," in *International Politics and Foreign Policy,* pp. 104–18; Henry A. Kissinger, "Domestic Structure and Foreign Policy," op. cit., pp. 261–75; and Spanier, pp. 86–97.

16. For a discussion of the court, its role in world affairs, and the American position regarding it, see Jones, pp. 536–40. See also Spanier, pp. 609–11; and William D. Coplin, "International Law and Assumptions about the State System," *World Politics* 17 (July 1965): pp. 615–34. One controversial case before the court involved the U.S. and Nicaragua. For a discussion of that case, see the entire issue on *"Nicaragua v. the United States* before the International Court of Justice," guest ed. Allan Gerson, *World Affairs* 148 (Summer 1985).

17. For historical background, see Walt W. Rostow, *The Diffusion of Power* (New York: Macmillan, 1972); and Bull and Watson. For a contemporary look at the new complexity of world politics, see William P. Bundy, "The 1950s versus the 1990s," in *America's Global Interests,* ed. Edward K. Hamilton (New York: Norton, 1989), pp. 33–81; Richard Rose, *The*

Postmodern President: The White House Meets the World (Chatham, N.J.: Chatham House, 1988); and Spanier, chapter 12.

18. For an introduction to these issues, see Spanier, chapter 11; U.S. Department of State, *Fundamentals of U.S. Foreign Policy,* (Washington: Government Printing Office, 1988); *New York Times,* 21 June 1988, p. A8; and Joan Edelman Spero, *The Politics of International Economic Relations,* 3rd ed. (New York: St. Martin's Press, 1985).

19. Bundy, pp. 58–59; and Dept. of State, *Fundamentals,* p. 6.

20. Donald S. Zagoria, "China-Soviet Détente: The Long March," *New York Times,* 22 May 1989, p. A17.

21. Bundy, p. 59. For an overview of this issue, see Robert G. Kaiser, "The U.S.S.R. in Decline," *Foreign Affairs* 67 (Winter 1988/9): pp. 97–113. For a discussion of what Gorbachev's changes imply for American foreign policy, see Graham Allison, "National Security Strategy for the 1990s," in *America's Global Interests,* pp. 220–29.

22. Rose, pp. 244–46.

23. See *World Bank Atlas 1988* (Washington: World Bank, 1988), p. 10.

24. Charles W. Kegley, Jr., and Eugene R. Wittkopf, *American Foreign Policy: Pattern and Process,* 2nd ed. (New York: St. Martin's Press 1982), pp. 168–69. On the issue of China in world politics, see June T. Dreyer, ed., *Chinese Defense and Foreign Policy* (New York: Paragon House, 1989). On the United States and China, see Banning Garrett, "China Policy and the Constraints of Triangular Logic," in *Eagle Defiant: United States Foreign Policy in the 1980s,* eds. Kenneth A. Oye et al. (Boston: Little, Brown, 1983), pp. 237–72.

25. See Dept. of State, *Fundamentals.*

26. Rose, p. 246.

27. C. Fred Bergsten, "Economic Imbalances and World Politics," *Foreign Affairs* 65 (Summer 1987): p. 790.

28. Rose, p. 253. See also OECD, "OECD in Figures," *OECD Observer* 152 (June/July 1988): supplement.

29. Ibid., p. 254. See also George R. Packard, "The Coming U.S.-Japan Crisis," *Foreign Affairs* 66 (Winter 1986/7): pp. 348–67.

30. See Bruce R. Scott and George C. Lodge, eds., *U.S. Competitiveness in the World Economy* (Boston: Little, Brown 1985); John Yochelson, ed., *Keeping Pace: U.S. Policies and Global Economic Change* (Cambridge, Mass.: Harvard Univ. Press, 1988); Catherine Stirling and John Yochelson, eds., *Under Pressure: U.S. Industry and the Challenges of Structural Adjustment* (Boulder, Colo.: Westview Press, 1985); Martin K. Starr, ed., *Global Competitiveness: Getting the U.S. Back on Track* (New York: Norton, 1988); and C. Fred Bergsten, "America in the World Economy: A Strategy for the 1990s," in *America's Global Interests,* pp. 82–112.

31. Rose, p. 3.

32. Henry A. Kissinger, "System Structure and American Foreign Policy," in *Perspectives on American Foreign Policy,* eds., Charles W. Kegley, Jr., and Eugene R. Wittkopf (New York: St. Martin's Press, 1983), p. 110.

33. See Rose, pp. 240–41.

2

American Foreign Policy

Presidential leadership abroad is contingent on presidential leadership at home. While it was easier during an earlier time for America's chief executive to make foreign policy without taking the preferences of the American people into account, today the first step in the foreign policy process is for the executive to generate at least tacit public support. America's experience in Vietnam was the turning point. The world's first televised war proved beyond a shadow of a doubt that the president who would shape attitudes and events beyond our own national borders first has to make foreign policy in his own backyard. This is not to say that the public is—or should be—aware of every venture in the realm of foreign affairs. It is to argue that with regard to the broad goals of foreign policy and major foreign policy initiatives, the president must have the people in tow.

The fundamental objective of foreign policy is to further the "national interest," which includes:

1. *security interests,* that secure the protection of the state and its citizens against threat from outside
2. *economic interests,* that enhance the national welfare through advantageous interactions with other nations
3. *ideological interests,* that protect and foster those values that the citizens of a nation share and believe to be universally good
4. *world order interests,* that maintain an international environment within which the state and its citizens can feel secure.[1]

Who exactly defines the national interest at a given point in time is, in good part, politically determined. For in reality—while security, economic ideological, and world order interests encompass the whole—particular interests are often conflicting and therefore need to be reconciled.

All presidents are, in any case, expected to further one or another form of the national interest all of the time—in ways that take the preferences of the American people into account. While the nature and composition of this constituency has changed significantly over the course of American history, in many important ways Americans have remained remarkably similar to what they were two hundred years ago. To gain a further understanding of who we are, and how that impinges on our foreign policy, we must turn to the particulars of the American experience.

THE WELLSPRINGS OF AMERICAN FOREIGN POLICY

History/Georgraphy.   Because America's history is still relatively short, because it was settled by emigrants from diverse places who were severed from their own roots, and because the U.S. has always been more oriented to the future than the past, Americans are a relatively ahistorical people. Yet the influence of history and also of the geography that shaped it have played important roles in determining how foreign policy problems are defined, alternatives viewed, and decisions ultimately made. America's formative experience, the Revolutionary War, has been an especially powerful and durable influence on our attitudes and actions in the foreign policy realm.

The Revolutionary War was facilitated by the expansive separation—an ocean divided them—between the military powers of Europe and the rebels who had left the mother country to make a new home in a distant land. The insurrection was motivated by our first foreign policy objective: a secure independence.[2] The war and all that precipitated it thus exacerbated the Americans' already extant tendency to resist political (although not necessarily religious) authority, to distrust all governments (including their own), to be suspicious of much that smacked of Europe's ancient regime, and above all to experience a strong sense of separateness from all the other nations of the world.

The fledgling Republic was geographically remote, in particular from the great European powers that were all-important in the late eighteenth century. It had broken new ground ideologically by putting into immediate practice ideas Europeans had heretofore embraced only in theory. And it was free of the old encumbrances—political, economic, and social—that in the past had determined the foreign policies of other countries. Their victory over the British, then, merely confirmed what the erstwhile colonists already thought anyway. They were at liberty to create an entirely new kind of foreign policy because their nation was distinct from—and morally and politically superior to—all those that had preceded it.

After liberty from Britain was gained, this sense of specialness, coupled with a privileged geography—which bestowed blessings that included abundant and diverse lands and resources, as well as isolation—continued to shape America's view of the world. In fact, from the time of George Washington until the First World War, United States foreign policy was designed in considerable part so as to keep the U.S. at a distance from what was happening elsewhere. President Washington had set the tone: "It is our true policy to steer clear of permanent alliances with any portion of the foreign world." And the framers of the Constitution had further cautioned against other countries influencing our government. As Hamilton wrote in *The Federalist Papers:* "One of the weak sides of republics . . . is that they afford too easy an inlet to foreign corruption."

But if the United States strove to keep out of international politics in so far as it reasonably could, when its interests were directly at stake, intervention became an option. The Monroe Doctrine was the clearest early signal that the U.S. fully intended to protect, and even further, its national interest. The American continents, President James Monroe declared in a message to

Congress in 1823, "are henceforth not to be considered as subjects for future colonization by any European powers." Moreover, any attempt by these powers to violate this precept would be considered by the U.S. to be "dangerous" to its "peace and safety." Since the Monroe Doctrine went on to reaffirm that the U.S. had no intention of interfering in the affairs of Europe, two distinct policies had been established: on the one hand, the U.S. would maintain its distance from the political affairs of Europe; but on the other, it would stand ready to defend if necessary its political *and* economic interests in the Western Hemisphere. It was this balance—between a preference for isolation and the willingness if need be to intervene—that characterized American foreign policy for almost two centuries.

For most of the nineteenth century, then, American activism was directed at: preserving freedom of the seas and America's right to undertake territorial expansion, pursuing economic interests in the Western Hemisphere and in Asia (beginning in the 1840s), and preventing any European state (or coalition of states) from occupying a position that might make it a threat to the military security of the North and South American continents.

It was not until our entry into the First World War and, after its conclusion, President Woodrow Wilson's plea for continuing American involvement in international relations through the League of Nations that our proclivity to isolation was really put to the test. But even then Wilson was ahead of his time. Due in part to his own poor political leadership, in part to the still considerable resistance at home to a greater U.S. role in world politics, and in part to the extreme partisanship and anti-Wilson animus exhibited by Republican leaders, the Senate defeated his proposal to join the League in 1919. The United States seemed poised to retreat once again to the isolationism that had characterized most of its history until then. But the retreat was only halfhearted. The First World War, during which for the first time thousands of American boys died on European soil, was evidence that the planet was shrinking and that the oceans, which had for so long been a buffer, could no longer protect the United States from events in Europe. As a result, despite its absence from the League of Nations proper, the United States played a growing role between the world wars in attempts to establish a more stable international order and give moral principles greater standing in international relations.[3] (For example, the U.S. signed a treaty in which all nations with interests in the Far East bound themselves to uphold the independence and territorial sovereignty of China, and it joined an international movement that culminated in the Kellogg-Briand Pact to "outlaw" war.)

And so the change from relative isolation to relatively greater involvement was gradually set in motion. World War II completed the transition. It led inexorably to America's permanent participation in world politics, making it impossible from that point on for the United States ever to return to its previous preference for keeping a safe distance.

The postwar period (1945–1950) was a watershed. By midcentury the United States was a superpower. Its military resources were superior to any in the world. Its national interests, again both political and economic, stretched around the globe. And there had been a profound change in attitude on America's proper role in world affairs. Whereas in the past those who would intervene in global politics were the ones who had to make their case, since Hitler those who counseled isolation were in the minority. The failure to stop Germany in the 1930s—as symbolized by British prime minister Neville Chamberlain's abject attempt to appease Hitler in Munich in 1938—came to be seen by the U.S. foreign policy elite as a ghastly mistake. As a consequence, in the postwar period, intent both on deterring future war and expanding American influence, U.S. policymakers increased America's involvement abroad to a level that had heretofore been unimagined. It was the U.S.—the soon-to-be-christened "leader of the free world"—to whom other countries, both friend and foe, now looked for leadership at the international level. Europe was in decline (East European countries rapidly became part of the Soviet bloc and West European countries had to do extensive rebuilding after the war); Japan had suffered a terrible defeat; China was in the throes of civil war; and the Soviet Union, even as it became militarily stronger, suffered under Stalin's dictatorial regime. That left the door wide open for the United States to forge a host of military alliances; to become in its own right a military superpower; to take the leading role in containing Soviet expansionism; to take the initiative in the restoration of Europe; to declare its interest in the Asian continent; and above all, to stake a claim at the international level to being morally right as well as rich.[4]

Ideology.   America's national belief system, particularly the faith Americans have had from the start in their own uniqueness and superiority, has inevitably had an impact on international relations. The U.S. government has made foreign policy on the assumption that it is its mission to spread—by example and, sometimes, by direct intervention—freedom and justice around the world. The massive immigration of the nineteenth century (particularly after 1865) reinforced this sense of national destiny: the United States was, and would always continue to be, a beacon, a "shining city on a hill." Whereas Europe stood for war, poverty, and exploitation, America stood for peace, opportunity, and democracy. The U.S. would set an example of a better way of life at home and morally superior behavior abroad.[5]

To this day—recent signs of national decline notwithstanding—most Americans still think of the United States as better somehow than the other nations of the world. Although the experiences of Vietnam and Watergate were profoundly disturbing, the fact is that the American people still retain an abiding faith in their own national virtue. The decades-long conflict between the United States and the Soviet Union, between capitalism and communism, only served to strengthen convictions in this regard.[6] Capitalism stood for individuality, freedom, and equality in all matters of social, political, and economic consequence; while during the cold war period, Soviet-style communism was considered in every way repressive and threatening and, indeed, inimical to the ideals Americans held most dear. As Ronald Reagan's first-term rhetoric testified, for years the impression conveyed was that the Soviet Union was an "evil empire" while the U.S., certainly in contrast, was a Garden of Eden. Indeed, the language that characterized the respective spheres of influence—the "Soviet bloc" versus the "free world"—further burnished the image Americans had of themselves as morally superior. To be sure, Mikhail Gorbachev and, in particular, his proclivity to *glasnost* (openness) and *perestroika* (reform) have impressed Americans. Significant and probably enduring changes in the U.S.-Soviet relationship have already occurred. But it is also true that the second half of this century has been characterized primarily by strong anticommunist attitudes at the highest levels of American government and by tendencies to see significant communist threats to American security, even in situations where they do not exist.

One policy outcome of the view Americans have had of themselves as better than the rest has been government action in the name of moral principle. George Kennan observed that these actions fall into two categories: "Those that relate to the behavior of other governments that we find morally unacceptable, and those that relate to the behavior of our own government."[7] With regard to the behavior of other governments, there are two moral imperatives we defend with special vigor: self-determination and peaceful change.[8] In theory at least, they top the list of reasons for American intervention in the affairs of other sovereign states.

Yet for all our self-righteousness, since the beginning of American history there has been a gap between our ideology and how we actually behave. Indeed, U.S. foreign policy has been characterized by what some consider to be an unfortunate discrepancy between the moral superiority that is implied in much of our national rhetoric and the pragmatism that is more typical of our national behavior. To take but one blatant example, throughout most of the nineteenth century Americans generally defined the policies pursued in quest of our "manifest destiny"—in particular the acquisition of Indian lands—as being outside the realm of foreign policy. To fight the Indians, Mexicans, and Spaniards was not seen as interventionist or expansionist, but merely as filling out the American union as God had intended.[9] While this particular rationale is unacceptable now, we still have a tendency to assume that our national self-interest and what is right, good, and true are one and the same.

Arthur Schlesinger, Jr., has written about Americans' propensity to ideology: "The Calvinist cast of mind saw America as the redeemer nation. It expressed itself in the eighteenth century in Jonathan Edwards's theology of Providence, in the nineteenth century in John Calhoun's theology of slavery, in the twentieth century in Woodrow Wilson's vision of world order and in John Foster Dulles's summons to a holy war against godless communism."[10] Schlesinger argues that the schism between this kind of ideologizing and America's practical streak has manifested itself in our approach to world affairs right from the start. On the one hand, the Founding Fathers were hardheaded and clear-sighted men who believed that states acted in their own national interest, who understood, for example, that the preservation of American independence depended on maintaining a balance of power in Europe. But on the other hand, they believed in a special mission for the United States and rather expected that in time the American experiment would redeem the world. Schlesinger concludes that the president who would take the lead in foreign affairs must take the tension between our ideology and our pragmatism into account.

> So two strains have competed for the control of American foreign policy: one empirical, the other dogmatic; one viewing the world in the perspective of history, the other in the perspective of ideology; one supposing that the United States is not entirely immune to the imperfections, weaknesses and evils incident

to all societies, the other regarding the United States as indeed the happy empire of perfect wisdom and perfect virtue, commissioned to save all mankind.

This schematic account does not do justice to the obvious fact that any American President, in order to command assent for his policies, must appeal to both reality and ideology—and that, to do this effectively, Presidents must combine the two strains not only in their speeches but in their souls. . . .[11]

The tension between what we profess to believe and what we actually do leads to certain inconsistencies. Consider the American attitude toward power and violence. Clearly we have a healthy respect for what Theodore Roosevelt once called "a big stick." Moreover, most of us are willing to concede that under certain circumstances that stick should be used. At the same time, there is deep concern, particularly since the war in Vietnam, over the potential abuse of American power. The question of when American intervention is justifiable or appropriate is endlessly debated among members of government and, indeed, resurfaces with special urgency as new situations arise.

During the 1980s, Central America has provided particularly interesting cases in point. For example, President Reagan sanctioned a brief invasion of the tiny island of Grenada to general acclaim. But when he wanted to stop communism as practiced by more formidable antagonists—as in Nicaragua— his path was often blocked. Indeed, because Congress wavered in its commitment to aid the (anticommunist) Contras, the Reagan administration resorted to covert action: to aiding and abetting the Contra cause in a variety of ways that were designed to be concealed.

However, the Iran-Contra scandal, which was largely about the issue of secret support for anticommunist rebels in Latin America, again dampened government enthusiasm for the use of even covert military power. Indeed, when George Bush became chief executive, a new era of caution dawned. In 1989, when President Bush sent troops to Panama, supposedly to intimidate Panamanian strongman General Manuel Noriega, he made clear to the audience at home that American boys had not in fact been sent there to fight; their rifles were in evidence merely for defensive purposes, to protect American civilians. Of course, our reluctance to actually use U.S. military power is attributable to more than just the American experience in Southeast Asia. In the Nuclear Age the application of any military force at all is generally considered risky—which still grates those Americans weaned on the midcentury conviction that the U.S. ought to fight to the finish for any cause it considers just.

To be sure, by and large our ideology is straightforward and unambiguous. For example, we have the hubris typically associated with great strength, and we believe, therefore, that national success is all-important. Americans want their country to be the "first" in the world: first in military might, first in economic prosperity, first in space exploration, and so on. There is an almost pathological fear of becoming a "second rank" power.[12] Similarly, we have strong convictions about the sanctity of the private sector, even when it impinges on the public welfare. Consider the relatively low level of governmental interference in the foreign operations of American corporations, even though their activities often have a negative impact on the U.S. economy.

Perhaps most obvious has been the high level of official tolerance for the shift in manufacturing—and jobs—from the U.S. to countries where labor is much cheaper. The government has a similar laissez-faire attitude to private-sector activities abroad that are morally questionable, for example the selling of chemicals and drugs outlawed at home. And note how sluggishly the federal government has responded to the widespread abuse of the environment by American industry. The Exxon *Valdez,* a tanker that ran aground and sprang a leak, spilling millions of gallons of oil onto the pristine shores along Alaska's coastline, is only the most infamous of countless cases in which, although a public good has been despoiled, it is the private sector that ultimately determines compensation.

In part, the government's reluctance to interfere with the private sector grows out of our faith in the virtue of economics. Put baldly: We believe that free-market economics in particular is good and politics bad. This attitude is attributable largely to a national experience shaped by millions of immigrants who came to the U.S. to seek a better way of life. In fact, America is still a symbol of free enterprise: the picture we carry is one of a country in which anyone willing to work hard can attain a comfortable standard of living and earn the respect of fellow citizens. It is hardly surprising then that the U.S. tends to think of solutions to international problems in economic terms. Individual economic achievement is identified in the American mind with group harmony and the welfare of all. Politics, on the other hand, is equated with trouble and strife. Thus, just as the "good" domestic society is the product of free competition, so the peaceful international society will be created by free trade.[13] In sum, our ideology is a product of how we have viewed ourselves from the start: as different from what had come before, as better than what had come before, as destined for greatness, and as a living exemplar of the maxim that capitalism and liberty go hand in hand.

American National Character. Although the concept of a national character remains somewhat controversial, there nevertheless is considerable agreement that national populations do have distinguishing characteristics (sometimes labeled differences in "national style").[14] For us this raises two questions: Which characteristics distinguish Americans from the citizens of other states? and How do these characteristics affect American foreign policy?

Michael Kammen had described Americans as a "people of paradox." Americans, he wrote, have managed to be "both puritanical and hedonistic, idealistic and materialistic, peace-loving and war-mongering, isolationist and internationalist, conformist and individualist, consensus-minded and conflict-prone."[15] The main reason for the tensions to which Kammen refers is the nature of the body politic. America is a nation composed of emigrants from other nations, from diverse backgrounds and cultures. We are different, therefore, not only from those who are not Americans, but also from each other. Unlike the homogeneous European lands to which most Americans can trace their heritage, this country is a heterogeneous collective that is less melting pot than mosaic.

Other social commentators struck a responsive chord by addressing the issue of how the American national character had changed over time. In *The Lonely Crowd,* for example, originally published in 1950, David Riesman argued that the national character that had dominated America in the nine-teenth century was being replaced in the twentieth by one of a quite different sort. Developing a typology between individuals who are inner-directed and those who are other-directed—other-directed types being depicted as too easily influenced by the opinion of others—Riesman prompted many Ameri-cans to take a hard look at what we had, as a collective, become.[16]

A similarly strong impact was made by a book published thirty years later, Christopher Lasch's, *The Culture of Narcissism*. Again, the topic was the American national character, in particular, changes that had afflicted it in the 1960s and 1970s. Like Riesman, Lasch was enamored of the past, per-suaded that what we had become was less good than what we once were. "Plagued by a sense of inner emptiness, the 'psychological man' of the twenti-eth century seeks neither individual self-aggrandizement nor spiritual tran-scendence but peace of mind, under conditions that increasingly militate against it. Therapists . . . become his principal allies in the struggle for compo-sure; he turns to them in the hope of achieving the modern equivalent of salvation, 'mental health.' "[17]

The tensions of which Kammen writes and the changes in national char-acter suggested by commentators such as Riesman and Lasch have policy implications. U.S. foreign policy is particularly prone to fluctuate. To take but one striking example from twentieth-century history: the 180-degree turn-around between the late 1930s and early 1940s when, in short order, the U.S. completely changed course from a hands-off foreign policy to one that sig-naled an all-out commitment to world war. Thus, sometimes the U.S. is disposed to act pragmatically; at others on the basis of moral principle. Sometimes it is inclined to intervene; at others to pull back. Sometimes Amer-ica employs force; at others it exercises influence through diplomatic chan-nels. Sometimes our national rhetoric is pitched toward protection against war; at others toward the achievement of peace. Sometimes America's domi-nant mode is confrontational; at others cooperative.

But if, in many ways, we are a people of paradox and if, in some ways, we change over time, as the preceding discussion on ideology suggests, there are nevertheless certain constants. In particular, Americans always have been, and continue to be, political optimists who are by and large satisfied with their lot. Even now we believe in ourselves, in our ability to do good in the world, and in a future rife with possibility. Thus, while there are swings in the pendulum, America's general orientation to foreign affairs is informed by the long-held and deeply rooted belief that we can, and should, shape the world in our own image.

AMERICAN FOREIGN POLICY IN THE POSTWAR PERIOD

Since the end of the Second World War, international relations have been characterized by the overriding importance of the conflict between the United States and the Soviet Union. Because of the continuing significance of the U.S.-Soviet relationship, we turn now to a very brief history of how this relationship has evolved over the past half century. It is this history that constitutes the backdrop against which all recent American presidents have tried to lead at the international level.[18]

The story of U.S.-Soviet relations must be viewed in the context of a past in which there was trouble from the start. Shortly after the Bolshevik revolution—which the U.S. government had opposed—the most fundamental source of conflict between the two nations became apparent: the ideological commitment of the Communist party leadership to the overthrow of capitalism—the political, economic, and social system traditional to American society. Thus, from 1917 on, the basic antagonism between the United States and the Soviet Union was grounded in their very different, and mutually exclusive, ideologies. (Tellingly, a full sixteen years elapsed before the U.S. finally recognized the Soviet regime.)

To be sure, there were moments when the antagonism between the two great nations abated. In particular, in 1941 Roosevelt and Stalin forged an alliance in common cause against the Nazis. But the events that took place during the final weeks of the war and in the immediate postwar period quickly destroyed any illusions that a new era of Soviet-American friendship was at hand. Above all, the Soviet Union's aggressive interventions into the domestic affairs of the countries of East Europe seemed to demonstrate in no uncertain terms that the Russians were a dangerous threat to world stability. As a consequence, there emerged in the late 1940s—in the East and in the West—those attitudes and opinions that came to be associated with the term *cold war*.

In order to demonstrate Western resolve and, in particular, to forestall the Soviet conquest of all Europe, the United States committed itself, in what was then considered virtual perpetuity, to the defense of West Europe. Moreover, after 1949, when China became a communist state, the U.S. declared itself ready to stop communist expansionism on the Asian continent as well. To buttress our Asian allies and to prove to militant anticommunists at home that the Democrats could stand up to the communists in Asia as well as Europe, when communist North Korea invaded South Korea, Harry Truman seized the moment.[19] Thus the U.S. entry into the Korean War was proof positive that a new pattern of American foreign policy had been established. For the first time it was taken as a given that we had permanent responsibilities well beyond the limits of the Western Hemisphere.[20] In fact, the U.S. would go so far as to assume the role of world policeman.

During the immediate postwar years there were four major innovations in American foreign policy: The first was the Truman Doctrine which, by establishing America's willingness to protect the independence of Greece and the territorial integrity of Turkey, demonstrated that the U.S. was committed to the defense of democratic nations everywhere against "direct or indirect aggression" and "subjugation by armed minorities or by outside pressure."[21]

The second innovation grew out of the first and came to be known widely as the *policy of containment*. While never officially formulated, it called for a halt to the territorial expansion of Soviet power beyond the line of military demarcation drawn at the end of the Second World War between the Soviet orbit and the Western world.[22] According to John Lewis Gaddis, containment was implemented through five different "strategies" adopted by a string of postwar presidents:

1. the original (1947–1949), and limited, strategy of containing Soviet influence at a few points (such as Western Europe)
2. global containment (1950–1953), to which America aspired after the start of the Korean War
3. the Eisenhower–Dulles "New Look" strategy (1961–1969), which shifted the burden of containment to nonnuclear means (such as the limited war in Vietnam)
4. the Nixon-Kissinger conception of détente (in the early 1970s), designed to "contain" and stabilize the Soviet Union by integrating it into the international system.

Gaddis demonstrates that while all postwar presidents maintained the overall goal of containing Soviet influence, each formulated a policy designed to appear different from that of his predecessors. Thus the history of American foreign policy vis-à-vis the Soviets since World War Two has been one of different approaches to achieving a common objective.[23]

Since the United States recognized that containment could not succeed while Europe remained weak, it undertook yet a third major foreign policy initiative, shortly after war, the Marshall Plan. The Marshall Plan was a vehicle for channeling billions of dollars into Europe over a four-year period to help it recover from the devastation of battle. (It should be noted that Europe was not the only beneficiary of America's largesse during this time; foreign aid was an important instrument for keeping the uncommitted nations of the world from tilting toward the Soviets.)

The fourth innovation in postwar foreign policy provides perhaps the most striking evidence of how completely the United States had given up on isolationism. Indeed, the string of new alliances between the U.S. and countries all over Europe and Asia testified to the fact that our traditional position vis-à-vis the international environment had been turned on its head. (These alliances included: the North Atlantic Treaty Organization, the Central Treaty Organization (Middle East), the Southeast Asia Treaty Organization, the Organization of American States, and ANZUS, a security treaty signed by the U.S., Australia, and New Zealand.) What we had, then, by the early 1950s was no less than a revolution in American attitudes toward foreign affairs. It was not that the national interest had changed, but that the international environment had. As a consequence, United States foreign policy had to change along with it.

Stanley Hoffmann has argued that the cold war, which at its most frigid lasted from roughly the mid-1940s to the early 1970s, was characterized by three distinct phases: "The era of President Truman, during which the policy of containment was initiated, a heated debate between Democrats and Republicans broke out over Asia, and McCarthyism spread; the Eisenhower phase, which lowered voices, dampened conflicts, and turned containment into routine; and a new Democratic period, which began as a revival of activism, fervor and 'vigor,' and ended in the Vietnam quagmire."[24] During the entire time, however, there was one constant: America felt beseiged. Virtually every Soviet move was experienced as a threat. And in fact communism did chalk up some very significant victories—in China, North Korea, Eastern Europe, and even ninety miles off the coast of Florida in Cuba.

The U.S. government's reaction to the stress of being world policeman was to protect its flanks. Alliances were forged. The nuclear arsenal grew dramatically in size. Allies were collected. A military presence was established in more than seventy countries,[25] and a worldwide network of U.S. air and naval bases was secured. America also invested in the United Nations. While the organization manifestly fell far short of the dream of a world community, the United States nevertheless learned to use it to at least intermittent advantage. Finally, the U.S. entered into several arrangements that solidified the economic stability of the noncommunist world. These included the World Bank, the International Monetary Fund, the General Agreement of Tariffs and Trade (GATT), and the Organization for European Economic Cooperation (OEEC).

Thus the substance of American foreign policy was shaped in the postwar period by our deep involvement in international relations. Driven by the fear of Soviet communism, the United States left isolationism behind, apparently forever, in favor of globalism which, by definition, implied full participation in world politics. The territorial threat that communism seemed to pose to the United States and its allies and the supposed intention of Communist party leaders to impose their ideological system worldwide legitimated American activism around the globe and supplied the rationale for a buildup of arms that was unprecedented in world history. In the international arena, Americans were in a fight, not for military conquest or for their own desire for territory, but for the preservation of their cherished and superior ideals of freedom and democracy.

> Thus the United States shaped or influenced the political profile of Western Europe and Japan, and obtained abroad the support it needed for its foreign policy. Far more than the American public realized, with its rather naive belief in the spontaneous convergence of autonomous forces, we recruited and shored up political clientels of "like-minded" people. Our favorite means were military and economic assistance, the most readily available and successfully tested American devices. Our emphasis on the similarity of values, visions, and techniques, our quest for a kind of universal pragmatism . . . all show that the "American empire," far more than the British, expressed a certain expansive notion of the ideal social order, not merely a mix of external realism and the will to preserve hard-won advantages.[26]

The fact that anticommunism drove U.S. foreign policy made life relatively simple for the foreign policy establishment. It encouraged the development of a near-consensus in elite and public opinion about what had to be done. The American foreign policy consensus was also encouraged by the legacy of Munich. Eager to avoid even a semblance of the appeasement strategy that was now considered such a dismal failure, America's policymakers were of one mind: to protect American interests and prevent another war, the Soviets had to be stopped.

This is not to say that the age of consensus on American foreign policy was entirely free from disagreement. Rather, it is to point out that during the two decades after the war, there were a number of fundamental propositions about the nature of the international environment, and America's proper role within it, that had broad support.[27] They included:

1. Global peace and stability were contingent on America's national security because the U.S. was the only nation strong enough to check Soviet expansionism.
2. The U.S. had the responsibility to be actively involved in creating a just and stable world order because it was so powerful and because it was the birthplace of a free and democratic society.
3. It was up to the U.S. to resist Soviet expansion and play a leading role in forging both peacetime alliances and a broad range of international organizations because the primary threat to a stable world order stemmed from the Soviet Union's efforts, either directly or by proxy, to alter the status quo by force.

VIETNAM AS A TURNING POINT

The war in Vietnam brought the era of consensus to a gradual close and thereby changed altogether the nature of the American foreign policy process.[28] During the cold war, power was in the political center and "the anti-Communist policy consensus was at the heart of centrism and gave it steadiness and direction."[29] But the long ordeal of our military involvement in Southeast Asia dispersed power out from the center and toward the political extremes. As a consequence, the forging of majorities became increasingly difficult. After polling almost five thousand leaders, Ole Holsti and James Rosenau concluded that by 1976 the cleavages in America were so deep that the post–World War II consensus on foreign affairs could only be described as shattered.

In fact, the differences of opinion extended well beyond Vietnam. Holsti and Rosenau divided the respondents into two main groups: supporters and critics. Supporters of the war, they found, tended to emphasize international security issues and such concepts as balance of power and containment. Further, they were more inclined than the critics "to regard force and subversion as means that have not lost their utility in contemporary world affairs."[30] As far as the Third World was concerned, supporters were like-minded as well; they wanted to see stable governments that subscribed to pro-American, or at least neutral, foreign policies.

Critics of the war, in contrast, believed that the most important goals of American foreign policy were arms control, international economic stability, and improvement of the standard of living in less developed countries. They were much less concerned than the supporters about the containment of communism and the global balance of power. In fact, the critics were quite skeptical about the utility of force in international relations under any circumstances.

The war in Vietnam had other effects on the American foreign policy process. For example, the war, more than anything else, removed foreign policy decision making from the purview of the Eastern establishment. In this case, the policy process began in Berkeley with the free speech movement and then spread eastward. The next step, protest from college and university faculties against the war in Southeast Asia, was first taken in the Middle West. Thus foreign policy issues began to fall in the domain of domestic politics, with areas far from the eastern seaboard now leading the way.[31] Moreover, as the war dragged on, the public's interest and active participation in the policy-making process increased dramatically. Indeed, before the conflict came to an end, it was clear that foreign policy was no longer the private domain of a select few. On those issues in which the American people clearly had a personal stake, they would make their differences with official policy known in no uncertain terms.

The differences over U.S. foreign policy were considerably more muted in the 1980s than they were in the 1960s and 1970s. In fact, one might reasonably argue that the main pillars of U.S. foreign policy remain largely unchanged and that overall, despite the fractious Vietnam experience, there has been a basic continuity in the main elements of America's diplomacy from President Truman through Bush. Still, there is clear evidence that a fundamental cleavage among members of the political elite persists. This disagreement runs to the very root of postwar strategy and still includes basic interpretations of the Soviet threat. "Since perceptions of the general situation vary so widely, with more than 20 percent of the sample on each end, 'hawk' and 'dove,' the chances for a unified or bipartisan policy are slim indeed."[32] Thus the propositions outlined above, which for two decades prior to Vietnam were regarded "as virtually self-evident truths" about international affairs, are now "among the most contentious points" in discussions of American foreign policy.[33]

This is not to say that no one has tried during the last twenty years to forge a new consensus. In particular, President Richard Nixon and Henry Kissinger, secretary of state under Nixon and Gerald Ford, attempted to develop broad support for détente, a policy based on establishing a more constructive relationship with the Soviet Union. But détente had strong critics, on the right and on the left. The Cold Warriors opined that the Nixon administration was soft on the Soviets and in any case had no business offering incentives (e.g., grain sales, access to American technology) in exchange for Soviet cooperation. Liberals, on the other hand, insisted that if the United States was really interested in a better relationship with the Soviet Union it should not attach threats to promises or interfere abroad unless our national interests were directly at stake. Of course the other reason détente had so little staying power—by the end of the Ford administration the term was actually in disfavor—was the Soviets' failure to respond as the Nixon administration had originally hoped. In particular, the Soviet Union's continued support of "wars of national liberation," and other Third World activities that the U.S. considered disruptive, alienated even some of those in the foreign policy establishment who had previously supported "constructive relations" with the Russians.[34]

But while some would simply complain that the old foreign policy consensus has given way to "paralysis and fragmentation,"[35] there are, as we noted earlier, strains in American foreign policy that remain constant, even over long periods of time. The "don't tread on me" agenda that Ronald Reagan formulated in the early 1980s (following the national humiliation endured as a consequence of Iran's prolonged seizure of American hostages during the administration of Jimmy Carter) may be seen, for example, as an echo of the Monroe Doctrine which, at a much earlier point in American history, proclaimed to the world that the U.S. would not be pushed around.

But if our national interests and priorities remain to a considerable degree stable, the domestic and international environments within which foreign policy is made and implemented have changed irrevocably. At home the policy-making system is far more open now than it was when a mere "handful of former classmates"[36] ran the show. And we are faced abroad with an array of global problems that were not even on the table a generation or two ago, such as terrorism, nuclear proliferation, global warming, and drugs. Moreover, changes in the Soviet Union and East Europe—particularly the abandonment of traditional communism—were so dramatic in the late 1980s and early 1990s that conventional cold war wisdoms that had prevailed for over forty years were, with startling alacrity, hopelessly outdated.

Finally, mention must be made of threats to America's economic interests that in recent years have become increasingly serious. In particular, the countries of Asia are proving to be formidable opponents in the international economic competition that is gradually becoming of paramount importance.

Of course United States foreign policy has been driven in good part by economic interests since the beginning of the Republic. But in the last quarter of the twentieth century the thriving countries of the Pacific rim and the growing interdependence of the national economies of the world have posed new challenges to American presidents. In particular, the increasingly interlocked relationship between the predominate U.S. economy and the economies of other nations has created an international environment in which whatever happens to the U.S. economy inevitably has a ripple effect abroad. To be sure, some have argued that worldwide economic interdependence enhances the prospects for global peace. While the evidence for this claim is mixed, it is in any case true that America is in a position to use its relatively strong economic position to advantage. Resources such as money, technology, energy, and food may all be seen as likely carrots in a global context in which big sticks (military force) have increasingly limited utility.

In short, while we no longer have a consensus on foreign policy, we seem to have replaced it with something more appropriate to late-twentieth-century international politics. Consensus is easy to obtain when the world is easy to explain. Now that the situation is more complicated than it was in the days of the cold war, agreement on all major issues is an elusive, and indeed probably inappropriate, goal. Rather, there are several key foreign policy questions that are quite properly open to honest debate. They include:

- What goals and strategies should govern America's changing relations with the Soviet Union and China?
- How should the demise of communism in Eastern Europe shape U.S. military, economic, and political policy toward the European continent more generally?
- Which arrangements should be established with the other industrial democracies on issues ranging from defense to trade?
- How should the U.S. relate to the less-developed nations so as to respond both to moral imperatives (which would imply generous assis-

tance) and the national interest (which might suggest a more cautious approach)?
- What should the U.S. foreign policy agenda be in a world struggling with rapid change and bedeviled by problems that can be addressed only at the international level, such as AIDS, acid rain, and terrorism?
- Under what circumstances should the United States apply military force to achieve foreign policy objectives?
- How should the United States respond to antidemocratic regimes abroad?[37]

Clearly, any president who would be a world leader faces an enormous task. At home he must master a foreign policy process that has become divided and politicized. And abroad he will inevitably confront problems inherent in finding areas of agreement with military and economic superpowers such as the Soviet Union, China, and Japan; in resisting the often-conflicting demands of restive allies; in promoting political stability and economic modernization in underdeveloped countries; and in addressing the challenges faced by a shrinking planet. At the same time, the executive is not without resources. In fact, as we shall see in the chapters that follow, there is reason to anticipate that presidents disposed to effect change at the international level will, if they play their cards right, realize their ambition.

Notes

1. Donald E. Nuechterlein, *National Interest and the Setting of Priorities* (Boulder, Colo.: Westview, 1978), pp. 4, 5.

2. Julius W. Pratt, *A History of United States Foreign Policy* (Englewood Cliffs, N.J.: Prentice-Hall, 1980), p. 2.

3. Howard Bliss and M. Glen Johnson, *Beyond the Water's Edge: America's Foreign Policies* (New York: Lippincott, 1975), p. 63.

4. For a brief discussion on change and stability in American foreign policy, see Charles W. Kegley, Jr., and Eugene Wittkopf, *American Foreign Policy* (New York: St. Martin's, 1987), pp. 7, 8.

5. John Spanier, *American Foreign Policy Since World War II* (New York: Holt, Rinehart, & Winston, 1985), p. 4.

6. Robert Dallek, *The American Style of Foreign Policy* (New York: Knopf, 1983), p. xvii.

7. George F. Kennan, "Morality and Foreign Policy," *Foreign Affairs* 64, no. 2 (Winter, 1985–86): p. 208.

8. Stanley Hoffmann, *Gulliver's Troubles or the Setting of American Foreign Policy* (New York: McGraw Hill, 1968), pp. 118–25.

9. Bliss and Johnson, p. 90.

10. Arthur Schlesinger, Jr., "Foreign Policy and the American Character," *Foreign Affairs* 62, no. 1 (Fall 1983): p. 2.

11. Ibid., p. 4.

12. Bliss and Johnson, p. 98.

13. Spanier, p. 8.

14. For a discussion of how the American national character impacts on leadership in this country, see Kellerman, *The Political Presidency: Practice of Leadership* (New York: Oxford University Press, 1984), chapters 1 and 3.

15. Quoted in Kellerman, p. 27.

16. David Riesman, Nathan Glazer, and Reuel Denney, *The Lonely Crowd* (New Haven: Yale University Press, 1950). Additional prefaces were written in 1961 and 1964.

17. Christopher Lasch, *The Culture of Narcissism* (New York: Norton, 1979), p. 42.

18. For a short chronology of presidential leadership vis-à-vis the Soviets, see James Schlesinger, "The Eagle and the Bear," *Foreign Affairs* (Summer 1985). For a chronicle of the East-West conflict from a psychological perspective, see Ralph K. White, *Fearful Warriors* (New York: Free Press, 1984).

19. Stephen E. Ambrose, *Rise to Globalism* (New York: Penquin, 1984), pp. 165 ff.

20. Hans Morganthau, "The American Tradition in Foreign Policy," in *Foreign Policy in World Politics,* ed. Roy C. Macridis (Englewood Cliffs, N.J.: Prentice-Hall, 1967), pp. 246–69. The following paragraphs are based on Morganthau's essay.

21. Morganthau, p. 249.

22. Ibid.

23. John Lewis Gaddis, *Strategies of Containment* (New York: Oxford University Press, 1982).

24. Stanley Hoffmann, *Primacy or World Order: American Foreign Policy Since the Cold War* (New York: McGraw Hill, 1978), p. 6. The following paragraphs are based on chapter 1 of Hoffmann's book.

25. Ibid., p. 9.

26. Ibid., p. 21.

27. This material is from Ole R. Holsti and James M. Rosenau, *American Leadership in World Affairs: Vietnam and the Breakdown of Consensus* (Boston: Allen & Unwin, 1984), pp. 218–20.

28. See, for example, Hoffman, *Primacy or World Order,* pp. 22 ff; and I. M. Destler, Leslie H. Gelb, and Anthony Lake, *Our Own Worst Enemy: The Unmaking of American Foreign Policy* (New York: Simon & Schuster, 1984), p. 19; and Holsti and Rosenau, passim.

29. Destler et al., p. 19.

30. Holsti and Rosenau, p. 103.

31. Robert Pranger, "Participatory Politics and Foreign Policy Coherence" (Paper prepared for the American Enterprise Institute, 1986), p. 3.

32. Richard Herrmann, "The Power of Perceptions in Foreign-Policy Decision Making: Do Views of the Soviet Union Determine the Policy Choices of American Leaders?" *American Journal of Political Science* 30, no. 4 (November 1986): p. 871.

33. Holsti and Rosenau, p. 249.

34. Ibid.

35. Howard J. Wiarda, "The Paralysis of Policy: Current Dilemmas of U.S. Foreign Policy-Making" (Paper prepared for the American Enterprise Institute, 1985), p. 11.

36. Pranger, "Participitory Politics," p. 6.

37. These questions are based in part on Holsti and Rosenau, pp. 255 ff. For an extended discussion of the debate on American foreign policy at the beginning of the 1980s, see Robert W. Tucker, "The Purposes of American Power," *Foreign Affairs* 59, no. 2 (Winter 1980–81): pp. 241–74.

3

The President's Role in the Foreign Policy Process

"I make American foreign policy," proclaimed Harry Truman in the Oval Office one day, holding forth in typically blunt fashion to a visiting group of Jewish War Veterans.[1] But while he personally was responsible for many of the major foreign policy decisions made during his presidency, his declaration nevertheless is misleading. For although Truman was able to leave a substantial mark on world politics, few executives in American history have been as influential. In fact, no less an authority then James Madison was of the opinion that by dint of its power to declare war—and, he might have added, to appropriate funds—it was Congress that shaped American foreign policy, with the president more or less limited to carrying out what the legislature had decided.[2]

The truth, of course, lies somewhere in between the views of Truman and Madison. As our recent history testifies, while presidents generally dominate the foreign policy process, there are nevertheless moments in time when power shifts away from the White House to Capitol Hill. For example, during the period immediately after World War II (1945–1955), the president and Congress actively cooperated on important foreign policy initiatives such as the United Nations, the Marshall Plan, and the North Atlantic Treaty Alliance (NATO). While Truman and, later, Eisenhower dominated the process, members of the House and Senate were nevertheless regularly involved, and there was comprehensive consideration by Congress of all the key measures. Later on, during the period 1955–1965, presidential influence over foreign affairs expanded significantly, with little apparent objection from Congress. The executive's obvious resources—for example, a large foreign policy bureaucracy to help him, and superior information and expertise—seemed, during the confrontations and crises of the cold war, to better equip him to protect America from foreign threat. In fact, during this time, Congress passed resolutions that gave the president "a virtually unilateral right to use American troops almost anywhere in the world, if he deemed such action to be wise and in the national interest."[3] But by the end of Lyndon Johnson's tenure in the White House, and continuing through Nixon's debacle with Watergate, the pendulum swumg the other way. For at least the next twelve years, until Ronald Reagan took office, the executive lost power to Congress. It is how the two branches of government vie with each other for the power to make American foreign policy that is the next subject of discussion.

THE EXECUTIVE VERSUS THE LEGISLATURE

Because the Constitution is vague on several important issues pertaining to foreign policy, there has been a continuing debate about where the power to make such policy actually lies. Few constitutional provisions deal with foreign affairs—which means that a definitive interpretation of the framers' intent is often impossible. As Richard Pious pointed out, this power vacuum has, over the years, enabled presidents to claim "the silences of the Constitution." They found a general "power to conduct foreign relations" for the nation and then assumed that whatever was not expressly assigned to the legislature could be exercised by the executive.[4]

Still, presidential license notwithstanding, the framers of the Constitution clearly intended that *virtually no international business should be conducted by the president alone.*[5] While the Constitution does expressly assign some specific powers to the president, each of these contains significant qualifications. Article II, section 2, provides that the chief executive shall have the power to make treaties, but only "provided two-thirds of the Senators present concur." Similarly, the president is awarded the title, "Commander in Chief of the Army and Navy of the United States," but it is Congress that has the right both to declare war and "raise and support armies."

The framers' belief that the power to make foreign policy should be shared by the legislative and executive branches (the judicial branch is by and large outside the foreign policy process) is evident in *The Federalist Papers.* John Jay wrote that the president *and* senators will "always be of the number of those who best understand our national interests . . . , who are best able to promote those interests, and whose reputation for integrity inspires and merits confidence. With such men the power of making treaties may be safely lodged."[6] In the same vein, Alexander Hamilton—who had initially argued for a virtual monarchy—now claimed that while in general the executive is the "most fit agent" to conduct foreign negotiations, treaties "plead strongly for the participation of the whole or a portion of the legislative body in the office of making them."[7]

Naturally, there are political implications to these constitutional constraints. Because the president's formal authority is circumscribed and because he can rarely count on the automatic support of a majority of both houses of Congress, he will typically have to exercise power or influence to get what he wants when he wants it. For example, the requirement that fully two-thirds of the Senate give its advice and consent on treaties generally obliges the president to lobby vigorously on behalf of a pact he particularly wants ratified.

Four general characterisics of the Constitution thus determine the conduct of American foreign policy:

1. the lack of specificity in assigning functions to the different agencies of government
2. the separation of powers, which allows the president and Congress to pursue, within limits, separate agendas
3. the system of checks and balances, which, also within limits, makes it

    possible for one branch of government to prevent another from pursuing its policies
4. the requirement that, under certain conditions, foreign policy can be executed only through the concerted action of both the executive and legislative branches.[8]

This is not to say that active, involved presidents—that is, those who really want to direct foreign policy without interference from Congress—have not found ways to circumvent the Constitution. As Hans Morganthau put it: "The president has a natural eminence in the conduct of foreign affairs from which constitutional arrangements and political practices can detract, but which they cannot obliterate."[9] For example, presidents who wish to disregard formal treaty procedures can employ "executive agreements." (The right to sign executive agreements has been validated by the Supreme Court, which has compared them to treaties.) Similarly, over the years executives have found ways of circumventing the congressional power to declare war. In fact, in only five of the eleven major conflicts in which the United States has been involved have there been formal declarations of war. And in each of these five cases Congress declared war only in response to the president's acts or recommendations.[10] (It should be noted, however, that the tendency of a government to avoid formal declarations of war is not peculiar to the U.S.)

One of the most notorious examples of evasion in this regard is also the most recent. The Gulf of Tonkin Resolution, passed by Congress in 1964 with only two dissenting votes, was used by President Lyndon Johnson to justify sending ground troops to South Vietnam and to order bombing attacks on North Vietnam. To be sure, the language of the resolution was sweeping, stating that Congress supported the president's right to "take all necessary measures to repel any armed attack" against United States forces and to "prevent further aggression." Nevertheless, as the war escalated, congressional critics protested that the president had exceeded the letter of the resolution and violated its spirit. Finally, in 1973, Congress retaliated by passing the War Powers Resolution, the legislature's most significant attempt to end the pattern of executive dominance in foreign policy that had existed since the end of the Second World War and which had even been expanded on in the decade before Vietnam.

It was hardly surprising that congressional activity in foreign affairs picked up in the wake of the war in Southeast Asia. For it was nothing so much as America's miserable experience in the jungles of Vietnam that persuaded many of its most concerned citizens that the traditional arguments in favor of presidential supremacy in foreign policy were overrated. These arguments included:

1. *unity*—the proposition that it would be easier for a single individual to manage the policy process than the hundreds of members of Congress
2. *secrecy*—the idea that the White House would also be better equipped to handle the covert aspects of foreign policy
3. *information and expertise*—resources considered to be more available to the executive than to the legislature
4. *decision and dispatch*—the hypothesis that the formulation and con-

duct of foreign policy would be executed more efficiently under White House, rather than congressional, control.

However, unity seemed illusory in the 1970s, a time when various departments, agencies, and individuals in the executive branch competed with each other for power and influence. The idea of secrecy was similarly absurd at a moment when the well-placed Washington leak was commonplace. As for superior information and expertise, the fact that the media now released more accurate information about the war in Indochina than did the government gave lie to the former, while the debacle of the Vietnam experience itself seemed to debunk the latter. Finally, with regard to decision and dispatch, the substance of American foreign policy suggested that perhaps there was more of a need for prudence than haste. Many Americans were thus left with little more than the memory of their previously held belief that the president was more suited to conduct America's foreign affairs than the Congress.[11]

Since Vietnam, Capitol Hill has further expanded its influence over foreign policy in the following ways:

- Congress has solidified its involvement in foreign affairs by expanding its staff and developing its own foreign affairs bureaucracy. This bureaucracy, while insignificant in comparison with its analogue in the executive branch, nevertheless constitutes an important resource.
- Congress has developed several new tactics. For example, the legislature's authority to control appropriations has been applied more often to limit or prohibit U.S. aid to other countries.
- Congress has demanded, and received, regular access to intelligence information. Whereas once the executive branch routinely withheld information from legislators on grounds that it was classified, today Congress insists on greater accommodation.
- The decline of the seniority system in Congress, and of party discipline, has made it easier for legislators to have an independent voice on foreign policy issues. No longer necessarily subservient to their political elders, members of Congress have more leeway to say what they want.
- Opposition to the Vietnam War taught legislators that at least some foreign policy initiatives were "magnets for media attention and popular recognition."
- Finally, there has been a strong upsurge in travel abroad, making "instant experts" out of legislators and, in a few cases, even giving them a taste for negotiating directly with foreign leaders.[12]

The most striking recent example of congressional assertiveness in the foreign policy realm occurred late in the Reagan administration. In November 1986, it was revealed that in the hope of securing the release of several American hostages, the National Security Council had secretly arranged to sell arms to Iran and then, also secretly and in violation of at least the spirit of American law, diverted profits from these sales to rebel (Contra) forces in Nicaragua. Congress was outraged. Within weeks the House and Senate were each conducting hearings in which the president's formulation and conduct of foreign policy were called to account.

The recent tendency toward legislative activism in the foreign policy field shows no signs of abating. None of the internal changes in Congress are likely to be reversed; moreover, the external pressures from, for example, interest groups and self-interested foreign governments further encourage members of Congress to be assertive. Thus the legislature will continue to undertake independent initiatives, to expand its role in the treaty-making process, and to keep a watchful eye on the range of our overseas commitments.[13]

Of course, whatever the balance of power between the president and Congress, there will always be those who root for one or the other to become more assertive. In a piece written for *Foreign Affairs* in 1972, in the heat of the domestic debate over Vietnam, Arthur Schlesinger, Jr., charged that both Lyndon Johnson and Richard Nixon had abused their power in the realm of foreign affairs: "If President Johnson construed the high perogative more in the eighteenth century style of the British King than of the executive envisaged by the Constitution, his successor carried the inflation of presidential author-ity even further. . . . President Nixon indulged in presidential war-making [expanding the war in Southeast Asia into Cambodia] beyond a point that even his boldest predecessors could have dreamed of."[14] Decrying Congress' apparent impotence, Schlesinger urged the legislature to vigorously reclaim what he considered its lost authority.

Conversely, Stanley Hoffmann focused on ways in which Congress has impeded the president over the years, arguing that it delayed processes that should have been swift and smooth; that its "inherent institutional conserva-tism" resulted in a "deadening of policy"; and that Congress had on occasion been downright destructive, particularly in the realm of foreign aid, either by cutting or rejecting requests for aid programs or by refusing to allocate for-eign aid to countries found guilty of "misbehaving."[15] Ironically, however, it was a senator who made the strongest case on behalf of presidential suprem-acy in foreign affairs. John Tower, a senator from Texas for over two decades, regretted that in the struggle for control over American foreign policy that took place in the 1970s, Congress won.

> . . . The balance between the Congress and the President has swung dangerously to the legislative side with unfavorable consequences for American foreign policy. If the balance is not soon restored, American foreign policy will be unable to meet the critical challenges of the 1980s. . . . It is my sincere hope that Congress will reexamine its role in the conduct of foreign policy and repeal or amend, as necessary, the legislation of the 1970s.[16]

What is clear is that, on paper, good arguments can be made for and against a greater congressional role in foreign affairs. More to the point, however, is the question of whether, even *if* one were persuaded that greater legislative participation in foreign policy were a good thing, Congress is up to the task. Indeed, one might reasonably argue that in the long run Congress is neither structured nor equipped to conduct America's foreign affairs. As a collective it is too large and unorganized; and as far as individual legislators are concerned, to be interested in foreign—as opposed to domestic—politics has not generally proved to be politically advantageous. Concern for foreign policy often goes unappreciated back home, which means, in turn, that members of Congress generally have little incentive to take a strong interest in international relations. As one member of the Senate Foreign Relations Committee commented: "It's a political liability. . . . You have no constituency. In my reelection campaign last fall, the main thing they used against me was that because of my interest in foreign relations, I was more interested in what happened to the people of Abyssinia and Afganistan than in what happened to the good people of my state."[17]

So far, in any case, few members of Congress have addressed the necessary implications of their demand for a position of equal partnership with the White House in foreign affairs. "Congress has supplied little evidence to show that it is prepared to adapt its own organizational structure and internal procedures to the demands of the active foreign policy role."[18]

Therefore, in spite of some significant constitutional constraints on the executive's freedom to act; in spite of a legislature that over two hundred years of American history has repeatedly tried, sometimes successfully, to wrest control over foreign policy from the executive; and in spite of a public that has frequently been highly critical; the president is dominant in the foreign policy realm. As Harold Laski stated: "The leadership provided by the president in foreign affairs is, without any doubt, the pivotal influence in framing foreign policy. Whatever part the constitution may assign to the legislative agency, the spirit of the presidential purpose, especially in a situation of gravity, is the overwhelming factor in forming the direction and the decision."[19] The chief executive is thus primarily responsible for undertaking an array of activity in the foreign policy and national security realms that includes: priority setting and program design, legislative and political coalition building, program implementation and evaluation, governmental oversight, and, if necessary, crisis management.[20]

PRESIDENTIAL DOMINANCE

The fact that a strong foreign affairs presidency has evolved over time is no accident. The main reasons for this development are: the president's preeminent position in the political system; the powers that have accrued in this century to the executive office; the president's political, informational, and bureaucratic resources; and the nature of the American foreign policy system in the late twentieth century.

Preeminent Position. The president is the only member of the federal government who is chosen in a nationwide election. All other federal officials are either appointed, elected by a regional or state constituency, or are members of the civil service. He is, therefore, the only individual who can legitimately claim the right to "speak" for the nation. We look to him to articulate the national purpose and to further the national interest. One might even argue that the president's leadership role is greater in the foreign policy realm than in the domestic one, for we typically lend at least passive support to the president on matters pertaining to our relations with other states. For example, during the late 1980s, a time of dramatic change in the Soviet Union and the countries of East Europe, Americans were quite content to let the White

House, first under Ronald Reagan and then under George Bush, shape the American response to what was, in effect, an entirely new international environment. Moreover, in times of international crisis, the president inevitably is the linchpin of our foreign operations.

Accrued Powers.   We alluded earlier to some of the executive's extraconstitutional, or accrued, powers. Along with his constitutional powers, they create an impressive arsenal of resources for leadership in foreign policy. Consider the following:

- *Executive power* has been construed as a writ to do almost anything in the name of national security. As Larry Berman points out: "As holder of the executive power a president can go beyond his enumerated powers and take whatever steps are necessary to preserve the country's security, even if his actions might be unconstitutional."[21]
- *Emergency powers* further expand the president's freedom to act. In general, emergency powers are invoked when presidents feel they can argue that the nation's survival requires nothing less than strong, unilateral, presidential action.
- *Executive agreements* allow direct negotiations with other countries. For example, executive agreements have allowed presidents to conclude arms deals with Israel and to provide military support to Saigon during the Vietnam War.
- *Executive privilege* is the implied or inherent (depending on which president you believe) power to withhold information on the basis of the claim that to release such information would affect either the national security or the president's ability to discharge his official duties.[22]

The executive thus claims the right to be the sole organ of communication with other nations and to control the activities and communications of all who officially represent the United States. He proposes formal alliances with other nations and, if the occasion demands, negotiates treaties without the prior advice of the Senate. Moreover, if the Senate refuses to ratify a treaty the president wants, he can resort to executive agreements. Indeed, the executive has some leeway to make commitments without formalizing them either as treaties or as executive agreements.

Political, Informational, and Bureaucratic Resources.   The president's political resources also include certain traditions, for example the pattern of leaving it to the executive to take the initiative on matters of foreign policy. To be sure, Congress and the public are ahead of the president on many issues. It was public opinion and subsequent congressional pressure, for instance, that compelled President Reagan to apply limited sanctions to South Africa, thereby expressing, at least in a modest way, the American people's disapproval of apartheid. Nevertheless, most specific foreign policy initiatives emanate from the White House, and most of the time the legislature is limited to meeting commitments already made by the executive.[23]

About the president's information base we need say little save that it is greater than anyone else's. As indicated above, his control of secret materials is based partly on the executive's power to classify documents deemed vital to the national security and partly on executive privilege, which can be invoked to withhold information from Congress and/or the judiciary. However, as recent history attests, a danger is posed by this privilege: to conceal information that would in some way embarrass them, some administrations have extended the claim to secrecy well beyond what more objective observers agreed was legitimate.

Yet another presidential resource is the foreign policy bureaucracies—for example, the Departments of State and Defense, the National Security Council (NSC), and the Central Intelligence Agency (CIA)—located in the executive branch under the chief executive's jurisdiction. To be sure, the bureaucrats who staff them are no easier to control than any other bureaucrats. Indeed, sometimes they engage in activities the chief executive never even knows about. Nevertheless, the president is their superior and as such he is generally in the best position both to draw on their expertise and skills and to exert influence over what they do. In fact, presidents who have a special interest in foreign affairs often infringe on their own appointees, preferring, for example, to serve as their own secretary of state. This can lead to a gap between how professional policymakers, especially those in the State Department, would like to perform and what they can actually do. "The secretary of state and the top officials in the department hope to control the conduct of diplomacy, with the secretary serving as 'chief negotiator' for the government. . . . [But] the top officials in State may not have much influence in negotiations, policy formulation, or even the management of crucial aspects of foreign relations."[24]

The question of who ultimately shapes and controls American foreign policy inevitably raises the issue of competition between the State Department and the NSC. The NSC was created after the Second World War for the purpose of advising the president on foreign policy. Unlike the Department of State, the NSC is not an independent arm of the government but a major component of what has grown into a highly influential in-house presidential advisory system. Members of the NSC—like all White House staff—are hired and fired by the president at his will and whim. Cabinet secretaries, in contrast, need to be approved by Congress, which means that these choices must sometimes be made according to political expediency and compromise and that the Cabinet is much more accountable to Congress than are members of the president's personal staff.

Because of his proximity to the president, the head of the NSC staff—the assistant for national security affairs—has become increasingly powerful over the years. In fact, there has been recurring friction in recent administrations between the national security assistant and the traditional authority figure in this area, the secretary of state. The national security assistant was at the apex of power during the early Nixon years when Henry Kissinger held the post. (Kissinger was subsequently named secretary of state.) But by the time of the Carter administration, the balance of power was restored and, as a consequence, turf battles resumed: Secretary of State Cyrus R. Vance and National Security Adviser Zbigniew Brzezinski clashed repeatedly over American policy on the Soviet Union and on other issues as well. Similarly, President Reagan's overhaul of the national security apparatus after the Iran-Contra affair did not resolve the strong and long-standing differences between the State Department and the more than sixty professionals who staff the NSC.

Reagan's secretary of state, George P. Shultz, was known to be forever complaining that the NSC was encroaching on his turf.[25]

Whatever the conflicts between the two foreign policy bureaucracies and the men who headed them, modern presidents have clearly liked having a foreign policy advisory system close at hand. Executives who take a special interest in international relations seem particularly inclined to draw on the National Security Council and even to grant greater access to the national security assistant than to the secretary of state. For better or worse, the NSC is now entrenched. It provides the president with information and advice, and once a decision on policy is made, it is frequently the national security assistant who is charged with implementing it.

The Nature of the American Foreign Policy System in the Late Twentieth Century.   Several changes have taken place in our foreign policy system over the last several decades, most of which further strengthen the president's hand in foreign affairs. For example, during the past forty years America has been, for the first time in its history, a major world power. As its strength and influence grew, so did the tendency to centralize the foreign policy process. It became increasingly clear that if the U.S. was to speak to the community of nations with one voice, that voice would have to be the president's.

To equip the executive to cope with the new array of foreign policy demands, in 1947 Congress approved the National Security Act. The act led to the establishment not only of a National Security Council but also of the Department of Defense and the Central Intelligence Agency. Moreover, it established the Joint Chiefs of Staff, whose members served along with the secretary of defense as key advisers to the president in national security affairs. Thus the president had powerful new weapons in his bureaucratic arsenal: organizations and individuals charged with assisting him in the formulation and conduct of foreign policy.[26]

Another contributor to a strong presidential role was the perception of the Soviet communist threat. As we have seen, since the end of the Second World War until only recently, the United States was highly wary of the Soviet Union and what it perceived to be that country's expansionist tendencies. The belief that communism was a clear and present danger was used to justify virtually every major foreign policy action in the postwar period and also the immense growth of the defense establishment. Moreover, where appropriations were required to combat communism, guidelines set by Congress were really only general directives given to the president. Specific implementation of policies was placed within the discretionary boundaries of executives who parlayed the Soviet threat into a stronger foreign policy role for themselves.

Presidential authority in foreign affairs has also been strengthened by the extension of foreign policy to new areas. The foreign policy realm is simply larger now than it used to be. In addition to traditional areas of concern, today it incorporates activities such as economic assistance, intelligence gathering, propaganda making, and scientific and cultural exchanges. The need to "pull together all of these disparate and often competing strands of foreign policy" further reinforced presidential primacy in international relations.[27]

Finally, the foreign affairs presidency is enhanced by the national security perspective, which in the last decade of the twentieth century has come to include economic and environmental as well as military interests. The single "natural security" outlook on the position of the United States in the international environment supported the already existing tendency to put the executive in charge of all aspects of our foreign relations. In particular, this fusion has contributed to the president's increased involvement in military affairs.

> The intimate involvement of the President, not only in determining the broad purposes for which military force is to be used but also in deciding tactical means by which those purposes are to be achieved, appears to have had a cumulative effect. More extensive involvement by the President has further increased the political component of the use of contemplated use of military force. Nearly every characteristic of nuclear weaponry . . . has been subjected to close presidential scrutiny, thereby entering the domain of presidential politics.[28]

To the question of around whom the United States government tries to build a coherent foreign policy, there is thus but one answer: the president. As I. M. Destler has observed, Congress can act as a restraint on the president, or it can be the source of useful albeit sporadic initiatives. But, in general, congressional influence is limited to constraining, modifying, or supplementing presidential and executive branch aims and actions, rather than imposing a coherence of its own. "Only the President has sufficient legal authority, prestige, and other bargaining advantages—plus sufficient motivation—for carrying out coherent and purposive policy."[29] We may conclude, then, that because the president is the preeminent player in the American political system; because he has a formidable array of constitutional and accrued powers; because he alone has access to a vast arsenal of political, informational, and bureaucratic resources; and because the nature of the foreign policy system at this time further strengthens his already dominant role; he will continue to be, for the indefinite future, "the overwhelming factor in forming the direction and the decision" of America's interest in world affairs.

THE PRESIDENT'S CONSTITUENTS

The president's preeminent role in foreign affairs raises the question of just how easy in actuality that role makes his leadership task. The fact is that for all his authority and power, in order to successfully direct the formulation and conduct of foreign policy, there are three key constituencies whose support the president must have: Congress, the foreign policy bureaucracies, and the American people. In order to reach each of these constituencies, the executive is increasingly dependent on the mass media. Therefore, this section will begin with a brief reflection on how the media and the president relate. Then we will turn to each of the three constituencies.

In the last three decades, the mass media has become an aggressive and independent player in both domestic and foreign politics. Indeed, since Vietnam, and later Watergate, American journalists have assumed something of an adversarial role toward their government. As a consequence, every president since Kennedy—who, occasional tiffs with journalists notwithstanding, was in fact unusually skilled at handling the press—has perceived himself as victimized by the media. Johnson felt hounded over Vietnam; Nixon was ultimately brought down by the legwork of two investigative reporters for the

Washington Post; Carter suffered through "a merciless accounting of his administration's meandering and sometimes contradictory policy path"; and while Reagan enjoyed a prolonged press honeymoon, after a time he too became an unwilling object of its unrelenting scrutiny, stung in particular by media speculation that he lacked a grasp of the substance of policy.[30]

The sense of persecution that Johnson particularly experienced was a product primarily of the electronic media. By the time he was in the White House, the president had become the single most important television story on a continuing basis. No matter how pedestrian his day had been, the chief executive was seen and heard on the nightly news with relentless regularity.[31] But, initially at least, Johnson did not understand the change that technology had wrought on the business of government. It took the war in Vietnam to drive home the point: it was no longer possible to keep the consequences of presidential policy from the public.

Changes in the print industry further accelerated the demystification of the president. Newspapers and magazines now had to compete for attention not only with each other but also with television and radio. As a result, sensationalism, rather than subtle discussions of public policy, became the order of the day. To boost ratings in TV or newspapers, a journalist had to discover the lurid or catch the president committing a gaffe—which made the executive's leadership task that much more difficult.

To be sure, in the contest of wills between the president and the press, the former retained some significant advantages. And once the special power of the electronic media became clear, presidents began to harness it to their benefit. Today no executive decision is made without gauging the likely media response; no information is disseminated from the White House without considering how the media will perform as messenger; and no presidential activity is scheduled without attending to the how, when, and where of media coverage.

Of course, not all presidents have been equally skilled as media performers. Television was not especially kind to Johnson, Nixon, Ford, and Carter, each of whom had their credibility lessened by the mere fact of poor performances. Kennedy and Reagan, on the other hand, were television naturals, and both exploited the medium to their political advantage.

As media strategist David Garth has observed: "Most people believe what they see in the unpaid media." It is for this reason that even in the more distant realm of foreign affairs, media coverage can, and has, influenced public opinion—sometimes in directions contrary to official policy.[32] If the media had not labored so hard to use new technology to bring the Vietnam War into American living rooms, would our involvement in Southeast Asia have ended when it did? If Gorbachev were not so telegenic, would he have persuaded so many Americans of his good intentions, thereby hastening the moderation of the U.S. government's traditional anti-Soviet position?

While the virtues of a presidency that is inextricably involved with the mass media are debatable at best—carefully staged media events being a poor substitute for real communication between the president and the people—executives who would be world leaders must learn to use this increasingly sophisticated technology to create desired impressions, to convey information, and to influence public opinion in ways deemed advantageous. As the twentieth century draws to a close, presidents can get and keep the attention of individuals and groups at home *and* abroad only through news organizations. Their capacity to harness them for their own benefit is therefore of enormous consequence.

Congress.   We have already discussed the fact that Congress is often engaged in a conflictual rather than cooperative relationship with the president on matters of foreign policy. Suffice it to reiterate at this point that in order to obtain congressional approval for White House policies that are in any way controversial, the president will have to lobby individual members of the House and Senate. Since even legislators from the president's own party can no longer automatically be counted as followers, it is politicking that will ultimately determine the executive's ability to lead Congress in foreign affairs.

Foreign Policy Bureaucracies.   The primary foreign policy bureaucracies are located in the executive branch and, as such, are under the president's jurisdiction. It would seem, therefore, that getting bureaucrats to follow the White House lead would be easy enough. But in this case, appearance deceives, for bureaucrats tend to resist rather than welcome direction and change. Moreover, the foreign policy bureaucracies are large and complex, which means that they are characterized by an elaborate division of labor and by the delegation of authority. This results in semiautonomous subunits, blurred jurisdictional boundaries, and conflicts that arise from the different values, experiences, and objectives associated with each of the different agencies.[33]

The president who would influence the foreign policy process thus has to take the dynamics of bureaucratic politics into account. Bureaucratic politics is the process by which the people within different agencies bargain with one another on complex policy questions. As I. M. Destler points out, this kind of negotiation is the inevitable result of two basic conditions: "One is that no single official possesses either the power, or the wisdom, or the time to decide all important executive branch policy issues himself. The second is that officials who have influence inevitably differ in how they would like these issues to be resolved."[34]

In fact, these differences, and the conflicts they inevitably generate, constitute perhaps the single most important aspect of bureaucratic politics in foreign policy. For what it means in practice is that even those presidents who are relatively successful in persuading others to go along can rarely be sure that everyone who needs to be is in line.

As Theodore Sorensen remembered of John Kennedy: "I can recall more than one occasion when it was necessary for the president to convince his own appointees before they would undertake to convince the Congress, the Soviets, or some other party."[35] Of course, there is an irony here: as more power has accrued to the executive branch over time, the president's capacity to make foreign policy has been complicated by the growing bureaucracy within the executive branch.

As indicated earlier, the most vivid examples of problems associated with foreign policy bureaucracies are provided by the State Department and the NSC. The State Department is large and complex and has had primary responsibility for conducting American foreign policy for two centuries. Its over three thousand Foreign Service officers represent the U.S. overseas, conduct negotiations with other governments, and analyze and report on events in particular countries. The NSC, on the other hand, is small, having been originally designed to serve only as a senior advisory forum. However, the NSC gradually became the president's link to the State Department and an alternative to it, at least on certain issues deemed especially important.[36] Taken together, then, the State Department and NSC have to be managed in terms of their size and complexity, the friction that recurs between them, and the issue of who has the authority to act in given situations.

Finally, to complete the picture of foreign policy bureaucracies that even the most competent president must struggle to control, we should note once more that there are other agencies that also play significant roles in the foreign policy process. The Departments of Defense and Treasury, the CIA, the Agency for International Development, and the United States Information Agency are further examples of organizations that have their own particular perspectives and priorities and that also participate in the making of American foreign policy.

The CIA is a particularly good example of an organization that has enjoyed a relatively high degree of autonomy—even from the White House— while at the same time playing an important foreign policy role. Ostensibly the agency is responsible for processing information gathered by technological collection systems; for carrying out covert operations designed to meet America's foreign policy objectives; and for assembling and analyzing political, economic, and military intelligence from *open* (that is, readily available) sources. By the late 1970s, it became clear that some CIA operations were actually at odds with official government policy. Thus presidents found themselves in a dilemma: effective intelligence gathering demanded secrecy. Secrecy, however, encourages institutional autonomy—which is not in the executive's interest. Yet, inhibitions on autonomy tend to violate secrecy and thereby reduce the agency's effectiveness.[37] The upshot of all this is a situation that can best be described as twisted. Sometimes it is the president who, in collusion with the CIA, maintains secrecy. In other words, the CIA and the president know something about which the Congress and public are kept in the dark. However, on other occasions the CIA alone has the secret knowledge, while the Congress, the public, and even the president remain ignorant.

Just as organizations have their own particular identities and interests, so do the people who staff them. Generally speaking, individuals in foreign policy agencies fall into two separate categories: career officials who maintain a long affiliation with government and typically have their own policies to promote and their own network of contacts, and "in and outers," political executives in Washington for only a limited time. Career officials are most heavily influenced by long-range professional objectives, which may or may not coincide with the president's agenda and which, in their case, is typically synonomous with the quest for promotion. Their ambition for professional advancement almost invariably leads career officials to support the organizations of which they are members, since they know that how they are judged by their superiors will depend in large measure on being viewed as furthering the interests of their agencies in particular.[38] In and outers, on the other hand, members of the professional foreign policy elite who are in government for only a fraction of their careers, have a different perspective. In general, they share the executive's perspective, and in general they also have a strong interest in seeing rapid results. It is up to the president, then, to recognize these two different types of foreign policy bureaucrats and to exercise leadership in ways that are responsive to the needs of each.

American People.   Public opinion on foreign policy issues does not ordinarily have a strong impact on the conduct of America's international relations. Citizens tend to go along with the president, even though the polling data suggests that the public's foreign policy goals are often different from those of the foreign policy establishment. For instance, while ordinary citizens profess to be most interested in protecting American jobs and maintaining the value of the dollar, the establishment's two top priorities are worldwide arms control and defending our allies.[39] Moreover, public opinion sometimes seems contradictory. With regard to Central America, for example, 80 percent of the American people want no more "second Cubas," no more Marxist-Leninist regimes close to home. But that same number also want no foreign aid, no covert actions by the CIA, and no commitment of American troops on foreign soil. Some would then ask: "How are we supposed to achieve the goals desired—no second Cubas—if none of the instruments (foreign aid, CIA involvement, military intervention) are permissible?"[40]

It does not follow, however, that public opinion plays no role at all in the foreign policy process.[41] In fact, public opinion matters in several ways: First, the public mood and its broad orientation toward world politics are an essential part of the climate within which foreign policy decision making takes place. As Herbert Kelman puts it: "Decision-makers are likely to be influenced by widespread sentiments within the population that may favor hostility or friendliness toward certain other nations, involvement in or withdrawal from international affairs, militancy or conciliation in response to external pressures, and expansionism or cooperation in the pursuit of national goals."[42] Similarly, Stanley Hoffmann believes that while public pressure on foreign policy issues is usually only indirect, there is, nevertheless, a kind of "ambiance" that affects the president in this area: "a vague, diffuse state of mind" that conditions the executive to respond in certain ways.[43]

The public also affects the American foreign policy process when opinion on a particular issue is strong. Some analysts consider increased public concern over foreign policy to be triggered primarily by negative sentiments. Hoffmann argues that the American public becomes mobilized on a foreign policy issue either when the United States had experienced "a traumatic defeat," such as after the Tet offensive in Vietnam, or when we are engaged in a situation in which there is an unsettling contrast between the effort and the results.[44] When over two hundred American marines were killed in a terrorist attack on their barracks in Lebanon in 1983, the cost was deemed too high relative to the perceived benefit. As a consequence, the Reagan administration withdrew as a player of consequence in the Middle East, more or less for the duration.

High motivation also fuels the activities of particular interest groups who seek to influence the course of American foreign policy. For instance, the American-Israel Public Affairs Committee (AIPAC), a pro-Israel interest group supported primarily by American Jews, has been able to make its voice heard in Washington on a range of issues affecting U.S. policy in the Middle

East. AIPAC has, for example, successfully lobbied the government to generously grant arms requests made by Israel, while, more often than not, turning a deaf ear to similar requests made by Arab states. This is not to imply that without AIPAC U.S. policy would have tilted toward the Arabs. In fact, America has many security, economic, and geopolitical reasons for its strong alliance with Israel. Moreover, the data do not support the notion that pro-Israel lobbyists are capable of imposing electoral sanctions on public officials who do not see things their way. Rather, it is to say that AIPAC is but one of a number of foreign policy interests groups that have proliferated in recent years and that have had some influence on the U.S. government's decision process.[45]

Large institutions in the private sector have also had an impact on the conduct of America's foreign affairs. In particular, multinational corporations, and the closely related private international financial institutions, have furthered their interests abroad. Indeed, both now possess a kind of autonomy that is sometimes exercised at the expense of a coherent U.S. foreign policy.[46]

Finally the American public is inclined to demand a voice when it has a clear basis for making a judgment—for instance, when it receives new information.[47] The astonishing 21 percent drop in President Reagan's approval rating in the wake of disclosures that his administration had secretly sold arms to Iran to raise money for the Contra rebels in Nicaragua was only the most recent evidence of a strong public reaction to presidential conduct in foreign policy.

It is fair to conclude, then, that the influence relationship between the president and the public on matters pertaining to foreign policy flows two ways.[48] Lyndon Johnson's ultimate debacle in Vietnam (chronicled in detail in chapter 6) is only the most striking example of presidential impotence in foreign policy in the face of militant public protest. This brings us back full circle to the point made at the start of this section: Despite the president's arsenal of resources and pivotal role, leadership in the foreign policy realm can be difficult. Moreover, the considerable costs of failing to persuade key constituents have been apparent in every administration from Kennedy to Reagan.

TURNING CONSTITUENTS INTO FOLLOWERS

Given the legal and political constraints on presidential leadership in foreign policy, there is clearly a premium on the president's political skills. In other words, his capacity to conduct American foreign policy will depend, in good part, on whether or not he is a skilled politician.

For the purposes of this discussion, we can say that in order to lead in the foreign policy domain, the president has resources at his disposal that fall into two categories: personal and political. His personal resources are quite simply those dimensions of personality that make him, in particular, will suited to the task of leadership in America. Presidents who would be successful leaders must have both a strong need for power (or influence) and the social skills necessary to see that power realized. For in order to exercise leadership in a political culture such as ours, one that has a proclivity to attitudes that can best be described as antiauthoritarian, leadership must be attempted. And to make this attempt in the first place, the would-be leader must be sufficiently motivated to invest assets such as time, energy, and prestige. Further, since presidents are unable to *command* key players such as legislators to follow their lead, they must be willing and able to engage in some of the interpersonal politicking that is the *sine qua non* of leadership in America. Thus the extraverted president will have an edge over the introverted one. By expending more energy on social activity and by being a more facile interpersonal actor, the extraverted president is more likely to be able to exercise political influence. (Certain social skills are a particular help in this regard. They include the ability to be ingratiating, the pointed use of humor, and speech fluency.)

The president's *weltanschauung* is also key. In the foreign policy realm in particular, the chief executive's view of the world can be a personal resource. This has been especially true of men who, on moving into the Oval Office, had histories of being hawkish in their attitudes toward the Soviet Union. Thus, Republican presidents such as Nixon and Reagan, their militant anticommunist credentials intact, manifestly felt more free to extend an olive branch to the communist superpowers, China and the USSR, than did their more dovish Democratic counterparts.

It should be noted that the same personal resources for leadership are applicable to practically all situations. That is, presidents will need to draw on more or less the same traits, skills, and dispositions in their relations with legislators, bureaucrats, and the American people. But *political* resources are something else again. Political resources—or, more precisely, political tactics—should be tailored, insofar as possible, to the particular audience. This is not to say that there is no overlap. Many tactics can be applied equally well to bureaucrats and legislators, and the media should be used in virtually all situations where presidential persuasion is at issue. But we will distinguish among them nevertheless, if only to point out that it is to the advantage of the president who would lead in the foreign policy realm to tailor his pitch to his audience. For instance, if he is out to persuade members of Congress to go along with his proposed initiatives, the executive will have to propose policies that most of them can at least tolerate and provide some evidence that he is capable of implementing those policies. To these ends the president has at his disposal a variety of political tactics that he can, and at one point or another almost certainly should, employ. Tactics to apply to *Congress* include:

- *Use of Cabinet and staff.* The president can enlist members of his cabinet and staff as foot soldiers on behalf of his foreign policy initiatives.
- *Personal appeals and access.* The president can pick up the phone or appeal face-to-face to legislators whose support he might need on a particular foreign policy bill.
- *Personal amenities.* The president can make friends and influence people by engaging in the social courtesies that enhance professional relationships. Such courtesies include small gifts and mementos, invitations to the White House or Camp David, personal notes, and VIP tours.
- *Services.* The president can provide a variety of services and favors so

as to create a general feeling of goodwill in Congress and also to win support on a specific issue. He might, for example, provide special access to executive branch documents or campaign on a legislator's behalf.

- *Bargaining.* The president can trade favors in order to win backing for his particular foreign policies and programs.
- *Arm twisting.* If necessary, the president can apply pressure, through the use of implicit or explicit threats, to get legislators to do what he wants them to do. The threat to veto a particular bill is, for example, garden variety "arm twisting."
- *Participation.* On occasion, the president can invite Senate and House leaders to become personally involved in the foreign policy process.
- *Compromise.* If necessary, the president can meet legislators part way in order to get them to accept something they otherwise would not. However, compromise has to be employed judiciously, at just the right moment and in just the right way, lest the executive appear weak.
- *Fait accompli.* The president proceeds to make a decision that other actors are, in effect, compelled to accept.[49]

Since another hallmark of a smoothly functioning foreign policy system is the effective management of the foreign policy bureaucracy,[50] the president must develop a policy-making process that enables him to obtain and analyze adequate information, to develop a wide range of policy options, to decide judiciously among them, and to plan for implementation.[51] (The president cannot personally implement the policies his administration formulates. But he is responsible for implementation, even in those situations in which there is a tension between his own imperative to formulate policy according to global designs and the preference for furthering their own more narrow agendas on the part of those departments charged with carrying out his policies.[52]) The question, of course, is how exactly can these managerial—as opposed to political—tasks be accomplished? What are the kinds of things a president can do to reduce the risk of poor foreign policy resulting from poor management?

The answer depends on the executive's managerial style. If the president has a formal approach to management, as Richard Nixon did, one in which a premium is put on orderly decision making through hierarchical channels, then he might benefit from deliberately establishing a machinery that is more fluid. If, on the other hand, the president's approach to management is, like John Kennedy's, collegial, if he has an in-group of advisors charged with problem solving, then he might look to institute a more formal structure (at least on routine matters) so as to concentrate his own energies and those of his most trusted advisors on the most prickly foreign policy issues. Finally, if the president's style is like Jimmy Carter's, one that encourages competition and conflict among his advisers, he might profit from establishing a few formal study groups—as indeed Carter did on the Middle East—that put a premium on careful staff work.

Whatever the president's managerial style, he should, in any case, provide for what Alexander George has called "multiple advocacy." Only by exposing himself to different options and arguments can he minimize the risk of a foreign policy disaster and maximize the probability that good policy will be made.

> Multiple advocacy is neither a highly decentralized policymaking system nor a highly centralized one. Rather it is a mixed system which requires executive initiative and centralized coordination of some of the activities of participants in policymaking. This management model accepts the fact that conflicts over policy and advocacy in one form or another are inevitable in a complex organization. . . . The solution it strives for is to ensure that there will be multiple advocates within the policymaking system, who, among themselves, will cover a range of interesting viewpoints and policy options on any given issue. The premise of the model is that multiple advocacy will improve the quality of information search and appraisal and, thereby, illuminate better the problem the executive must decide and his options for doing so.[53]

Finally, since the foreign policy bureaucracy, like the Congress, is vulnerable to political considerations, presidents who would lead will once again want to employ political tactics in order to gain, and retain, control. Tactics to apply to *bureaucrats* include:

- *Advance planning.* During the transition period, or at least early in his first term, the president might address questions such as: Who will constitute policy-making groups for particular foreign policy issues? How will information be disseminated?[54] What will be the balance between the State Department and the NSC?
- *Building coherence.* Coherence in foreign policy is typically achieved by a small group of presidential advisers. The individuals who constitute this key group can help the president carry out his foreign policy responsibilities. This help should not, however, result in uncritical loyalty or in decisions made outside regular channels.
- *Administrative checks.* At regular intervals, the president can make certain that his top appointees, in particular the secretary of state and national security advisor, are performing in accordance with their job requirements.
- *Lesser ploys.* A variety of political maneuvers can also be used to keep foreign policy bureaucrats in line. For example, the president might directly address the concerns of executive branch staff. Or he might show top bureaucrats the courtesy of informing them of his foreign affairs agenda before it is made public, thereby giving them the opportunity for review and accommodation.

Finally, in order to shape the foreign policy process, the president must court not only legislators and bureaucrats but also the American people. To be sure, most of the time most of the citizenry is rather uninterested in the specifics of foreign affairs. This removal gives the president considerable leeway to make policy as he sees fit. But some issues are important to some people, and a very few issues are important to many people. It is generally in the president's best interest, then, to provide the American public with a clear indication of his foreign policy direction and design, and then to enlist public support.

To these ends, too, there are political tactics presidents would do well to employ, in particular toward interest groups that have a strong stake in particular foreign policy issues. Tactics to apply to the *public* include:

- *Formulation.* The president produces the best, most rational policy possible so that the policy is supported on its own merits—simply because it promotes the nation's goals abroad.
- *Education.* The president serves as a teacher-leader who educates and mobilizes the American people on behalf of his foreign policy agenda.
- *Impression management.* The president creates the impression that he in particular is qualified to be a world leader. He should persuade the public that because of both his office and persona, he deserves support on major foreign policy issues.
- *Timing.* The president is sensitive to the mood of the moment. The right moment in foreign affairs depends on the situation at both the national and international levels.
- *Public appeals.* The president can use the mass media, particularly television, to take his case directly to the people. But he should appear on television only infrequently; otherwise his presence will become overly familiar and the audience will become bored.
- *Manipulating information.* The president can generate public support by releasing or withholding information calculated to strengthen his case. Moreover, the well-timed "leak" can be used to further strengthen the administration's agenda and even to cast opponents in an unfavorable light.
- *Vagueness and detachment.* The president can typically use language that is somewhat vague so as to maximize his flexibility. Moreover, he can refrain from identifying himself too closely with the most vulnerable parts of his foreign policy. Failed initiatives can thus be considered victims of circumstance rather than the result of the executive's incompetence as a leader.

What we see, then, is that while the task of mastering the American foreign policy system is enormous, presidents are by no means rendered impotent in their quest for followers in Congress, in the foreign policy bureaucracies, or among the American people. Chief executives have an array of personal and political resources at their disposal, some of which can be used genuinely to persuade and others to manipulate their constituencies. In either case, these resources, if aggressively and intelligently employed, will enable presidents to control the system's tendencies toward fragmentation and resistance. What it comes down to finally is this: Does the president have the will to become a powerful player in the foreign policy process? And does he have the skill to maximize his resources? The executive's ability to be a world leader depends ultimately on the answers to these deceptively simple questions.

PRESIDENTIAL POLITICS

The image of the foreign policy leader as professional politician is pertinent here, for we conclude this discussion on the president's role in the policy process by noting that, in recent years, foreign affairs have become politicized. From the vantage point of the executive branch, in any case, domestic and foreign politics are now heavily entwined. As Mortin Halperin observed: "Presidents and their associates frequently come to determine their [foreign policy] stands largely in relation to problems of maintaining effective power and getting reelected."[55] Indeed, some of the more vocal critics of American foreign policy charge that the process has become so politicized that it has resulted finally in nothing less than a foreign policy breakdown.[56]

Recent presidents, in particular, have been guilty of playing politics with America's foreign affairs. Truman and Eisenhower were prepared to make politically unpopular decisions to further policies they considered in the national interest. Since Kennedy, however, politics have repeatedly intruded on what should be a judicious and, ideally, bipartisan foreign policy process. John Kennedy's decision to invade Cuba in 1961, in response to the Soviet deployment of missiles (Bay of Pigs), was taken in part because of his own militant campaign rhetoric and subsequent fear of being accused of being soft on communism. Lyndon Johnson's conduct of the war in Vietnam was shaped by domestic political concerns as far back as the 1964 presidential campaign. Richard Nixon oversold the American people on détente, thereby concealing deep problems in the Soviet-American relationship that persisted in spite of the new climate. To appease the Republican right in 1976, Gerald Ford decided to scratch the word *détente* from his vocabulary. By controlling the news, in so far as possible, during the 1980 presidential campaign, Jimmy Carter tried to limit the damage inflicted by the Iranian hostage crisis, in particular, to protect himself from the challenge to his candidacy by Senator Edward Kennedy. And to appease the American farmer, Ronald Reagan lifted the grain embargo against the Soviet Union—even as he pressed our allies not to sell industrial products to Moscow.[57]

But if presidents must be held accountable for foreign policy decisions more political than wise, it must also be said that the system has contributed to pushing them in this new and disquieting direction. For example, today's overly long presidential campaigns exhaust candidates and therefore make them appear less intelligent and more self-serving then they actually are. Issues are raised in ways that make little or no sense, responses to questions are often embarrassingly vague or ill informed, and campaign rhetoric is prone to excess—which leads inevitably to swings between depictions of America as weak and disheartened on the one hand and the "myth of American omnipotence" on the other. Moreover, sometimes the legacy of such campaigns is "ideological, doctrinaire behavior by new presidents in their first year in office. The new leader is all the more convinced that a 'new' approach is needed to rectify the terrible errors of his predecessor."[58]

Today's foreign policy-making system is further politicized by being more participatory than it ever was before.[59] There are an array of new players demanding to be heard, including what is now a large, complex, and fractious bureaucracy; a public that, since Vietnam, has been emboldened to speak out on those issues about which it particularly cares; and powerful interest groups who typically are adroit at organizing, lobbying, and collecting monies on their own behalf. Moreover, information is now transmitted around the globe with dazzling speed, thereby enhancing the capacity of the outside world to impinge on the American foreign policy process. Finally, the tendency to democratize the making of foreign policy is fueled by the media, which is much more now than just an objective source of news. The media exposes, feeds on, and ultimately fosters a foreign policy system that functions noisily and in public, rather than quietly and behind closed doors.

Not surprisingly, while there are some obvious gains to this broadened participation, there are also costs. Indeed, some would argue that it has resulted in a foreign policy process characterized by division and paralysis rather than cohesion and progress. The situation, in any case, is one in which foreign policy–making increasingly resembles domestic policy-making. Everybody plays a political game, which means that if the president is to come out on top, he will simply have to play harder and better than everyone else.

Despite the pitfalls and problems that now constrain presidential leadership at the international level, presidents continue to be drawn to foreign affairs. They seem persuaded that their reelection prospects, as well as the judgment passed on them by history, will be vitally affected by their performance in foreign policy. Apparently they also believe that presidential leadership is easier in foreign than in domestic affairs, if only because foreign policy actions can always be sold as being in the interest of national security. Foreign policy issues are, in any case, useful mechanisms not only for exercising power but also for expanding it. Therefore, presidents are tempted to turn to foreign affairs when domestic problems become intractable, or when domestic failures pile up, or when they have only weak electoral mandates.[60] To be sure, this is a time-honored political ploy. Even Shakespeare had Henry IV advise Prince Hal to "Busy giddy minds with foreign quarrels." Finally, presidents are preoccupied with foreign affairs because of the objective reality of the U.S. position in the world: America now has global responsibilities that make it virtually impossible for any chief executive to ignore international relations.

But to repeat: For all the differences between the foreign and domestic policy–making processes, in terms of the exercise of presidential leadership it is the similarities that are most compelling. In both, the president is preeminent. In both, he relies most heavily on close advisors and political appointees. And in both, his success in reaching a particular goal depends on constituent groups who, if dissatisfied, will simply balk. What this means is that in the foreign affairs presidency, as in the domestic affairs presidency, the president who would be a leader will have to be, above all, a practicing politician.

Notes

1. Quoted in Louis W. Koenig, *The Chief Executive* (New York: Harcourt Brace Jovanovich, 1981), p. 211.

2. Ibid.

3. Randall B. Ripley, *Congress, Process and Policy* (New York: Norton, 1975), p. 283.

4. Richard M. Pious, *The American Presidency* (New York: Basic, 1979), p. 333.

5. James A. Nathan and James K. Oliver, *Foreign Policy Making and the American Political System* (Boston: Little, Brown, 1987), p. 131. See chapter 5 for a full discussion of the concept of shared power in foreign affairs.

6. *The Federalist Papers* (New York: New American Library, 1961), p. 391.

7. Ibid., p. 451.

8. Hans J. Morganthau, "The American Tradition in Foreign Policy," in *Foreign Policy in World Politics*, ed. Roy C. Macridis (Englewood Cliffs, N.J.: Prentice-Hall, 1967), p. 262.

9. Ibid., p. 451.

10. Koenig, p. 216.

11. This paragraph is based on Arthur M. Schlesinger, Jr., *The Imperial Presidency* (Boston: Houghton Mifflin, 1973), p. 273.

12. Koenig, pp. 221, 222.

13. See Cecil V. Crabb, Jr., and Pat M. Holt, *Invitation to Struggle: Congress, the President and Foreign Policy* (Washington: Congressional Quarterly, Inc., 1989), chapter 8 for a fuller discussion of the issues surrounding congressional assertiveness in foreign affairs.

14. Arthur Schlesinger, Jr., "Congress and the Making of Foreign Policy," in *Perspective on the Presidency*, ed. Aaron Wildavsky (Boston: Little, Brown, 1975), p. 251.

15. Stanley Hoffmann, *Gulliver's Troubles or the Setting of American Foreign Policy* (New York: McGraw Hill, 1968), pp. 255–57.

16. John Tower, "Congress versus the President: The Formulation and Implementation of American Foreign Policy," *Foreign Affairs* 60, no. 2 (Winter 1981/82): pp. 230, 246.

17. John Spanier and Eric M. Uslander, *American Foreign Policy Making and the Democratic Dilemmas* (New York: Holt, Rinehart, & Winston, 1985), p. 96.

18. Crabb and Holt, p. 252.

19. Harold J. Laski, *The American Presidency* (New Brunswick, N.J.: Transaction, 1980), p. 171. (The original edition copyright is 1940 by Harper & Bros.)

20. Thomas Cronin, *The State of the Presidency* (Boston: Little, Brown, 1980), p. 155.

21. Larry Berman, *The New American Presidency* (Boston: Little, Brown, 1987), p. 56.

22. This paragraph is based on chapter 3, ibid.

23. This paragraph is based on chapter 10 in Pious.

24. Pious, p. 359.

25. See "At the Foreign Policy Helm: Shultz vs. the White House," *New York Times*, 26 August 1987, p. 1.

26. Howard Bliss and M. Glen Johnson, *Beyond the Water's Edge: America's Foreign Policies* (Philadelphia: Lippincott, 1975), p. 139.

27. Ibid., p. 140.

28. Ibid., p. 143.

29. I. M. Destler, *Presidents, Bureaucrats, and Foreign Policy* (Princeton: Princeton University Press, 1972), p. 84.

30. Nathan and Oliver, p. 234.

31. Roderick P. Hart, *The Sound of Leadership: Presidential Communication in the Modern Age* (Chicago: University of Chicago, 1987), p. 111. These paragraphs are based on chapter 4 of the book. Also see Michael Baruch Grossman and Martha Joynt Kumar, *Portraying the President: The White House and the News Media* (Baltimore: Johns Hopkins University Press, 1981).

32. Nathan and Oliver, p. 236.

33. James A. Robinson and Richard C. Snyder, "Decision Making in International Politics," in *International Behavior*, ed. Herbert Kelman (New York: Holt, Rinehart, & Winston, 1965), p. 449.

34. I. M. Destler, *Presidents, Bureaucrats, and Foreign Policy: The Politics of Organizational Reform* (Princeton: Princeton University Press, 1972), p. 52.

35. Theodore Sorensen, *Decision Making in the White House* (New York: Columbia University Press, 1963), p. 26.

36. I. M. Destler, "National Security II: The Rise of the Assistant (1961–1981)," in *The Illusion of Presidential Government*, eds. Hugo Heclo and Lester M. Salamon (Boulder, Colo.: Westview, 1981), p. 263.

37. Henry T. Nash, *American Foreign Policy: A Search for Security* (Homewood, Ill.: Dorsey, 1985), p. 244. See all of chapter 7 for a detailed discussion of "Intelligence, CIA, and Foreign Policy."

38. Spanier, p. 171.

39. Morton H. Halperin, *Bureaucratic Politics and Foreign Policy* (Washington, D.C.: Brookings, 1974). This paragraph is based on Halperin's chapter 5.

40. Howard J. Wiarda, "The Paralysis of Policy: Current Dilemmas of U.S. Foreign Policy Making" (Paper prepared for the American Enterprise Institute, 1986), p. 3.

41. Herbert C. Kelman, "Social-Psychological Approaches to the Study of International Relations," in *International Behavior,* ed. Kelman.

42. Ibid., p. 581.

43. Hoffmann, p. 233.

44. Ibid., p. 236.

45. Events also affect public opinion toward presidential conduct of foreign policy. On the impact of war on public opinion, see John E. Mueller, *War, Presidents and Public Opinion* (New York: Wiley, 1973).

46. See Nathan and Oliver, chapter 8, for more on "Private Power and American Foreign Policy."

47. Valerie Bunce, "Presidential Leadership of Public Opinion: The Hardening of American Attitudes toward East-West Relations" (Paper prepared for Annual Meeting of the American Political Science Association, New Orleans, 1985).

48. This paragraph is based on Bunce, pp. 44ff.

49. For more on presidential politicking, see Barbara Kellerman, *The Political Presidency: Practice of Leadership* (New York: Oxford University Press, 1984), especially chapters 4 and 5.

50. For a list of the organizational pitfalls common to foreign policy bureaucracies, see Alexander George, *Presidential Decisionmaking in Foreign Policy: The Effective Use of Information and Advice* (Boulder, Colo.: Westview, 1980), pp. 112, 113. For a list of small group flaws, see George, p. 121 ff.

51. Ibid., p. 10.

52. Erwin C. Hargrove and Michael Nelson, *Presidents, Politics, and Policy* (Baltimore: Johns Hopkins University Press, 1984), p. 247. For more on policy implementation, see George C. Edwards III, "Problems in Presidential Policy Implementation," in *The Presidency: Studies in Policy Making,* eds. Steven A. Shull and Lance T. LeLoup (Brunswick, Ohio: Kings Court, 1979), pp. 271–94; Steven A. Schull, *Presidential Policy Making: An Analysis* (Brunswick, Ohio: Kings Court, 1979), pp. 261–81; and George C. Edwards III and Stephen J. Wayne, *Presidential Leadership: Politics and Policy Making* (New York: St. Martin's, 1985), pp. 349–87.

53. George, p. 193.

54. For further questions that should, ideally, be part of a planning process, see ibid., p. 99.

55. Haperin, p. 63.

56. I. M. Destler, Leslie H. Gelb, and Anthony Lake, *Our Own Worst Enemy: The Unmaking of American Foreign Policy* (New York: Simon & Schuster, 1984), p. 13.

57. Ibid., pp. 22, 23.

58. Ibid., p. 37.

59. For much more on the sources of American foreign policy, see Charles W. Kegley, Jr., and Eugene Wittkopf, *American Foreign Policy: Pattern and Process,* 3rd ed. (New York: St. Martin's, 1987), passim; Nathan and Oliver, especially chapters 6, 7, 8; and Nash, especially chapter 1.

60. This paragraph is based on Bunce, pp. 44 ff.

4

The President as World Leader

One question a book such as this inevitably poses is whether or not presidential leadership makes a difference: Can an individual actor, no matter how personally powerful or how well positioned, have a demonstrable impact on world politics?

Clearly the premise underlying this particular investigation is that, indeed, American presidents can, and sometimes do, bring about change in world affairs. We hold that chief executives have the capacity to strongly influence U.S. foreign policy, and that this capacity is likely to be a function of who they are as well as of the office they hold. To be sure, it is, as we pointed out earlier, one thing to shape American foreign policy and quite another to effect change at the international level. Our claim, nevertheless, is that presidents willing and able to capitalize on their personal and political sources of power will have a fair chance of getting others, both at home *and* abroad, to follow their lead.

Our search for a clearer understanding of how America's chief executives approach the daunting task of world leadership begins with a general discussion of the individual actor in the international environment. Then we explore the president's particular role in world politics, and how he might exercise power and influence to his advantage. Finally, we consider some of the ways in which psychological factors, at the level of both the individual and the group, impinge on America's foreign relations.

THE INDIVIDUAL IN THE INTERNATIONAL ENVIRONMENT

For centuries, people have argued over whether or not a single individual can change the course of history. On one side of what is still called the "hero in history" or "great man in history" debate are those who claim that great men (and, increasingly, women) can literally determine political outcomes: Without Moses, the Jews would have remained in Egypt. Without Churchill, the British would have been defeated in 1940, and Hitler would have conquered all Europe. And without Rosa Parks and, subsequently, Martin Luther King, Jr., African-Americans might still be forced to sit at the back of the bus. Others take the opposite view, holding that a great leader is merely the product of a particular time, place, and circumstance—an expression, if you will, of the mood of the moment.[1] Though recent leadership theories consider and give some accommodation to both arguments, the question of how much an individual matters on the stage of world history has not been answered to everyone's complete satisfaction.[2]

Remarkably, the impact of individuals on the course of world politics has been given short shrift in the literature on international relations. One exception to this general rule is Herbert Kelman's work, some of which focuses on the role of key players in world politics. Kelman is persuaded that "the analysis of international politics should be centered, in part, on the behavior of those whose actions are the actions of the state, namely the decision-makers."[3] To hone in on the individual decision maker does in fact have several methodological advantages. In particular, it curtails the tendency to conceptualize the state itself as if it were a human being, and it helps to focus the analysis of the complex processes that ultimately produce state behavior.[4] To those who would argue that the study of individuals is misguided, Kelman thus responds:

> We sometimes tend to forget that it is individual human beings who make the decisions and carry out the actions that constitute international relations. It is individuals who threaten and feel threatened, who perceive and misperceive, who give and withhold support, who compete and cooperate, who kill and who die. . . . Individuals constitute the ultimate locus of action. Individual decision-makers act and speak for the nation-state; individual citizens, by their actions or failures to act, set the limits and define the mood within which decision-makers can operate; and individual actors carry out the official and unofficial interactions of which international relations consist.[5]

If some individuals are important some of the time, the key question is: When is an individual most likely to make an impact? The issue was addressed some years ago by Fred Greenstein, who formulated three propositions that indicate those circumstances under which the actions of individuals are "likely to be links in a chain of further events":

1. The likelihood of personal impact varies with the degree to which the actions take place in an environment that permits restructuring.
2. The likelihood of personal impact varies with the location of the actor in the power structure.
3. The likelihood of personal impact varies with the actor's peculiar strengths and weaknesses.[6]

We have expanded on Greenstein so as to point to those circumstances under which the *individual's impact on world politics* is likely to be significant:

- The individual's impact on world politics will vary to the degree that the international environment permits restructuring. The more ambiguous and unsettled it is, the more likely he is to have an impact on world politics.
- The individual's impact on world politics will vary according to the extent of his power, authority, and influence in his own state. The more power, authority, and influence he has, the more likely he is to have an impact on world politics.

- The individual's impact on world politics will vary according to the nature of his role. The more his role demands an orientation to foreign policy, the more likely he is to have an impact on world politics.
- The individual's impact on world politics will vary according to the personal strengths, weaknesses, and proclivities of the individual actor. In particular, the more competent, ambitious, and self-confident he is, and the keener his interest in foreign affairs, the more likely he is to have an impact on world politics.
- The individual's impact on world politics will vary according to how important foreign affairs are to the domestic politics of his own state. The more important foreign affairs are, the more likely he is to have an impact on world politics.
- The individual's impact on world politics will vary according to the size, power, and strategic importance of the country in which he is located. The stronger and more important it is, the more likely he is to have an impact on world politics.

These six propositions suggest that those individuals most likely to have an impact on world politics are national leaders. They also imply that personality is likely to be important to the study of international politics only with regard to those at the very top of the political hierarchy—primarily, again, national leaders.[7] Moreover, certain objective factors, such as the size and power of the state, play a role in determining individual impact. Obviously, leaders are important to world politics only if they are involved in foreign affairs. Indeed, under certain circumstances, the impact of a powerful personality with a passion for, or even obsession with, world politics can overwhelm objective factors such as the size of the state. Libya's strongman since 1969, Muammar Qaddafi, and Iran's Ayatollah Khomeini, who dominated his country throughout the late 1970s and 1980s, are vivid examples of national leaders who have had an impact on world politics far beyond what anyone could have predicted based on the prominence of their states.[8]

To be sure, there remain sound reasons why even powerful individuals can have a difficult time making an imprint on world politics. Nevertheless, it seems clear that national leaders are likely to be important variables in international relations at least some of the time. In particular, the leader is likely to be a factor in world affairs if the international environment admits of restructuring; if he has a large measure of power, authority, and/or influence in his own state; if the requirements of his role dictate an orientation to foreign policy; if he is energetic and also motivated to play a role on the international stage; if foreign politics are important to domestic politics; and if his nation is in and of itself a significant power at the international level.[9]

THE PRESIDENT IN THE INTERNATIONAL ENVIRONMENT

Machiavelli pointed to the political advantage to be gained from foreign adventure. "There is nothing," he wrote, that brings a prince "such repute as great exploits and rare trials of himself in heroic acts."[10] While Machiavelli was interested in how to use the relationship between war and personal heroism to the ruler's benefit, in today's world national leaders can profit from the "flight" to foreign affairs without demonstrating personal bravery. As the following list suggests, presidential involvement in international relations can be politically advantageous:

- Intervention in international politics can have a quick political payoff. For example, the Reagan administration's military operation in Grenada, a modest undertaking by any standard, nevertheless gave the president's popularity a significant boost.
- Blaming external forces for internal problems is an easy—which is not to say illegitimate—way to deflect responsibility. For decades, since the start of the cold war, the Soviet military buildup was used to justify America's high defense budget. Thus the Soviets were held responsible for the fact that presidents often felt compelled to spend for guns rather than butter.
- A clear and present danger abroad fosters consensus at home. A bipartisan foreign policy that enjoys widespread public support is relatively easy to attain when the president can point to a particular individual or nation that appears to embody a threat to America and its way of life.
- Presidents often come to believe that their place in history will be secured by how they conduct themselves in foreign affairs. As we will see in the case studies that follow, Ronald Reagan is only the most recent example of a chief executive who looked for the kind of foreign policy breakthrough that would ultimately be labeled "historic."

All of this is not to suggest that the extent to which the U.S. is engaged in world affairs is a function only of presidential self-interest. Executives have loftier motives as well. Jimmy Carter's involvement in the politics of the Middle East, for example, was fueled by his missionary drive to bring a measure of peace to this troubled area. Yet advantages can, and often do, accrue to presidents as a consequence of their involvement in international relations. As a result, it is in their political interest first to control the foreign policy process at home and then to oversee implementation abroad.

This first step—controlling the foreign policy process—is, as we have seen, a complex and difficult task. In order to effect a particular outcome, the president must provide policy direction, staff and manage the foreign policy bureaucracy, coordinate decision making, and maintain at least tacit public support for his conduct of foreign affairs.[11] Moreover, as discussed in chapter 3, in order to accomplish these tasks, there are at least three constituencies the president must have in tow: Congress, the foreign policy bureaucracies, and the American public. What we concluded, therefore, was that in order to overcome the foreign policy system's tendencies toward fragmentation and resistance, the president would have to be a highly skilled political operator.[12]

But can we simply assume that presidents who in fact manage to direct the foreign policy process at home will be similarly effective abroad? Obviously some national leaders have managed to play significant roles in world politics.[13] Surely, then, the president of as great a power as the United States can shape the course of international relations—or can he?

Of course, we know full well that chief executives are often frustrated by their inability to determine what happens in foreign affairs. We also know that although national power and wealth would appear to be important resources for world leadership, the president has often seemed muscle-bound in recent years, incapable of getting what he wants when he wants it, despite American's great military and economic strength. Why did Lyndon Johnson sink in the quagmire that was Vietnam? Why was Jimmy Carter humiliated for over a year—and finally defeated at the polls—by the Iranian hostage crisis? And why, after six years of riding high, was Ronald Reagan's Teflon shield ultimately pierced by foreign policies gone badly awry?

We can approach these questions from several directions. The traditional bipolar explanation suggests that the president has lacked the capacity to do what he wanted to do because of his fear of triggering an unwelcome response from the Soviet Union. In other words, to see the international environment primarily through the lens of East-West relations—as most Americans in fact did from the mid-1940s to the late 1980s—is to assume that whatever the president does might be construed as hostile by his Soviet counterpart (which is not to deny that even during the cold war the U.S. and USSR cooperated when it suited them both).

But for a more sophisticated understanding of how difficult it is for the American president to lead in world politics, we would do well to focus more narrowly on the unit that since the mid nineteenth century has dominated international relations: the state. We know that states are collectives bound by social, political, economic, ideological, historical, and territorial ties. We also know that all states have their own particular interests, some of which inevitably conflict with the interests of other states. The American president must try to lead, therefore, in an environment in which 174 independent states strive for goals that are often mutually exclusive.

The bottom line is that tribal, or international, competition is virtually impossible to eradicate, for only if *every* state choses the way of peace can all states live in peace. If only one opts for expansion and conquest, then all the others are obliged—if they want to remain independent—to resort to power themselves.[14] Therefore, so long as the international environment remains fragmented, and so long as we do not have world government to mandate global law and order, the quest for national power and security must characterize international relations.

Inevitably, it is the national leader who plays the dominant role in this quest. In fact, it can be argued that the national leader's most important charge is to protect his state from physical, political, economic, and cultural encroachment by anyone from outside. (This does not mitigate against the growing recognition by national leaders that global problems, such as pollution, require global solutions.) Thus his concerns are focused almost entirely on the needs and wants of *his* followers, rather than on those of humankind more generally. In fact, the stronger any national leader's bond to his people in particular, and the more urgent his need to see them (and thereby himself) prevail, the weaker his impulse to consider the well-being of anyone else (that is, of "foreigners," "aliens," "outsiders," "the other"). In this sense the bond between national leaders and their followers may be said to be at the root of all international conflict. It enables leaders to justify—to themselves, to their domestic constituences, and to the rest of the world—their quest for ever greater national power and wealth. Thus we have a world politics fueled by passions that are parochial rather than ecumenical and conducted by leaders who are so bonded to the citizens of their own state that they are relatively oblivious to the welfare of others.[15]

The impact of this nationalistic leadership on the capacity for world leadership—even the capacity of one so relatively powerful as the American president—is clear. Since the international environment is populated by national states that are often in competition and sometimes in conflict, and since international institutions such as the United Nations and World Court remain peripheral in most situations, these states are inevitably led by men (and, in rare cases, women) who do what they can to enhance the power of their realms in particular. If one state's goals chance, therefore, to coincide with another's, international leadership is relatively easy. An initiative by one leader will be favorably received by other leaders who also stand to gain. But if national goals conflict, indeed even if there is merely indifference, the leader's task is difficult. For in the final analysis, no national leader has any legal authority over any other national leader—which means that in order to lead at the international level, heads of states must exercise either power or influence. (Of course, precisely how national leaders interact depends on personal characteristics and also on a range of objective factors over which they have little or no control. For example, are the states they embody allies or adversaries, or are they neutral toward each other? Clearly the American president's relationship to the prime minister of England will be quite different from his relationship to the general secretary of the Communist party of the Soviet Union. The genesis of this difference is role determined, which means that it persists no matter who sits in the White House, 10 Downing Street, or the Kremlin.)

PRESIDENTIAL POWER AND INFLUENCE AT THE INTERNATIONAL LEVEL

The exercise of presidential *power* implies access to military and/or economic resources that can be used to punish or reward other national leaders to compel compliance. The exercise of presidential *influence,* on the other hand, suggests the use of personal resources so as to persuade other national leaders to support—or at least not to resist—his particular initiatives. Thus the distinction between power and influence lies primarily in the degree of voluntarism involved. While both power and influence are employed in relationships in which the president gets others to do something they would not do otherwise, the notion of power generally implies a level of coercion that the notion of influence does not.[16]

Ordinarily, then, when we refer to the president's ability to compel compliance in the international environment, what we have in mind is the access he has, through his office, to the military and economic resources of the U.S. government. But bear in mind that the president's persona is also relevant to the use of power, for his willingness to employ—or even to threaten to employ—these same military and economic resources are dimensions of *his* personality in particular. Some American presidents have been very cautious about the use of force, even though they had large arsenals at their disposal. Others have been disposed to take risks, even though their power positions were relatively weak. Similarly, some executives were inclined to try to shape the course of world history. Others were less interested in what transpired beyond America's borders.

The traditional view of power at the international level has, in any case, emphasized the role of the military, especially so far as the superpowers are concerned. Military power can be exercised in a variety of ways. It can be applied directly, in battle, or indirectly, such as through an increase in the military budget or by mobilizing the reserve. Indeed, military power is often exercised in a nonaggressive fashion for defense purposes only. For example, U.S. presidents typically justify America's great military strength on the grounds of "national security."[17]

Thomas Schelling has made a useful distinction for the Nuclear Age between brute force and coercion. There is a difference, he observed,

> between taking what you want and making someone give it to you, between fending off assault and making someone afraid to assault you, between holding what people are trying to take and making them afraid to take it, between losing what someone can forcibly take and giving it up to avoid risk or damage. It is the difference between defense and deterrence, between brute force and intimidation, between conquest and blackmail, between action and threats. It is the difference between the unilateral, "undiplomatic" recourse to strength, and coercive diplomacy based on the power to hurt.[18]

Others have been similarly intrigued by the conception of "coercive diplomacy" as appropriate to the Nuclear Age. The point is to "affect the enemy's will rather than negate his capacities." In other words, the use of force to achieve political objectives is rejected in favor of the *threat* to use force; and if the threat does not work, such force as is employed is applied in a limited and selective manner, and in discrete and controlled increments.[19] Ronald Reagan's decision to send in the military to protect shipping in the Persian Gulf, particularly from assault by the Iranians, is a good example of a controlled and selective show of force.

One fact, in any case, is clear: Recent history has changed the ways in which American presidents think about, and employ, military power. This is not to deny that in the last half century the use of armed forces has sometimes been an effective way for executives to achieve near-term foreign policy objectives.[20] It is to suggest, however, that nuclear weapons are virtually unusable; that such "successes" as have been enjoyed tend to erode over time; that the American experience in Vietnam made it painfully clear that military power cannot be relied on to accomplish difficult and complex foreign policy objectives; and that recent developments, like the greater willingness of less-developed countries to employ methods of aggression and resistance such as guerilla warfare and terrorism, and the increasingly vocal devaluation of war (especially in the U.S. and Europe), have restricted still further the president's capacity to exercise, or even to threaten to exercise, military power. Clearly, then, there is no longer a simple equation—if, indeed, there ever was one—

between America's military strength and the president's capacity to get other national leaders to do something they would not do otherwise. (Ironically, constraints on executives actually increase in situations in which the U.S. is pitted against a much weaker adversary. Superior military powers, although they have the capacity to inflict massive destruction on less-developed countries, find effecting submission more difficult than it used to be. In the late twentieth century victors cannot readily recruit new, viable governments willing to accept defeat, and military occupation is likely to be costly and difficult. Moreover, it simply is not acceptable any longer for a great power to overwhelm a much smaller one, unless the provocation is very great indeed—as George Bush claimed in 1989 when he ordered American soldiers into Panama to overthrow the resident strongman, General Manuel Noreiga.

Because the traditional military approach to exercising power at the international level is of decreasing utility, and because international economic interdependence is of increasing importance, economic power is now considered to be a significant tool of statecraft.[21] Economic power relies primarily on resources that have a reasonable semblance of market price in terms of money.[22] Like military power, economic power can be exercised either by bestowing (or promising to bestow) rewards or by inflicting (or threatening to inflict) punishments. Rewards and punishments associated with economic power fall into two categories: trade and capital. Positive trade sanctions include: favorable tariff discrimination, granting "most-favored nation" treatment, direct purchases, and subsidies to exports or imports. Positive capital sanctions include: providing aid, investment guarantees, and encouragement of private capital exports or imports. Negative trade sanctions include: embargos, boycotts, tariff increases, and quotas. And negative capital sanctions include: freezing assets, control on exports or imports, and expropriation.[23]

Like military power, then, economic power can be exercised to threaten, weaken, or strengthen another state. Of course, a distinction must be made between the capacity for power and the actual use thereof. American presidents have possessed nuclear weapons in their arsenal for decades now, but no chief executive has come close to using them. Nevertheless, deterrence has worked because of the fear of what would happen if the unwritten prohibition against the use of nuclear arms was violated. Thus while military and economic power constitute potentially important resources for leadership, the ways in which these resources can actually be employed to full effect—the ways in which presidents can draw on them to coerce other national leaders into going along—are in fact fewer than they might at first appear to be.

Because the use of power is fraught with potential problems such as provoking other nations to respond in kind, presidents who want to lead in the international environment are almost invariably at less risk when they try to do so by exercising influence. As we have seen, *influence* is the ability of one party to change the behavior of another without directly drawing on military or economic resources. This is not to say that military and economic power have no bearing on "influence relationships." On the contrary, exerting influence is easier if you have access to something somebody else fears or wants. It is, however, to affirm that the capacity to exert influence, as we are using the term here, is the capacity to be personally persuasive and, thereby, to get compliance on a voluntary basis.

Although influence has received much less attention than power in the literature on politics, it has in fact always played a significant role in international relations. The mutual, although often asymmetrical, flow of influence is an important aspect of the quiet relations among many small countries, of relations between great powers and small countries, and particularly of the relations among allies or friendly countries. After all, most international discourse is the stuff, not of high drama, but of interactions on a range of relatively unexciting issues. It is on these routine matters that influence relationships tend to be significant.[24]

Essentially, presidents influence important players in world politics in three ways: by proxy, through diplomats charged with negotiating on their behalf; by personal diplomacy, in which they themselves participate in international negotiations; and by the use of propaganda, which, at the international level, can win support for their particular agendas.

In the late twentieth century, American diplomats still continue to serve as symbols of the country they represent, as legal agents of the U.S. government, and as personal emisaries of the executive for whom they are conducting foreign relations.[25] But it is also true that the nature of diplomacy has changed over the years, especially perhaps in the last two decades. Among the more significant developments in modern diplomacy are the growing number of diplomatic channels, the louder public voice in the foreign policy debate, the universalizing of international deliberations, and the broadened range of participants in international negotiations, including technical experts.[26] Yet the basic point still applies: in foreign affairs the American president generally communicates through stand-ins, appointees such as ambassadors who try to exercise influence over diplomats from other states on his behalf.

The president himself meets face-to-face with other national leaders only relatively infrequently. But when he does, on occasions other than those that are strictly ceremonial, the interaction that ensues tends to be unfamiliar. By definition, other national leaders are the products of alien cultures; moreover, they are political actors over whom the president has no authority of any kind. Thus the president is negotiating with foreigners who are, at least in term of international law, his equals.

While all summits tend to have considerable symbolic significance, in fact their nature varies depending on whether the president's counterpart is a German chancellor, Jordanian king, or Costa Rican president. Of course, the most dramatic summits are those that transpire when the leaders of two powerful countries with a history of discord between them—such as the U.S. and the USSR—get together. Some Soviet-American summits have manifestly been failures. The John Kennedy–Nikita Khrushchev encounter in Vienna (1961) did not, to put it charitably, further the cause of world peace. Similarly, Ronald Reagan's brief meeting in Reykjavik (1986) with Mikhail Gorbachev was widely considered something of a fiasco.

But more often than not, Soviet-American summits are in one or another way productive, even if only at a symbolic level. Lyndon Johnson's meeting with Aleksei Kosygin in 1965 produced the benevolent, if short-lived, "spirit of Glassboro." In his three conferences with Leonid Brezhnev, Richard Nixon forged a relationship with the Soviet leader that, had Watergate not intervened, would almost certainly have continued to bear fruit, particularly in the area of arms control. By the time Reagan left office, he had met Gorbachev five times, thereby achieving what many regard as a breakthrough in postwar Soviet-American relations. And George Bush was in office less than a year before he met Gorbachev at sea, off the coast of Malta, at a summit that was stormy so far as the weather was concerned, but in political terms nothing if not tranquil. It should be noted as well that Bush's personal diplomacy extends to the telephone—he regularly talks to allied leaders such as Margaret Thatcher of England, Helmut Kohl of West Germany, and François Mitterand of France—and to handwritten notes. The December 1989 Malta summit was first proposed by Bush to Gorbachev in a handwritten note sent in July and finalized in two other personal notes from the White House to the Kremlin. One might reasonably argue, then, that intelligently planned and executed diplomacy at the highest level affords the American executive—and his counterpart—a singular opportunity to exercise influence at the international level.[27]

Of course not all leadership in world politics falls into conventional categories. Once in a great while a national leader shapes history by making a bold departure from past patterns of diplomatic practice. Janice Gross Stein describes just such an initiative, taken by Egyptian president Anwar Sadat in 1977:

> To break the psychological barrier Sadat chose to do the daring, the imaginative, the dramatic, the unprecedented, and indeed, the inspired. . . . Sadat publicly asked to address Israel's parliament. With alacrity [Israeli prime minister Menachem] Begin issued the invitation and within days, the context and dynamics of the Arab-Israeli dispute were fundamentally and permanently altered. . . . Sadat captured the attention and the imagination of the world, fired Israel's public opinion, and challenged fundamental assumptions of Israel's leaders about their Arab neighbor. The president succeeded not only in shattering the old but, more importantly, in putting new rules in place: the conflict between Egypt and Israel was normalized and made negotiable.[28]

As Stein points out, the history of the Middle East was forever changed by Sadat's single stroke. His visit to Jerusalem, which was motivated in part by objective factors such as Egypt's increasingly grave domestic problems, led the next year to the historic meetings at Camp David during which President Jimmy Carter alternately cajoled and browbeat the Egyptian and Israeli leaders into signing the Camp David accords.*

While this particular sequence of events was set in motion by one individual, and while Sadat provides a striking example of how one national leader single-handedly changed the configuration of the international environment, we should nevertheless not be misled. Such an outcome is clearly an exception to the rule that most of the time national leaders cannot in fact effect major change overnight.[29]

Finally, a word on the president's capacity to exercise influence at the international level by shaping world opinion—that is, the opinion of national publics other than the American public. To attain this elusive end the executive has always had only two resources at his disposal; words and deeds. But

---

*See chapter 8 for an analysis of Jimmy Carter's leadership role in the Camp David peace process.

today there is a difference; advances in technology make it possible for the American president to be heard and seen around the globe virtually instantaneously. Thus the president now has a considerably greater opportunity to influence world opinion than he ever did before. While there is scant evidence that even the most recent presidents have fully understood the dimensions of this change, they will probably come to recognize in the not too distant future that the revolution in telecommunications provides them with an important new weapon in the fight to win the hearts and minds of all those who people the global village.

THE PSYCHOLOGICAL DIMENSION

As indicated in the Preface, the definition of *leadership* used in this book is rather narrow. That is, we employ two basic measures of presidential leadership in world politics:

1. Did the president shape the American foreign policy process with regard to at least one major initiative?
2. Was he able to affect attitudes and events pertaining to this initiative beyond America's borders?

Remember, too, that our particular focus is not on *reactive leadership*—leadership in response to an external stimulus. Rather, our concern here is with *directive leadership* in which the president, acting on his own initiative and on the basis of his own deliberations and convictions, attempts to engage followers so as to bring about significant change in the status quo. (This is not to suggest that reactive leadership is trivial or that all change is to the good. Rather, it is to distinguish between two different kinds of leadership and to reiterate the locus of this investigation.)

Of course, even those presidents who do not meet the criteria of effective leadership typically have a modest impact on the course of world politics. For whatever the executive's personal capacities and proclivities, as we saw earlier there are objective reasons for the president's involvement in foreign affairs and for his starring role on the international stage.[30] But to the extent that strong presidential leadership at the international level is contingent on the executive's capacity to exercise power and influence, the president's personality is, virtually by definition, an important variable in international relations.

How exactly personality matters is less clear. Drawing a straight line between presidential personality (cause) and a particular political outcome (effect) is difficult if not impossible to do.[31] Nevertheless, basing their work on the reasonable assumption that in one way or another presidential personality is of consequence to foreign affairs, researchers have made several attempts to explore what exactly the linkage is.[32] Most of the literature that forges explicit ties between personality and world politics is biographical. Psychobiographies, or psychohistories as they are sometimes called, draw on both history and psychology to shed light on how private experiences influence behavior in public life. Consider this sampling of four of the presidents scrutinized later in this book: Lyndon Johnson, Richard Nixon, Jimmy Carter, and Ronald Reagan.

Throughout *Lyndon Johnson and the American Dream,* Doris Kearns suggests that Johnson's early feelings and experiences determined his actions as president. Moreover, she makes a specific connection between Johnson's personality and his decisions with regard to the Vietnam War.

> The influence of Johnson's personality on the decision-making in Vietnam is [easy] to observe in his conduct of the war—[particularly] in the decision to conceal its nature and extent from the American people. . . . This decision was Lyndon Johnson's decision. It is easy to imagine another president, less concerned with domestic reform, more capable of choosing between goals, less confident of his ability to move in contradictory directions at the same time, less experienced in the art of secrecy, deciding differently. Indeed, this decision seems almost to sum up the character of the man. The very qualities and experiences that had led to his political and legislative success were precisely those that now operated to destroy him.[33]

Richard Nixon's persona has also provided fertile soil for psychobiographers. Like Kearns, Bruce Mazlish, in his work *In Search of Nixon: A Psychohistorical Inquiry,* explored the ways in which a president's family and early life contributed to his later political behavior. The following excerpt indicates how private motives are seen as shaping presidential choices in the foreign policy realm. Mazlish is writing here about Nixon's new China policy, in particular about his remarkable decision—given his virulent, long-standing anticommunism—to journey to Beijing.

> Have his feelings about the international conspiracy of communism changed? Such a reading would . . . fly in the fact of our fundamental view of Nixon as an extraordinarily ambivalent man. Nixon, I suggest, still projects his personal unacceptable feelings onto an external enemy, in this case, communism. But . . . he also sincerely believes in working for peace. . . . The roots of this conviction lie deep in the Nixon family. . . . I am prepared to believe Nixon when he says he has "an obsession on this point."[34]

Jimmy Carter has been subjected to similar scrutiny by Betty Glad, who proposed that his type of personality is prone to develop a highly idealized self-image. As a consequence, shortcoming and failures are dismissed, leaving a kind of fictionalized (perfect) self to function in the real world. Glad spells out the impact of this on American foreign policy by suggesting that many of Carter's problems in this area stemmed from his particular concern for keeping up appearances. The idealized self-image had to be kept intact: "In his handling of the Iran and Afganistan crises he choreographed a series of dramatic responses, mobilized national sentiment behind them, and created a demand for results that his policies could not satisfy."[35]

Glad also wrote a psychobiographical essay on Ronald Reagan. His personality, she proposed, had a perceptible effect on his view of, and consequent behavior toward, the Soviet Union. She argued that his basic tendency to see the world in terms of a battle between the Americans and Russians, between the forces of light and the forces of darkness, are rooted in "deeper psychic needs." In particular, Glad claimed that since Reagan has difficulty in expressing anger in controlled ways, his "stereotyping of [a] culturally approved out-group, the communists, as well as his manifest tendencies to show aggression in fantasy and verbal attack upon them, suggest he has projected anger outward to a safe target."[36] (Clearly, Glad was addressing the first term Ronald Reagan, who was openly hostile to the Soviets. The second term Reagan, who was able to forge a relationship with Mikhail Gorbachev, was far more conciliatory.)

James David Barber developed another approach to the issue of how presidential personality impacts on political outcomes by postulating that all presidents may be categorized along two crucial dimensions of personality:

active → passive and positive → negative

The first dimension addresses the question of how much energy the president invests in his job, and the second how he feels about what he does. John Kennedy, for example, was described as an active-positive personality who, because of his high level of energy and because he enjoyed being president, was able to "incorporate" the lessons learned during the Bay of Pigs fiasco and use them to good effect during the next Cuban affair—the 1962 missile crisis. Richard Nixon, on the other hand, was classified by Barber as an active-negative type, for whom power was a "core need." Thus, under Nixon, foreign policy planning, publicity, and execution were "a closely held White House responsibility." Moreover, Barber traces Nixon's more specific policy decisions—such as the decision in 1970 to invade Cambodia with U.S. troops—to a personality type that was ready to fight to maintain control.[37]

Still another approach to the question of how psychological factors impact on international relations focuses on the decision-making process. For example, Robert Jervis's work on perception and misperception in international relations grew out of his concern about the poor quality of decision making in the foreign policy realm. His focus was primarily on how information is processed ("leaders tend to fit incoming information with their existing theories and images") and on how other actors in the international environment are perceived ("leaders tend to see other states as more hostile than they really are").[38]

Irving Janis was similarly disturbed by the quality of decision making in government. In particular, he questioned how policymakers who were ostensibly the best and the brightest could have been responsible for the miscalculations and fiascos that plagued American foreign policy in the 1960s (e.g., the Bay of Pigs, Vietnam). Janis concluded that it was the small-group dynamic that was deeply flawed. He found that when the president's closest advisors were deeply engrossed in problem solving, their drive for consensus—so as to preserve friendly intragroup relations—overrode what otherwise was their capacity to appraise alternative courses of action realistically. Janis coined the group's unhealthy impulse to unanimity "groupthink."[39]

Like Jervis and Janis, Alexander George focused on how policymakers make decisions. George concluded that the chief constraints on rational decision making under routine conditions are value complexity (the presence of competing values and interests embedded in a single issue) and uncertainty, particularly as a consequence of inadequate information. Under crisis conditions, stress tends to further impair performance.[40]

George's work on the relationship between the psychological and structural aspects of decision making in the White House is particularly useful. For
instance, the way in which the president structures his office and manages his
staff is a reflection of his personality and of how he in particular is comfortable conducting the decision-making process. John Kennedy was at ease with
the conflictual aspects of politics. His sense of efficacy included confidence in
his ability to manage the interpersonal relations of those around him, and his
cognitive style led him to participate actively in the policy-making process.
George concludes that "these personality characteristics contributed to forging a collegial style of policy making based on teamwork and shared responsibility among talented advisers. Kennedy recognized the value of diversity and
give-and-take among advisers, and he encouraged it."[41] Richard Nixon, in
contrast, favored a highly formalistic system, a preference that was shaped by
some of his particular personality traits, including intense conscientiousness,
a pronounced sense of aloneness and privacy, and a distaste for conflict in
face-to-face situations. Nixon's managerial system was thus characterized by
a high degree of centralization and tight structure, which allowed him to
protect his personal control over, among other things, foreign policy.

What we are arguing, then, is that the serious investigator of the president's impact on foreign affairs cannot afford to ignore totally the psychological dimension. In particular, aspects of personality such as worldview, cognitive style, political style, level of interest in foreign affairs, and life history
clearly shape presidential behavior in the international environment.[42] As
well, group dynamics, especially those that characterize small groups empow-
ered to make big decisions, shape political outcomes. It comes down then,
finally, to this: there is a relationship between individuals (particularly national leaders), either acting alone or in concert with a few others, and political outcomes at the international level. Our focus on the role of the American
president in world politics is therefore a necessary corrective to what we have
in the past either forgotten or ignored: that foreign affairs are fueled by the
passions of real men and women who ultimately determine how nations
behave.

PRESIDENTS AS WORLD LEADERS

Richard Rose has observed that the difference between the modern and
postmodern presidency is that a postmodern president can no longer dominate world politics. While we would argue that even the "modern" president
never could, Rose would seem to have a point. Relatively speaking, in recent
years the U.S. has become weaker and other nations stronger, certainly in
comparison with countries such as Japan. However, the same could not be
said of our power position in relation to the Soviet Union. The dramatic
collapse of communism in East Europe and the Soviets' own abandonment of
the communist monopoly of power have underscored the inability of the
Marxist-Leninist model to match democracy's capacity to fuel economic development. The global scope of America's commitments make the U.S. vulnerable to trouble abroad. This means that the resources of the White House
are no longer sufficient to meet all of the president's international responsibili-

ties. He has no choice, therefore, but to cooperate with foreign governments to achieve America's major economic and national security goals.[43]

It is impossible to pinpoint exactly when the international environment became so difficult for the president to manage. Rose proposes that it was the Vietnam War that heralded the arrival of the postmodern president by signaling that the time had arrived when executives were failing to accomplish what they had set out to accomplish. "Whereas President Truman's dispatch of troops to defend South Korea was a success, efforts by Kennedy, Johnson, Nixon, and Ford to defend South Vietnam finally met defeat. . . . Jimmy Carter has the unenviable distinction of being the first completely postmodern president."[44]

What is clear, in any case, is that the international context within which the president would exercise leadership is replete with constraints on his ability to act. The system is anarchic, at least to the extent that no single state is so powerful as to be able to dominate—either militarily or economically—the others; and there is no world government to impose law and order. Moreover, the major concerns are well beyond the control of any single national leader. That is, they are global in nature—for example, monetary and fiscal stability, a steadily growing population in the face of limited resources, pollution, the proliferation of nuclear weapons, and huge discrepancies in income among the world's peoples, especially along the North-South axis. Finally, the stage on which the president must now perform in order to get others to do what he wants them to do—from *initiation* of a policy goal all the way through to *implementation*—has expanded almost beyond recognition. The interdependence among nations and the revolution in telecommunications referred to just above make it imperative that the president be as attentive to the audience in Paris, France, as he is to the one in Paris, Illinois. In sum, presidents can no longer do their job simply by staying at home. To be effective world leaders, they must politick actively at the international level and confront the imperatives that govern a host of other sovereign states.[45]

This brings us to the tales of five recent presidents who tried to exercise leadership in world politics: John Kennedy, Lyndon Johnson, Richard Nixon, Jimmy Carter, and Ronald Reagan. In Part II, "Close-ups," we will take a hard and close look at one particular initiative, at the context within which it was carried out, and at the players—leader and followers—who were involved. To repeat what was said at the start: Our interest is in how well these five presidents led the nation and the world with regard to a foreign policy goal in which they were heavily invested. In particular, we ask whether the president's goal was clearly articulated and communicated; how energetically he used his authority and exercised power and influence; which tactics of power, authority, and influence he employed; what motivated domestic and foreign constituencies to accept, or reject, his attempt to lead; which sources of power, authority, and influence were most effective; and whether implementation was in fact ultimately accomplished.

We do not claim that these five chronicles render final judgments on Kennedy, Johnson, Nixon, Carter, and Reagan as world leaders. Foreign affairs are too complicated, and the leadership task too daunting, for conclusions based on a single case. At the same time, they are stories with lessons to teach—one of which is that, constraints at home and abroad notwithstanding, presidents who are so inclined can, *if* they are lucky *and* play their cards right, make an impact on international relations.

Notes

1. For more on the "hero in history debate," see Part I of *Political Leadership: A Source Book,* ed. Barbara Kellerman (Pittsburgh: University of Pittsburgh Press, 1986).

2. For a detailed discussion of theories of leadership, see Bernard M. Bass, *Stodgill's Handbook of Leadership* (New York: Free Press, 1981), chapter 3. Also see Barbara Kellerman, *Leadership: Multidisciplinary Perspectives* (New York: Prentice-Hall, 1984), passim.

3. Quoted in Herbert C. Kelman, "Social Psychological Approaches to the Study of International Relations," in *International Behavior,* ed. Kelman (New York: Holt, Rinehart, & Winston, 1965), p. 586. For one of the early efforts in this area, also see Joseph de Rivera, *The Psychological Dimension of Foreign Policy* (Columbus, Ohio: Charles E. Merrill, 1968).

4. For a recent case study of how individuals matter in foreign policy decisions, see Philip D. Stewart, Margaret G. Hermann, and Charles F. Hermann, "Modeling the 1973 Soviet Decision to Support Egypt," *American Political Science Review* (March 1989): pp. 35–39. The article focuses on how group processes mediate individual differences.

5. Herbert C. Kelman, "The Role of the Individual in International Relations: Some Conceptual and Methodological Considerations," *Journal of International Affairs* 1 (1970): pp. 1–4.

6. Fred I. Greenstein, *Personality and Politics: Problems of Evidence, Influence and Conceptualization* (Chicago: Markham, 1969), p. 42.

7. For more on the national leader's personality, see Barbara Kellerman and Jeffrey Z. Rubin, eds., *Leadership and Negotiation in the Middle East* (New York: Praeger, 1987).

8. For Alexander George's definition of personality, see *Presidential Decision Making in Foreign Policy: The Effective Use of Information and Advice* (Boulder, Colo.: Westview, 1980), p. 6.

9. Now that the word *leadership* has become fashionable, it appears frequently in the titles of books, especially books on the American presidency. Authors especially sensitive to the leadership process include James MacGregor Burns (virtually his entire oeuvre), Richard Neustadt (especially his classic *Presidential Power*), Fred I. Greenstein (particularly his more recent publications), and Bert Rockman (*The Leadership Question*).

10. The quote is from chapter 21 of *The Prince.* Machiavelli is quoted by Jean Blondel, on whose ideas this paragraph is based. See Blondel's *Political Leaders* (Beverly Hills, Calif.: Sage, 1987).

11. Ryan J. Barilleaux, "Evaluating Presidential Performance in Foreign Affairs," in *The Presidency and Public Policy Making,* eds. George C. Edwards et al. (Pittsburgh: University of Pittsburgh Press, 1985), pp. 114–29.

12. For more on the tie between leading and politicking, see Barbara Kellerman, *The Political Presidency: Practice of Leadership* (New York: Oxford University Press, 1984), especially chapters, 1, 3, and 4.

13. For a discussion of how African leaders have affected world politics, see Timothy M. Shaw and Naomi Chazan, "The Limits of Leadership: Africa in Contemporary World Politics," *International Journal* (Autumn 1982): pp. 543–54.

14. This argument is taken from Andrew Bard Schmookler, *The Parable of the Tribes* (Berkeley, Calif.: University of California Press, 1984).

15. For more on the motivations of followers, see Barbara Kellerman, ed., *Political Leadership: A Source Book* (Pittsburgh: University of Pittsburgh Press, 1986), Part II.

16. For a more detailed discussion of the way in which social scientific conceptions of power pertain to international relations, see David A. Baldwin, *Economic Statecraft* (Princeton:

Princeton University Press, 1985), pp. 18–24. Baldwin draws particularly on the pioneering work in this area of Robert Dahl.

17. The discussion that follows borrows heavily from Klaus Knorr, *The Power of Nations* (New York: Basic, 1975), especially chapter I.

18. Thomas Schelling, *Arms and Influence* (New Haven: Yale University Press, 1965), pp. 2, 3.

19. Alexander L. George, "The Development of Doctrine and Strategy," in *The Limits of Coercive Diplomacy*, ed. Alexander L. George, David K. Hall, and Willian E. Simons (Boston: Little, Brown, 1971), p. 18. For a discussion of coersion and diplomacy as they applied to the conflict in Vietnam, see Wallace J. Thies, *When Governments Collide* (Berkeley, Calif.: University of California Press, 1980).

20. For examples and a full discussion, see Barry M. Blechman and Stephen S. Kaplan, *Force without War: U.S. Armed Forces as a Political Instrument* (Washington: Brookings, 1978).

21. Robert O. Keohane and Joseph S. Nye, *Power and Interdependence: World Politics in Transition* (Boston: Little, Brown, 1977).

22. Baldwin, p. 14.

23. Ibid., pp. 41–42. It should be noted, however, that the experience of recent years suggests that economic power, like military power, is of only limited utility in achieving foreign policy goals.

24. Knorr, p. 310.

25. Hans Morganthau, *Politics among Nations* (New York: Knopf, 1963).

26. Elmer Plischke, *Diplomat in Chief* (New York: Praeger, 1986).

27. For more on presidents and summits see Plischke. For presidents at Soviet-American summits since 1960 see Barbara Kellerman, "Leaders and Leaders: Nine Soviet-American Summits," in *Essays in Honor of James MacGregor Burns*, Thomas Cronin and Michael Beschloss, eds. (New York: Prentice-Hall, 1988).

28. Janice Gross Stein, "Leadership in Middle East Peacemaking," *International Journal* XXXVII, no. 4 (1984): pp. 538–39.

29. Richard Nixon, who, as the Watergate scandal recedes, is being credited with considerable understanding of international relations, counseled the virtue of patience in presidential diplomacy. He once wrote that for the benefit of his successors, he would like to carve onto the wall of the Oval Office ten rules of negotiation. They are: (1) Always be prepared to negotiate, but never negotiate without being prepared. (2) Never be belligerent, but always be firm. (3) Always remember that covenants should be openly agreed to but privately negotiated. (4) Never seek publicity that would destroy the ability to get results. (5) Never give up unilaterally what could be used as a bargaining chip. (6) Never let your adversary underestimate what you *would* do in response to a challenge; never tell him in advance what you would *not* do. (7) Always leave your adversary a face-saving line of retreat. (8) Always carefully distinguish between friends who provide some human rights and enemies who deny all human rights. (9) Always do at least as much for our friends as our adversaries do for our enemies. (10) Never lose faith. In a just cause, faith can move mountains. Faith without strength is futile, but strength without faith is sterile. These ten aphorisms are quoted in Plischke, p. 477.

30. For more on the foreign affairs presidency, see Thomas E. Cronin, *The State of the Presidency,* 2nd ed. (Boston: Little, Brown, 1980), pp. 145 fg.

31. For more on this, see Margaret Hermann, "The Role of Leaders and Leadership in the Making of American Foreign Policy," in *Readings in American Foreign Policy* ed. Charles Kegley and Eugene Wittkopf (New York: St. Martin's, 1988).

32. For one interesting such effort, see Alexander George, "The Causal Nexus between Cognitive Beliefs and Decision Making Behavior: The Operational Code Belief System," in *Psychological Models in International Politics*, ed. Laurence S. Falkowski (Boulder, Colo.: Westview, 1979), pp. 95–124. Also see Stewart et al., p. 43.

33. Doris Kearns, *Lyndon Johnson and the American Dream* (New York: Harper & Row, 1976), p. 393.

34. Bruce Mazlish, *In Search of Nixon: A Psychohistorical History* (New York: Basic, 1972), pp. 138–39.

35. Betty Glad, *Jimmy Carter: In Search of the Great White House* (New York: Norton, 1980), p. 505.

36. Betty Glad, "Black and White Thinking: Ronald Reagan's Approach to Foreign Policy," *Political Psychology* (March 1983): p. 68.

37. The quotes in this paragraph are from James David Barber, *The Presidential Character: Predicting Performance in the White House* (Englewood Cliffs, N.J.: Prentice-Hall, Inc., 1972), pp. 12, 13.

38. See Robert Jervis, "Hypotheses on Misperception," in *International Politics and Foreign Policy,* ed. James N. Rosenau (New York: Free Press, 1969), pp. 239–54; and *Perception and Misperception in International Politics* (Princeton: Princeton University Press, 1976).

39. Irving I. Janis, *Groupthink: Psychological Studies of Policy Decisions and Fiascos* (Boston: Houghton Mifflin, 1982).

40. George, *Presidential Decision Making,* p. 57.

41. Ibid., p. 157.

42. Margaret Hermann, "Effects of Personal Characteristics of Political Leaders on Foreign Policy," in *Why Nations Act: Theoretical Perspectives for Comparative Foreign Policy Studies,* Maurice A. East et al., eds. (Beverly Hills: Sage, 1978); Charles W. Kegley, Jr., and Eugene R. Wittkopf, *American Foreign Policy* (New York: St. Martin's, 1987), especially pp. 526–31; and Paul M. Sniderman, *Personality and Democratic Politics* (Berkeley: University of California Press, 1975).

43. Richard Rose, *The Postmodern President: The White House Meets the World* (Chatham, N.J.: Chatham, 1988), pp. 2–7.

44. Ibid., p. 26.

45. Ibid., pp. 29, 38.

Part II

CLOSE-UPS:
Case Studies of
Presidential Leadership
in World Politics

5

John F. Kennedy's
Initiative in
Latin America

*Let every nation know, whether it wishes us well or ill, that we shall pay
any price, bear any burden, meet any hardship, support any friend, oppose any foe to assure the survival and the success of liberty.*
—Inaugural Address, January 20, 1961

BACKGROUND

Although in many ways John Kennedy can be considered the first modern president—he was, for example, the first to use television to maximum
advantage—in terms of foreign policy he still held most of the attitudes and
opinions that prevailed during the cold war. As the Inaugural quote cited
above suggests, he believed that the United States had the responsibility and
capacity to be actively involved in creating a just and stable world order.
Moreover, like his two predecessors, Harry Truman and Dwight Eisenhower,
he saw the world as essentially divided into two spheres: one dominated by
the United States and the other by the Soviet Union. The United States was the
leader of the "Free World" and the Soviet Union was the "Red Menace."

The picture of a young politician still engaged with old ideas emerged
very clearly during the 1960 presidential campaign. Kennedy argued that
America should be rallying the Free World against the Soviets "without war
or surrender."[1] Recognizing that the nation's confidence had been under-
mined by Sputnik (seen as evidence of the Soviet Union's advantage in space),
the U-2 incident (in which a supposedly invincible American spy plane was
shot down by the Russians) and Castro's victory in Cuba, Kennedy boldly
asserted that under Eisenhower the U.S. had passed from a position of
strength and respect to one of weakness and shame. He hammered at the
existence of a "missile gap" and said he would close it; he insisted that there
be a clear answer to communism and promised to provide it; and in the
closing days of the campaign, he asserted that "we can check the Communist
advance, that we can turn it back, and that we can, in this century, provide for
the ultimate victory of freedom over slavery."[2] In short, in a variety of ways
he was staking out a position more stridently anticommunist than that of his
predecessors. While the motivation for this posture was in part political, and

79

while clearly Kennedy saw the necessity for peaceful coexistence between the superpowers, he was in fact more a product of, than a deviant from, cold war thinking.

Theodore Sorensen, Kennedy's closest aide (after his brother Robert), has written that foreign affairs always interested the president more than domestic: "They occupied far more of his time and energy as President. They received from him far more attention to detail, from the shaping of alternatives, to the course of a proposal from origin to execution."[3] The main reason for this probably lies in his life history. Far more than most American presidents, John Kennedy was exposed to foreign cultures and international politics at an early age. Conversations at home during the early years, especially when his wealthy father Joseph P. Kennedy was in residence, were often about world affairs, and the education of young John Kennedy included a liberal number of trips abroad. During his college years, Kennedy made three trips to Europe; in all, during the forty-eight months that passed while Kennedy was enrolled at Harvard, he spent twelve months outside the U.S. Yet he was hardly an ordinary student out to see the world. Once his father was appointed ambassador to England, Jack Kennedy had access to the British establishment. Thus the trips provided him with another kind of education: a broad and substantial knowledge of European geopolitics, society, and customs.[4]

John Kennedy's exposure to the world beyond his own national borders did not stop with his experiences as a college student. During World War II he saw combat in the South Pacific. Later he had a brief foray into journalism, during which he covered the opening meeting of the United Nations and the British elections. And a short time thereafter, while he served in the House of Representatives for Massachusetts' 11th District and later as senator, he made additional trips to Europe, as well as to Asia and the Middle East. In fact his senatorial positions on such foreign policy issues as Vietnam (years before it became a public obsession), Algeria, the Third World, and the Soviets foreshadowed his views as candidate and president—which brings us back to the apparent contradiction between Kennedy as cold war warrior and Kennedy as herald of Camelot—the idealized name by which the Kennedy administration came to be known, especially after the president's death. (Camelot is the legendary English town where King Arthur had his court and Round Table.)

Not surprisingly, the real Kennedy was an amalgam of pragmatist and idealist. The same Inaugural Address that spoke to America's willingness to pay any price to defend liberty, also affirmed that while the U.S. ought never to negotiate out of fear, it ought never fear to negotiate. In fact, by the time he became president, Kennedy's views on foreign affairs were a mix of vigorous anticommunism and cautious realism. As a result, one chronicler accused him of fanning the flames of the cold war, another of being blind to the threat of communism. One critic called his Inaugural and first State of the Union messages alarmist, another naive. A religious leader who was pleased with the president's efforts on disarmament but unhappy with his emphasis on a strong defense, advised him; "Don't try to do two opposite things at once." The president replied, with an analogy to the rhythmic expansion and contraction of the heart: "All of life is like that—systole and diastole."[5]

Kennedy's management style was a logical extension of his eclectic, and sometimes even contradictory, world view. Since he felt altogether at ease with the conflictual aspects of politics and policy-making, since he had confidence in his ability to manage the interpersonal relations of those around him, and since he enjoyed participating directly in the policy-making process, he forged a style of decision making based on teamwork and shared responsibility. Characteristics of the president's decision-making style included his position at the center of the process, group problem solving, an information flow into the executive's team from various points lower in the bureaucracy, advisers who acted as generalists, and a typically informal decision process.[6]

Kennedy's leadership style tended to place relatively less emphasis on the traditional foreign policy bureaucracy, particularly the State Department, and more on his own personal staff. In fact, it has been said that his major organizational contribution in the area of foreign policy lay in the creation of a strong foreign policy staff and in the way he used this personal cadre of experts.[7] His relations with the State Department were often testy, and Dean Rusk, his secretary of state (known around town as "everybody's second choice for the job"), was never an administration insider. In contrast, his relationship with McGeorge Bundy, the special assistant to the president for national security affairs who was Kennedy's personal choice, was excellent. Bundy was a "crisp, terse, intellectual operator, accustomed to the chaos of a university faculty. He was close to an aggressive, pragmatic President whose style meshed well with his own."[8] Thus it was the strong foreign policy staff rather than the State Department that developed into the president's prime "agent of coordination" for foreign affairs—a fact that, not unnaturally, caused resentment among many long-time career officials.

There were considerable virtues to Kennedy's approach to foreign policy. It put him in touch with a wide range of information and opinions; it provided him with a roster of exceptionally fine aides; and, above all, it took into account the fact that foreign policy–making is inherently a political process that will respond to a chief executive with strong political skills.

There were disadvantages to Kennedy's style as well. It discouraged the emergence of a primary policy leader other than the president himself; it failed to draw on institutional memory; it exacerbated tensions between the traditional foreign policy bureaucracy and the White House foreign policy staff; and, as a consequence, it frequently resulted in a lack of coordination among the various elements of the foreign policy–making system. In fact, both the advantages and disadvantages of Kennedy's approach to the making of foreign policy were evident in the first two years of his administration, which were characterized by several dramatic episodes in the realm of international relations.

Two of the most remarkable took place during the first several months of Kennedy's tenure in office. The worst disaster, perhaps of the entire Kennedy presidency, was what has come to be known simply as "the Bay of Pigs." A force of some fourteen hundred anti-Castro Cuban exiles—organized, trained, armed, transported, and directed by the U.S. Central Intelligence Agency— landed at the Cuban Bay of Pigs, only to be crushed in less than three days by troops fighting under Kennedy's nemesis, Fidel Castro. While in retrospect it became clear that Kennedy was only proceeding with a scheme that had its origins in the Eisenhower administration, his decision to forge ahead was hasty.

The plan of attack was never subject to the rigorous scrutiny of the Kennedy administration, and to this day the incident stands as an exemplar of how not to operate in the foreign policy realm.

The Bay of Pigs was immediately recognized as a debacle. At home it signaled an early end to the euphoria that had characterized the first hundred days of the Kennedy administration; abroad there was widespread astonishment and disillusion. The president, however, took responsibility for the fiasco. "We got a big kick in the leg," he acknowledged. "And we deserved it. But maybe we'll learn something from it."[9] Many observers have in fact commented that when the next Cuban crisis broke—the missile crisis—the lessons learned the first time around seemed to stand Kennedy in good stead.

Kennedy's second major foray into international politics, however, was also something less than a brilliant success. His trip to the summit with Soviet premier Nikita Khrushchev, a mere four months after Inauguration Day, accomplished little. While the agenda contained at least three complex and critical items—the communist encroachment of Laos, test ban negotiations, and the divided city of Berlin—preparations for the Soviet-American talks were meager. As a consequence, no progress was made at the 1961 Vienna conference on either Laos or a test ban treaty, and on Berlin the only step taken was a step back. Moreover, the fact that the missile crisis was precipitated a little over a year after the Vienna summit lends credence to the view that their meeting may actually have hindered understanding between the two leaders. In particular, some commentators concluded that Khrushchev came to view the young American president as naive and indecisive. No less astute an observer of the Soviet-American relationship than George Kennan opined that the Vienna summit may actually have done the cause of peace harm: "I felt that [Kennedy] had not acquitted himself well on this occasion and that he had permitted Khrushchev to say many things that should have been challenged right there on the spot. . . . I think [the Soviets] thought that this is a tongue-tied young man who is not forceful and who doesn't have ideas of his own."[10]

The third major episode during John Kennedy's eventful first year as president was the conflict between East and West over Berlin. Khrushchev seemed convinced that he could acquire West Berlin; Kennedy was determined to defend it against Soviet incursion. In the president's words: "We cannot negotiate with those who say: 'What's mine is mine, and what's yours is negotiable.' " Still, the communists went ahead in August 1961 and built the infamous Berlin Wall. They thereby divided the city, eliminated the escape hatch for East Germans, ended West Berlin's usefulness as a "showplace for Western capitalism," and violated Berlin's quadripartite status.

The Soviet action precipitated a major policy disagreement among Kennedy's advisers. On the one hand were the hard-liners who considered the Russians to be engaged in an offensive move in Berlin that posed serious dangers to the entire Western position in Europe. And on the other were those who held a less ominous view of Soviet intentions, who believed that Khrushchev was engaged in an essentially defensive operation in Berlin, aimed only at consolidating Soviet control over its current holdings in East Europe, which included East Berlin.

Kennedy's response demonstrated his growing sophistication as a world leader and his creative use of conflicting opinions and advice. He did not react by resisting the erection of the wall with bulldozers and tanks. But he did communicate to Khrushchev in no uncertain terms that the West was resolved to defend the beleaguered German city. Kennedy's effort in this regard succeeded. West Berlin not only did not wither, it flourished. And when John Kennedy visited the city in 1963, it was the scene of one of the most overwhelming receptions of his career. Before a crying, shouting, cheering crowd of four hundred thousand Berliners, Kennedy proclaimed, "All free men, wherever they may live, are citizens of Berlin, and therefore as a free man, I take pride in the words: *Ich bin ein Berliner.*"

Since the Cuban missile crisis is one of the most widely covered international incidents in the academic literature, here we need only point out that the episode is widely perceived to be the high point of Kennedy's brief career as a world leader.* After what was manifestly a rocky start in foreign affairs, the president had in fact made some substantial gains in 1961 and early 1962. Not the least among these was a growing reputation as an international star. His mere presence on any scene turned the event into a media spectacular and his several trips abroad, especially when accompanied by his beautiful and fashionable wife, were, at the least, a public relations triumph. In terms of Kennedy's stock, then, the missile crisis came at a fortuitous time. It enabled him finally to demonstrate that he was a man of substance as well as of style.

The Caribbean confrontation between the U.S. and the USSR lasted thirteen days and when it was over it was Khrushchev who had backed down. The U.S. had warned the Soviet Union against placing missiles in Cuba; if they were permitted to remain, therefore, American credibility would be worthless. Thus Kennedy was in a situation in which he felt that he could under no circumstances afford to lose. To be sure, the risks this time around were extraordinarily high. Had neither side turned back, a violent clash, and possibly even a nuclear war, might have ensued. But Khrushchev did, in the words, of Dean Rusk, "blink first," which meant both that the crisis passed and that Kennedy emerged the stronger for having coped with a situation of unprecedented tension and anxiety, and indeed for having stood his ground vis-à-vis his Soviet counterpart.

Although Kennedy had been considering the idea of a test ban for some time, the missile crisis provided it with new impetus. In December 1962, Kennedy was surprised and pleased to receive a letter from Khrushchev in which he agreed that the time had "come now to put an end once and for all to all nuclear tests." Nevertheless, the path to agreement on this issue between the Americans and the Soviets continued to be rocky. This time around, however, Kennedy was undaunted by Soviet recalcitrance. In the late spring of 1963 he took three important steps in search of an accord with the Soviets: he joined with the British prime minister Harold Macmillan in proposing new talks on a test ban treaty; he decided that the U.S., once its present series of tests had ended, would not be the first to resume nuclear tests in the atmosphere; and he delivered a path-breaking speech at American University that amounted to a loud and clear departure from the cold war rhetoric that had

---

*However, in recent years some revisionist historians have refuted that view, arguing that Kennedy brought the world unnecessarily close to the brink of war.

prevailed on both sides for well over fifteen years.[11] Six weeks after the American University address, the test ban treaty between the United States and the Soviet Union was concluded and initialed. By all accounts it was one of John Kennedy's finest achievements.

It will be apparent from this review of some of the major episodes punctuating foreign policy during the Kennedy years that they generally entailed reactive leadership—leadership (or managership) in response to events imposed from outside. Of the events touched on in the foregoing discussion only the test ban treaty was the product of directive presidential leadership. That is, the treaty constituted a goal toward which President Kennedy deliberately and self-consciously led the American people. It was largely the product of *his* vision and initiative, and it was *his* energy and conviction that turned the dream into reality. But there was another major Kennedy initiative that fits all our criteria of directive presidential leadership. In fact, since the Alliance for Progress was the realization of a foreign policy goal that predated John Kennedy's time in the White House, it can reasonably be seen as his most considered claim to being a world leader.

NATIONAL LEADERSHIP: PRESENTING THE CASE AT HOME

John F. Kennedy considered the Alliance for Progress—a huge ($20 billion) economic and social development program for South and Central America—the "most important element of his Administration's foreign policy."[12] A "vast cooperative effort . . . to satisfy the basic needs of the American people for homes, work and land, health and schools," the Alliance no doubt satisfied the president's humanitarian impulse. But John Kennedy was also a determined counterrevolutionary.[13] By initiating an aid program for democratic modernization in Latin America, Kennedy sought to nip communism, new Fidel Castros, in the bud—counterrevolution through "democratic revolution." He sought, in other words, to address his own campaign charge that under the Republicans too little had been done to eliminate local sources of communist success.

Kennedy's particular interest in Latin America had its roots in his days as a student when he took a South American tour, one of several trips abroad that were arranged by his father.[14] During his early years, he also became convinced through his studies that the Democratic party had contributed to the growth of a special relationship between the countries of Latin America and the U.S. He took note, for example, of Franklin Roosevelt's Good Neighbor Policy and Sumner Welles's organization of an anti-axis wartime front in the hemisphere. As an aide to Kennedy recalled much later, the president was determined to build on these achievements of his Democratic predecessors.[15]

The process began in 1958 when the stoning of Vice President Richard Nixon in Peru and Venezuela prompted Senator Kennedy to urge that our own hemisphere be given greater priority in U.S. foreign policy. He went on to endorse several specific proposals, including loans to encourage land reform and the expansion of programs of cultural and educational exchange.[16] Soon U.S. policy toward Latin America would figure prominently in the senator's campaign for the presidency, as he repeatedly accused the Republicans of failure with regard to that area of the world.

In fact, it was during the 1960 presidential campaign that the Alliance for Progress was conceived: Kennedy instructed his expert on Latin America, Richard Goodwin, to prepare a speech outlining key objectives toward the region. That speech was delivered in front of the county courthouse in Tampa, Florida, in October 1960. It reached a crescendo when Kennedy declared his belief "in a Western Hemisphere where all the people—the Americans of the South and the Americans of the North . . . are joined together in an alliance for progress—*alianza para progresso.*"

More specifically, the aspiring president explained that the alliance would introduce a number of departures in U.S. policy toward Latin America, including:

- "unequivocal support to democracy" and opposition to dictatorship
- provision of "long term development funds, essential to a growing economy"
- aid to "programs of land reform"
- stimulus to private investment and encouragement to private business "to immerse themselves in the life of the country . . . through mixing capital with local capital, training local inhabitants for skilled jobs, and making maximum use of labor"
- expansion of technical assistance programs.

Because the outdoor crowd appeared restless, Kennedy decided against delivering the entire prepared text. But he told Goodwin that he considered the speech of major importance and that he wanted it released in full as a statement.

Once elected, Kennedy left no room for doubt that he attached great importance to his plan for Latin America. Apparently persuaded that the funds were available—Kennedy was far less hemmed in by concerns over the dangers of robust federal spending than Eisenhower—in his Inaugural Address he affirmed to the nation: "To our sister Republics South of the border, we offer a special pledge . . . a new alliance for progress."[17] And on March 13, 1961, in an animated speech in the East Room of the White House, the new president formally proposed the program to members of Congress and to the Latin American diplomatic corps.[18]

The next day he brought his case before the legislature. He began by asking that $600 million be specifically earmarked for the Alliance. He noted that millions of Latin Americans "are struggling to free themselves from the bonds of poverty and hunger and ignorance," looking to the "modern science" of North America to bring "a better life for themselves and their children." Latin Americans, he continued, are the "inheritors of a deep belief in political democracy." At the same time, he warned that the desperate problems of the region made it particularly vulnerable to "communism or other forms of tyranny."[19] This last point was repeated a month later; addressing the public in a television interview, the president again raised the spectre of communist expansion in Latin America.[20]

Kennedy was also involved in personally lobbying on behalf of the Alliance. In fact, he decided not to go to the August conference in Punta del Este, Uruguay, that would formally launch the Latin American initiative because he thought it in the "best interests" of his program that he stay in Washington and work for its passage by Congress.[21] The president was particularly solicitous of members of the Senate. While the Senate was considering Kennedy's request for funds, he sent individual senators personal messages, stressing the importance of his initiative.[22]

In the main, Kennedy's politicking bore fruit: the $600 million originally requested was approved by Congress. And Congress also authorized spending on development loans up to $7.2 billion over five years. While this was less than the $8.8 billion the president originally requested, and while authorizations would have to be approved by Congress each year, the monies that would now be funneled to Latin America represented a significant victory for the president.[23]

Indeed, a defeat in Congress would have seriously embarrassed the administration for at the same time the president's five-year borrowing and lending program was being deliberated, the United States was making a long-term commitment at the conference in Punta del Este. Virtually certain that Kennedy's foreign aid program would be approved by Congress in roughly its original form, Treasury Secretary Douglas Dillon in effect pledged the U.S. to a ten-year program of assistance to Latin America, running at approximately $1.1 billion annually and marked by loans "up to fifty years and at very low or zero rates of interests."[24] In welcoming Dillon back to Washington, Kennedy first told the public that the conference—at which the Alliance for Progress was signed by the U.S. and nineteen Latin American nations—had been the country's "most important" foreign policy event in months and then vowed to uphold the commitments Dillon had made there.[25]

In striving to keep his promise, Kennedy undertook an initiative that at least one authority has described as decisive in gaining congressional support for the alliance. In his book on the Kennedy presidency, Lewis J. Paper stated that Kennedy realized from the outset that the Alliance would not attract the required congressional support unless Latin American countries indicated "a willingness to join in the fight against the spread of communism."[26] As the president wrote to Goodwin just after the Punta del Este conference: "It is going to be increasingly difficult to get the money from Congress unless we can find some interest on the part of the other Latin American countries to do something about Communism."

Accordingly, the administration pressured the Organization of American States (OAS) to take some action to demonstrate Latin America's commitment to democracy. Responding to American pressure, the OAS foreign ministers voted in January 1962 to institute an immediate arms embargo to Cuba and to exclude Cuba from the Inter-American System. It should be noted that the OAS instituted these measures despite their apparent violation of its own charter. Legal "formalities" were superceded by the necessity of sending a clear anticommunist signal to Congress.

For his part, Kennedy ensured that this signal did not go unnoticed.

Before accepting questions at his January 31, 1962, news conference, he explained what the OAS had done and expressed "satisfaction" that the organization had "taken explicit steps to protect the hemisphere's ability to achieve progress with freedom."[27]

However, just seven months after the Punta del Este conference, the administration had to retreat somewhat from the pledges it had made there. To be sure, more than $1 billion in loans and grants to Latin America had already been committed by March 1962,[28] keeping pace with the Punta del Este promise. But in his foreign aid message to Congress on March 17, 1962, Kennedy requested $3 billion for the Alliance over the next five years,[29] markedly less than what the U.S. had virtually pledged in Punta del Este.

Despite Kennedy's successful engineering of the OAS signal to Congress, there was good reason for his modified request. There was an influential body of opinion in Washington that held that the Alliance would "open the door to incompetent liberals who would bring about inflation, disinvestment, capital flight and social indiscipline and would eventually be shoved aside by the communists."[30] Moreover, there was growing sentiment that the Alliance was a mere check-writing program that would do little to push for land reform or remedy the continuing financial disorder in many Latin American countries. Several congressmen went so far as to declare that "you have got to let a few of these countries go to the communists so they and the others will understand that the United States will not be milked by simply posing the threat that they might go Communist if the aid is withheld."[31] Even Senate majority leader Mike Mansfield, long an advocate of aid to Latin America, stated that the United States should refrain from long-range commitments to Brazil because that country's regime had been unable to govern effectively and make good use of financial assistance to date.

Although it was such skepticism that presumably prompted Kennedy to modify his request to Congress, he remained vigorous in his appeals for what was still substantial aid to Latin America. In a forceful March 14, 1962, news conference, the president asserted that the Alliance "is just as important as our national defense." He even went on the offensive, suggesting that those who advocated the deepest cuts in foreign aid were either misguided or hypocritical: they were the same ones who "make the most vigorous speeches against Communism and call for a policy of victory." In a final thrust at those who would prune his new aid request, the president made clear that any opponent of the bill would have to live with his conscience: "If anyone feels that . . . it doesn't make any difference if Latin America is taken over . . . by Communists, and if they are not interested in this fight, they should cut it."[32]

Of course, Kennedy also stressed the achievements the Alliance had made in its first seven months. For example, his March 13, 1962, address on the first anniversary of his proposal of the Alliance evolved into a full-fledged panegyric. He told members of Congress—"on whom we depend so much in guiding and supporting and stimulating and directing our policies in this hemisphere"—that the Alliance had ushered in a "dramatic shift in the thinking and the attitudes . . . in our Hemisphere."[33] He then referred to a variety of groups within Latin American society, declaring that they "have accepted the goals of the Charter [of Punta del Este] as their own personal and political commitments."[34] In terms of concrete accomplishments, the president cited, among other developments, "better food for the children of Puno in Peru, new schools for people of Colombia, new homes for campesinos in Venezuela," and tax and land reform laws "on the books."[35] Then, close to the conclusion of the speech, Kennedy declared that the U.S. was, through the Alliance, finally accepting "its full responsibilities to its sister Republics."[36]

When confronted with questions from the press regarding the pace of progress of the Alliance, Kennedy counseled patience. At his March 14, 1962, news conference, for example, he urged "some sense of perspective" about the Alliance. "The organization took place only months ago. We should have some understanding of how complicated this task is and give this child a chance to build some strength before we psychoanalyze him."[37] Similarly, at his June 14, 1962, press conference, the president stated that he was "hopeful that the United States would be persistent in supporting the Alliance for Progress and not expect that suddenly the problems of Latin America, which have been with us and with them for so many years, can suddenly be solved overnight. . . ."[38]

The president's efforts and manifest personal interest in the Alliance would result in some success with the legislature. Title VI of the 1962 Foreign Assistance Act singled out the Alliance in a separate authorization bill, thus marking Congress's formal adoption of the president's hemisphere program.[39] Since funds would now be appropriated to the Alliance separately from development funds for general use in other areas of the world,[40] the president's Latin American initiative was accorded special status.

However, instead of authorizing $3 billion over five years, as requested, the bill authorized only $2.4 billion over four years.[41] More important, Congress again exercised its institutional prerogative by stipulating that the administration would have to request appropriations annually.[42] This measure posed a particular obstacle to the Alliance's goal of facilitating long-term development planning on the part of recipient countries. Indeed, the day after Kennedy's foreign policy priority had been formally recognized and funded by Congress, the president sounded less than pleased at a news conference when asked his thoughts on the Alliance: "Measured against all that has to be done, I think we have to do much better."[43]

This appraisal reflected Kennedy's own very high standards for his foreign policy priority, as well as his desire to give Congress the message that more would, in fact, have to be done. In addition, Congress's insistence on yearly appropriations requests was, to be sure, a serious setback to the Alliance's goal of long-term planning. Indeed, in his public statements on the Alliance during the several months immediately following the enactment of Title VI, Kennedy mainly spoke of the difficulties facing the program, maintaining they were greater than those that had confronted the Marshall Plan.[44]

Nonetheless, during Kennedy's January 14, 1963, State of the Union Address, he once again spoke buoyantly of the Alliance.[45] And it was true that, setbacks notwithstanding, his particularly high investment of political capital in the program had brought returns. In 1961–1962, Latin America's share of the U.S. foreign assistance budget was 25 percent, as compared with a mere 7 percent for the period 1946–1960. In 1962, U.S. economic assistance to Latin America amounted to a per capita commitment of $4.82. By comparison, obligations to the Near East and South Asia amounted to a per capita commitment of $2.73; the Far East, $2.71; and Africa, $2.50.[46]

Withall, by the summer of 1963, it was becoming increasingly clear that the lofty goals of the Alliance were far from being met. In early August, Kennedy again publicly acknowledged that "we have a long, long way to go and in some ways the road seems longer than it was when the journey started."[47]

But what is clear is that the problem did not lie in Kennedy's failure to mobilize the legislature. For until Kennedy's death, Congress did in fact enable the U.S. to keep pace with its Punta del Este commitment. From August 1961 to November 1963, the U.S. provided Latin America with $2.3 billion in aid.[48] Moreover, for fiscal year 1964, Congress appropriated for the Alliance approximately $852 million of the $902 million Kennedy had requested. As the *New York Times* reported: "At a time when Congress is increasingly impatient with foreign aid, this is a sensationally high batting average."[49]

WORLD LEADERSHIP: IMPLEMENTING THE POLICY ABROAD

In 1962, few Latin American republics exceeded the Punta del Este goal of a 2.5 percent increase in annual per capita income.[50] By 1963, however, eight Latin American countries attained increases in per capita income of nearly 5 percent.[51] Moreover, by August 1963, the Alliance could claim credit for the addition of 140,000 new homes (or family dwelling units); 8,200 classrooms; 4,000,000 textbooks; 160,000 agricultural loans; 700 community water systems and wells; and 900 hospitals and health centers.[52] In addition, the Alliance enabled one out of every four school-age children in Latin America to enjoy an extra food ration.[53]

On the other hand, there were reasons to doubt that the Alliance was in the process of creating the "lands of hope and progress" that Dillon foresaw at Punta del Este,[54] or the "development of an entire continent" that Kennedy spoke of hopefully just four days before his death.[55] The disappointment was in large part attributable to economic woes in Brazil and Argentina,[56] which together accounted for about half of Latin America's population, as well as half its industrial and agricultural production.[57]

Moreover, land and tax reforms were bottled up in conservative legislatures all across Latin America. While by July 1963, land reform laws were on the books in ten countries, virtually no substantial progress had been made in practice.

Neither did the Alliance prove to be a boon for democracy. In 1962, the governments of both Argentina and Peru were toppled by military coups; in 1963, four more governments—Guatemala, Ecuador, the Dominican Republic, and Honduras—fell under military control.

Finally, there was growing disenchantment with the Alliance in general among the peoples of Latin America. Politicians and neighborhood leaders throughout the region, reflecting public sentiment, explained that the Alliance was losing its struggle against corruption, underdevelopment, and ignorance.[58]

The question then is, where did things go wrong? How did it come to pass that Kennedy's relative success with Congress failed to translate into long-term gains? The problem did not lie with Kennedy's failure to articulate his goals. Indeed, from the outset Kennedy made a point of being personally involved in communicating the message of the Alliance not only to Americans but to Latin Americans as well. On March 13, 1961, it will be recalled, the president himself formally introduced the program to the Latin American diplomatic corps; moreover, he himself had gone over Goodwin's draft of the prepared speech with particular care. The address was idealistic, but it was delivered with vigor and conviction and it animated the audience despite underlying doubt and cynicism.[59] A month later, speaking to a session of the OAS, Kennedy took some time to remind the delegates of the program he had proposed the previous month, which would give "substance to the hopes of our people."[60] Kennedy himself was not present at the August Punta del Este conference that formally organized the conference because, as indicated above, he felt the Alliance's interests would be better served if he remained in Washington and campaigned for his foreign aid package. But a speech was read in his name, which was marked by words that "no President of the United States had ever spoken . . . to Latin America before."[61]

Moreover, after the Punta del Este conference had formally set the Alliance in motion, the president made a point of meeting personally with Latin American leaders with an unusual degree of frequency.[62] Between September 1961 and October 1963, there were no less than eleven such private meetings with individual Latin American leaders, all of which resulted in joint statements pledging continued commitment to the Alliance.[63] In addition, he took the opportunity presented by the first anniversary of his proposal of the Alliance to praise the program at length before an audience of Latin American ambassadors and members of the OAS and to stress that Latin Americans themselves would have primary responsibility for the future of the initiative.[64] He also seized every occasion to hail Latin American leaders whom he deemed particularly cooperative in implemeting the program.[65]

Kennedy further recognized the importance of personally communicating his message to other influential groups within Latin America. For example, in talking to the Third Inter-American Meeting of Educators in August 1963, he spoke of the "great goals" and "common hope for the future" represented by the Alliance.[66] Finally, Kennedy also delivered his message in person to the masses in Latin America, despite the discouragement of State Department officials, who remembered the violently hostile crowds that Nixon had encountered three years earlier.[67] In December 1961, he visited Caracas, Venezuela, and Bogotá, Colombia. In Venezuela he spoke bouyantly of the Alliance before crowds at the airport and later at La Morita Resettlement Project, where he spoke at some length about "the gigantic new steps that are now being taken."[68] In Columbia, at both the airport and at a housing project, he sounded the same themes.

The following two years Kennedy continued to appear personally before the Latin American public on behalf of his hemisphere program and the "democratic revolution" that it was supposed to usher in. In March 1962, the site was a housing project in Mexico City.[69] In March 1963, he visited Costa Rica, where he also spoke at a housing project and at the University of Costa

Rica.[70] Everywhere the president was greeted by throngs that gave him tumultuous welcomes[71] and by all accounts he was enormously popular with both the leaders and the publics in Latin America.[72] At the same time, however, there were good and ample reasons why Kennedy's hemisphere program fell short of reaching the heights that his personal popularity did.

It was widely recognized among both U.S. and Latin American officials that bureaucratic inefficiency was seriously hampering the hemisphere program. Andrew E. Rice, special assistant to Under Secretary of State Chester Bowles, stressed the problem in a March 28, 1962, memorandum to Bowles. The success of the alliance, he argued, would require:

> streamlining of our own administrative structure so that we can *execute* programs rapidly and flexibly. In Latin America I heard one sad story after another about the endless delays in getting replies from Washington. . . . It seems obvious that we must give greater autonomy to the field if we are to move with dispatch. Similarly, we must speed up Washington's decisions when decisions have to be made here.[73]

During the same period, another U.S. official, reporting from La Paz, Bolivia, sent a telegram to the State Department describing Bolivia's frustration over "delays and evasions being made by the American bureaucracy in administering aid programs."[74]

Latin Americans saw the need for an autonomous agency which, like the Peace Corps, would be separate from the Agency for International Development (AID) and much closer to the president. Two former Latin American heads of state, writing reports on the Alliance in June of 1963, strongly urged such structural reformation. Former Brazilian president Juscelino Kubitschek de Oliveira stated that it is "indispensable that the mechanism for coordinating the Alliance for Progress be improved and strengthened by an autonomous agency . . . with direct access to the President."[75] The former president of Colombia, Alberto Llerus Camargo, maintained that the alliance "has been administratively relagated to a subordinate position—separated from its author and most vigorous defender, the President himself, by a number of steps in the bureaucratic hierarchy."[76] Even former White House aide Arthur M. Schlesinger, Jr., one of Kennedy's most sympathetic biographers, agreed in retrospect that it was "probably a mistake to set up the Alliance within the Agency for International Development." With the benefit of hindsight, Schlesinger writes: "If the Alliance had been established, like the Peace Corps, as a separate agency, the resulting states and independence would, I believe, have increased its effectiveness. But the proponents of bureaucratic tidiness won out."[77]

Among other things, bureaucratic delays meant that loans and grants that had been committed to Latin America were not disbursed in timely fashion. By the middle of March 1962, for example, of the total of more than $1 billion that had been allocated, only an estimated 25 percent had actually been distributed.[78] In addition to slowing the achievements of the alliance, such bureaucratic delays also weakened morale. Lleras reported that the "sense of urgency that persuaded the meeting in Punta del Este" gave way to a "slow process of bureaucratization."[79] Rice wrote that the slowness in Wash ington made it a "little embarrassing to be trying to tell the Brazilians how to improve their personnel practices."[80]

Kennedy himself expressed serious concern that bureaucratic inefficiency was impeding progress. Teodoro Moscosco, AID deputy for Latin America, recalled that the president continually pressed him, "asking why they couldn't do more and do it faster."[81]

In late October 1963, Kennedy "was more troubled than ever by the organization of Latin American affairs within our own government."[82] He returned to an idea that had first been proposed by an aide in 1961 and had eventually been rejected due to bureaucratic opposition: the creation of an under secretary of state for the Bureau of Inter-American Affairs, embracing both the Alliance and the political responsibilities of the assistant secretary. He dictated a memorandum to Secretary of State Dean Rusk, stating that he wished now to establish the new undersecretariate. He did not receive a response, and renewed the message to Rusk shortly before his death.

Hence, up to the end, "proponents of bureaucratic tidiness won out," as Schlesinger put it. To be sure, a vigorous presidential effort would have been required to overcome the resistance to significant change in the existing bureaucracies. But as Lleras explained, the Alliance was "an exceptional movement that required, perhaps, exceptional organs and more dexterous procedures than those that prevailed when the great effort was initiated."[83]

Successful implementation of the Alliance also demanded devotion to the president's program among Foreign Service officers both in Washington and Latin America. Indeed, the president was warned by Schlesinger early on that there was a lack of dedication to the Alliance in the Foreign Service—in part, no doubt, because they recognized the task could not be done with the resources available. In a memorandum dated June 27, 1961, the White House aide reported to Kennedy on "a long talk" he had had the previous day with Dr. Arturo Morales-Carrion, deputy assistant secretary of state for Inter-American Affairs. On the basis of the discussion with Morales-Carrion, Schlesinger informed the president that the Foreign Service officers involved in Latin American affairs were "predominantly out of sympathy with the Alianza."[84] Quoting Morales-Carrion, he reported that " 'Among this group there is no joy, no purpose, no drive. . . . They form a sullen knot of resistance to fresh approaches.' "[85]

Despite this early warning, the record suggests that Kennedy failed to take the requisite measures to rectify the situation. An April 1962 Foreign Service dispatch from Brazil, for example, was forthright in acknowledging that most Brazilian workers and labor leaders regarded U.S. officials there as insufficiently committed to the goals of the Alliance.[86] A staff report issued in the summer of 1962 stated: "Direct influencing of the public by senior officials of our mission is not attempted to the extent that it probably [could be]."[87] Several months later, in a memorandum to Ralph Dungan, a special assistant to the president, Schlesinger expressed his concern over "the kind of men we are sending as Ambassadors to Latin America . . . men who have no particular sense of identification with the Kennedy Administration and who could live (and in some cases did live) quite as happily with the Eisenhower–Latin American policy."[88] Finally, writing to Kennedy in September 1963, Goodwin confirmed that there had been little improvement since Schlesinger's initial warning more than two years earlier: "The Alianza has the same trouble as the Washington Nats—they don't have the ballplayers. . . . The reasons for this are many but include: complete lack of a good recruiting effort. . . ."[89]

To be sure, there may have been many other reasons why the Alliance was not served well by many of the officials assigned to work on its behalf,[90] and Kennedy did on occasion attempt to infuse his Foreign Service officers with a measure of zeal.[91] But the "incomplete lack of good recruiting effort"—the lack of Foreign Service officers assigned to Latin America who were committed to the goals of the Alliance—was surely a serious hinderance to the implementation of the program.

There was also a consensus among close observers of the Alliance that the U.S. was not doing enough to create a "mystique" for the Alliance that would inspire Latin Americans and facilitate implementation of the program. For example, in a February 1962 letter to the executive vice president of the Inter-American Development Bank, the vice president of Vision, Inc., Alexander Nimick, Jr., began by arguing that vigorous public relations campaigns stopped a swing toward communism during the early days of the Marshall Plan and thwarted a Nazi attempt to win over Latin Americans in the 1940s. He concluded that such an information program was vital for the Alliance:

> We are attempting to launch the Alliance *without* any information program at all! I submit that this is impossible. The only hope of making the Alliance something more than just another U.S. aid program—of giving it an emotional, ideological appeal (a mystique as you have called it)—is by a major, imaginative information campaign.[92]

There is evidence to suggest that Kennedy was made aware of such arguments, as they were also expounded within his administration. In his March 1962 memorandum to Bowles, for instance, Rice urged the creation of "an Alliance 'mystique' which makes each element of society feel it has a part in the success of the grand design."[93] He also proposed a number of means by which this "mystique" could be created.[94] Similarly, a staff report issued in the summer of 1962 called for the U.S. to begin "development and influencing of indigenous government information programs."[95] It, too, offered a number of specific suggestions as to how such a campaign might be undertaken.[96]

Indeed, during this period the media had also seized on the lack of a vigorous information program. The *New York Times,* for example, reported: "Almost no full-time attention has been given to the political and psychological aspects of 'selling' the Alliance to a Latin America that is still half skeptical about United States intentions. . . ."[97]

The Kennedy administration did not, however, act on these public relations concerns. To be sure, the president continued to make numerous trips to the region. But as to a full-fledged information campaign, there is no evidence to suggest that the situation had changed since the first half of 1962, when administration officials expressed their concern and when the *New York Times* offered its critique. As late as November 1963, Brazilian foreign minister Joao Augusto deplored Kennedy's political leadership in the Alliance because the American president had, he charged, turned the program into an essentially economic machinery with little appeal to the hemisphere's masses.[98]

Finally, implementation of a central Alliance objective—democratic revolution—appears to have suffered because of its inherent incompatibility with another one of Kennedy's chief aims: containing communist revolution. Although Kennedy's goal of democratic revolution depended largely on pro-democratic leaders, he greatly increased American aid to the traditionally antidemocratic Latin American military because it was a safeguard against communist insurrection. Indeed, U.S. military assistance to Latin America during the 1960s jumped 50 percent per year over that allocated during the 1950s.[99]

To be sure, Washington's embarrassment over this contradiction was mitigated by several considerations: the military was frequently pro-U.S.; it was often quite efficient in its efforts to modernize; and it occasionally had at least tacit public support.[100] Nevertheless, the marked increase in U.S. aid to the Latin American military hardly fostered the Alliance's aim of strengthening democratic institutions in the hemisphere. Instead, as noted above, there were six successful coups in 1962–1963 alone in which U.S.-backed counterinsurgency units often played a key role.

Moreover, it was only after the takeovers in the Dominican Republic and Honduras in the fall of 1963 that Kennedy resolved to take concrete measures against such usurpations; he removed missions and suspended U.S. aid indefinitely. In the meantime, the U.S. had given the impression that it was "quite prepared to accept military dictatorship in Latin America." Such was the observation of none other than Schlesinger—following Kennedy's decision to renew military aid to the Peruvian junta even after its 1962 coup.[101]

Perhaps the president's dual aims of promoting democratic revolution in Latin America and containing communism there at the same time were inherently irreconcilable. In that case, the rise in Latin American militarism in 1962–1963 may be seen as a development the Alliance was simply powerless to prevent. On the other hand, it is at least possible that had Kennedy quickly and clearly conveyed the message that military coups were unacceptable, their numbers would have been checked without any concomitant rise in communism.

Of the fact that the president displayed some of the same conviction and energy abroad that he did at home there can be little doubt. His tactics, however, clearly left something to be desired—in no small part because he seems not to have recognized what had to be done in order to get where he wanted to go. These issues will be explored more fully in the following section, as will the larger problem of the inherent limitations of any American president undertaking leadership at the international level. Indeed, the Alliance made these limitations abundantly clear.

KENNEDY AS WORLD LEADER

For President Kennedy's ambitious Latin American program to be realized, he would have to lead effectively both at home and abroad. At home he would have to persuade the American people, especially their representatives in the Congress, that spending large sums of U.S. money on Latin America was justified on humanitarian grounds and in terms of our own self-interest as well. He would, moreover, have to motivate those Americans who were charged with implementing the Alliance for Progress to put their best efforts into a plan that many of them believed had only a remote chance of being successful. Abroad, the president's task was even more daunting. For in order to really accomplish what was originally imagined, no less than massive social and political change in Latin America would be required.

It seems fair to say that the president thought at the start that the Alliance for Progress would in fact kill two birds with one stone. As we have seen, in terms of his views on foreign policy, Kennedy was still a product of the cold war. Thus one of the primary purposes of the Alliance: to make the countries of Latin America more resistant to the appeal of communism. The memory of Castro's victory in Cuba was still fresh, and the drive to prevent another country south of the border from a similar fate was powerful. At the same time, the Alliance spoke to another strong American impulse: to see itself as doing good in the world. The prospect of infusing countries in our own hemisphere that were beset by poverty and underdevelopment with monies from our coffers was a gratifying one; it could only gladden the hearts of those many Americans who continued to believe the U.S. had a moral mission to help those less fortunate than themselves. Finally, there was the personal element. Kennedy had long had a general interest in foreign affairs and a particular interest in Latin America. The Alliance would give him a chance to act on these more personal concerns.

And so it is not in any way surprising that even before he was elected president, the Alliance for Progress had started to take shape. Moreover, as soon as he took office, it was clear that this program would in fact have a prominent place on the presidential agenda. Within weeks Kennedy was asking for money for the Alliance from Congress.

What can we say, then, about step one in the leadership process: conception? In other words, how carefully was this daring initiative thought through *before* it was undertaken? While this is not the place for a detailed evaluation of Kennedy's Latin American program, we can say that it was not, in any case, a resounding success. Even before Kennedy's death it had become quite clear that the program would fall woefully short of its lofty goals. More than anything else the reason for this failure was the inability to recognize early on that for such a program to succeed a leadership role would have to be played by one or another group within Latin America itself. But, on the whole, no group qualified for, or even wanted to take on, this overwhelming task. The oligarchs in the region clung to their property and power. The goals of the basically conservative middle class were not, as it turned out, those of the Alliance. And the masses had no mechanism whatsoever by which to participate in the democratic revolution. Indeed, as Bruce Miroff points out, Kennedy's invocation for the masses to actually participate in implementing the Alliance had something of a hollow ring.[102]

The failure to think through who in fact would carry the banner of the Alliance Latin America was only one aspect of Kennedy's plan of action that can be faulted. Moreover, this particular defect was of no mean significance— all of which raises the question of whether any initiative that is sloppily conceived will eventually fail. We will return to this question at the end of the chapter. At this point it will suffice to observe that, at a minimum, poor planning at the start will have to be compensated for later on.

We can in fact say that Kennedy's articulation of what he was hoping to achieve was convincing. Both at home and abroad he was able, at least at the start, to convey to his various audiences the virtues of his Latin American initiative. With regard to the Alliance, Kennedy did what a good leader should do: he spoke passionately, persuasively, and often about where it was he wanted to go. He used language to push the right buttons. Americans were promised that the Alliance would further democracy and at the same time satisfy people's basic needs for homes, work, land, health, and schools. And Latin Americans were told in buoyant if vague terms of how gigantic new steps were being taken to improve their lot in every way. The president's rhetorical efforts paid off. Early in Kennedy's presidency the Alliance was widely heralded as one of those New Frontier programs (like the Peace Corps) that had the perspicacity to combine the American penchant for both idealism and pragmatism.

Moreover vis-à-vis some groups at least, Kennedy was unusually willing to politick on behalf of what he wanted. John Kennedy was not known to enjoy lobbying even for those programs in which he was heavily invested. He preferred to remain outside the fray whenever possible, leaving the wheeling, dealing, and horse-trading to others. To get backing for the Alliance, however, the president departed from his usual practice. He involved himself personally in adminstration efforts to get key groups to go along. At home he was especially attentive to Congress, which, after all, held the purse strings. He took it on himself to make personal contact with leading members of the House and Senate. And he had other members of his administration put their very best efforts into getting Congress to pass his foreign aid program, part of which included the Alliance for Progress. It is instructive in this regard to listen to the voice of the chairman of the House subcommittee in which the 1961 foreign aid appropriation bill originated. A strong opponent of Kennedy's foreign aid program, Otto Passman nevertheless was impressed with the vigor of the administration's effort in this regard. "Never," exclaimed Passman, "has there been so much propaganda and so much money spent on lobbying."

> First, the Administration requested an excessive amount of foreign aid. . . . Second, the Democratic party was . . . sending wires to Democratic officials all over the country trying to get them to exert pressure on Congress in behalf of the program. Third, an epistle from [the secretaries of state and treasury] blowing up the reasons for the program was sent to all Members of Congress. Fourth, the program was talked up at State Department briefings for editors. Fifth, the President of Pakistan was invited here by [Vice President] Johnson to give a pep talk for foreign aid. Sixth, the Citizens' Committee for International Development was organized to exert further pressure. Seventh, I was interviewed on "Meet the Press" by hostile questioners who I think tried to make me look silly. Eighth, [the House majority leader] was elected to write 2,400 mayors across the U.S.A.—including some in my own district—on behalf of the program. Ninth, [the Peace Corps director] made a personal visit to every office on the Hill. . . . [Finally] the White House kept contacting business groups all over the country until 2 A.M. in the morning of full committee action asking businessmen to pressure Committee Members into reversing the Subcommittee cuts. . . . [103]

Passman's description is one of an administration doing virtually everything it could to politick on behalf of something considered a priority. The

effort paid off. As a direct consequence, no doubt, of Kennedy's heavy investment in the outcome, and of his ability finally to persuade Congress that it
was in our own self-interest to pump money south of the border, his program
received a generally favorable hearing. The cuts Congress inflicted on his
foreign aid requests, in 1961 at least, were far less drastic than those experienced by his predecessors, going as far back as 1951. Moreover, in 1962, Title
VI of the Foreign Assistance Act singled out the Alliance in a separate authorization bill, thereby formally adopting the president's hemisphere program.
And for fiscal year 1964, Congress still appropriated a good measure of the
$902 million the president had requested specifically for the Alliance. His
record, then, vis-à-vis the Congress is quite impressive, especially given the
fact that as far as Latin America was concerned, his appetite was large. The
president wanted to increase U.S. foreign aid to this region of the world no
less than threefold.

While it is somewhat more difficult to assess Kennedy's track record
abroad, the evidence suggests that, initially in any case, the political and
economic elites of Latin America also responded well to the president's initiative. One has a sense that the chief executive's interest in the region did not go
unappreciated, nor did his effort to touch base personally with Latin American leaders go unnoticed, Moreover, his journeys to the area were, by any
measure, personal triumphs. He was enormously popular with the masses, his
own good looks and considerable charm enhanced on more than one occasion by the grace and beauty of his young wife. What we can say then is that
by and large President Kennedy was able to draw on both his own considerable resources and those of his administration to market and sell the Alliance
for Progress within and beyond American borders. He succeeded in communicating his vision of a better world, and he demonstrated energy, commitment,
and conviction in his efforts to persuade both U.S. and Latin American audiences to follow him to the promised land.

The problems started when the initiative actually had to be implemented.
They began, in other words, when it came time for the dream to be realized.
To understand why the Alliance ran into trouble so fast, it is important once
again to look to what happened both at home and abroad.

It seems fair to say that President Kennedy never fully appreciated the
fact that throwing American money at the problem simply would not be
enough. He would have to have a cadre of dedicated Foreign Service professionals to implement the programs that Congress had funded. Moreover, he
would almost certainly also have to have some bureaucratic mechanism,
possibly one devised just for the Alliance, that would facilitate program planning and execution. As it turned out, however, bureaucratic barriers were
never overcome. The innate resistance and skepticism of traditional Foreign
Service officers was not adequately addressed, nor, despite the advice of key
individuals both at home and abroad, was an autonomous agency established
that would have more effectively met the Latin American challenge.

It was not that the president was oblivious to the sluggish systemic
response. He knew it was a problem because he was repeatedly so informed.
But either he never really recognized its magnitude or in the press of the
presidency, he never made it a priority. The fact that Kennedy tended to favor
working with White House staff rather than the traditional foreign policy

bureaucracy almost certainly worked against him on this issue. The testiness of his relations with the State Department and his distance from the secretary of state (particularly in contrast to the national security adviser) put him in a relatively poor position to recognize that State's poor attitude toward the Alliance would eventually cost it dearly. Moreover, his collegial style of management, while it allowed good ideas to float to the top, was not especially well suited to the administrative demands of an initiative such as the Alliance, which required, among other things, good coordination among the various elements of the foreign policy system. In the event, it seems fair to conclude that in view of the importance of the American bureaucracy in implementing an enterprise such as the Alliance for Progress, President Kennedy did too little too late to address what in the end turned out to be bureaucratic barriers of no mean significance.

The problems of implementing the Alliance were even greater abroad than they were at home. In fact, it was with regard to implementation in Latin America itself that the conceptual problem referred to above was most obvious. We said earlier that the president failed to think through who would carry the banner of the Alliance for Progress on the scene—which Latin American groups or individuals could be counted on to put the program into effect on their own turf. But there were a number of other ways as well in which the failure to consider the problem of implementation early on manifested itself.

For example, it was apparently not understood at the outset that the administration might be caught between a rock and a hard place with regard to the Latin American military. On the one hand, the democratic aspirations of the Alliance dictated that the Americans should keep their distance from the military, which was associated in the minds of many, for good reason, with authoritarianism and repression. On the other hand, fear of the left, of a revolution from the left as opposed to democratic reform, made the military an easy ally for an administration that wanted, perhaps above all, to preclude even one more Cuba south of the border. Thus the tack the president took was to increase American aid to the traditionally antidemocratic Latin American military. But there was a price to be paid. Over time, the Alliance was viewed by many as just one more example of American self-interest at work. In its zeal to avoid a major social and political upheaval in Latin America, and in its dedication to preserving America's foreign investments in the area, the Kennedy administration became, finally, too much like its predecessors: an object of suspicion.

Thus the situation in Latin America was one in which the problems were many but the saviors few. The 2 percent of the citizenry that owned more than 50 percent of the wealth saw no reason to undermine a system that served them well. The middle class, which was quite closely tied to the upper class, tended as well to defend the status quo. The military was, at best, an ally with an albatross around its neck. And the masses, whose numbers grew at the staggering rate of 10 million a year, were simply not equipped (or expected) to play a leading role.

Moreover, after its initial splash, the Alliance for Progress lost its panache. While Congress continued on the whole to support Kennedy's initiative, as time went on the problems in the executive branch became clear and the obstacles abroad unmistakable. In fact, in relatively short order the gap between the magnitude of the task the president had originally set forth and his capacity to carry it out became obvious. This gap, this sense of lost illusion, finally reduced the administration's investment in the program. Indeed, the administration's failure to create a "mystique" that would have propelled the Alliance forward can probably be traced to a deeply felt loss of self-confidence.

We said early on that any leadership analysis hinges on three components: the leader, the followers, and the situation. We can see that, in this case, while the leader was ready and willing, too many of the followers were not. Too many Foreign Service professionals in this country kept their distance, and too many players abroad never signed on in the first place. Moreover, the situation in Latin America, the overweening problems in the region, presented the kind of challenge that only the most brilliant, committed, and persistent effort could have even begun to meet.

We learned earlier that President Kennedy was more interested in foreign than domestic affairs. "They received from him far more attention to detail," Theodore Sorensen wrote, "to the shaping of alternatives, to the course of a proposal from origin to execution." We also learned that Kennedy had long had a particular concern for Latin America and that he hoped as president to build on the achievements in this region of some of his Democratic predecessors. But while the Alliance for Progress confirmed his interest in foreign affairs, and especially Latin America, it also testifed to the fact that as a leader in world politics he left something to be desired. A year or two after its inception the bright hopes that accompanied the founding of the Alliance had all but dissolved. Growth rates for the Latin American economies were still low. Land and tax reforms remained a dim hope. And democratic institutions all across the region suffered repeated setbacks.[104]

There were at least three big problems that beleaguered the president's Latin American initiative: First, the fact that Kennedy was both a vigorous anticommunist and a cautious idealist complicated what, sometimes at least, should have been simple choices. We have seen, for example, that Kennedy's fear of the left drove him into the arms of the right. Second, Kennedy turned out to have been a poor manager. He never seemed to fully understand the critical role that would have to be played by those on the front lines; he never was able to vault over the bureaucratic obstacles that, from the American side, held his program back. Finally, he failed to think through at the start what the Alliance would really entail. He did not understand that only major structural reform in Latin America would enable him to get to where he wanted to go. And he failed further to see that such reforms would require groups or individuals to assume indigenous leadership roles.

All of this is not to say that the Alliance was a failure in every way, nor is it intended to underestimate the daunting task of implementing on foreign soil an agenda that was little short of revolutionary. But because Kennedy ultimately lacked the power, in particular the economic power, that *might* have enabled him to realize his lofty goals, the Alliance was, in the end, unrealistic. In this sense, Kennedy's initiative was doomed from the start.

One could argue that President Kennedy should not be faulted for aiming high. Indeed, his vaulting ambition reflected the general American overconfidence of the time as well as cold war precepts such as militant anticommunism, the benefits of foreign aid, and the conviction that the U.S. had a moral responsibility to create a just and stable world order. But Kennedy's experiences with the Alliance can nevertheless be seen as an object lesson for future chief executives who would be world leaders. Understand that to lead at the international level, you will have to be in control both at home and abroad. Understand that good management is a requisite of good leadership. And understand that implementation, while not necessarily the most glamorous stage of the leadership process, is nevertheless an integral part of it. In short, if you play the game, play to win, lest you waste precious political capital on what history will regard as a failed effort.

Notes

1. See discussion on Kennedy's campaign rhetoric in I. M. Destler, Leslie H. Gelb, and Anthony Lake in *Our Own Worst Enemy: The Unmaking of American Foreign Policy* (New York: Simon & Schuster, 1984), pp. 50 ff. For more on Kennedy as cold warrior, also see Henry Fairlie, *The Kennedy Promise: The Politics of Expectation* (New York: Doubleday, 1973).

2. Quoted in Destler et al., p. 51.

3. Theodore Sorensen, *Kennedy* (New York: Harper & Row, 1965), p. 509.

4. Joan and Clay Blair, Jr., *The Search for J.F.K.* (New York: Berkley Medallion, 1976), p. 49.

5. Sorensen, p. 512.

6. This paragraph is based on Alexander George, *Presidential Decisionmaking in Foreign Policy: The Effective Use of Information and Advice* (Boulder, Colo.: Westview, 1980), p. 157.

7. I. M. Destler, *Presidents, Bureaucrats, and Foreign Policy* (Princeton: Princeton University Press, 1974), p. 99.

8. Destler, et al., p. 184.

9. Arthur Schlesinger, Jr., *A Thousand Days* (Boston: Houghton Mifflin, 1965), p. 290.

10. Quoted in Louise Fitzsimons, *The Kennedy Doctrine* (New York: Random House, 1972), pp. 89–90.

11. Sorensen, pp. 729, 730.

12. *New York Times*, 12 March 1962. See also *ibid.*, 16 November 1963; Schlesinger, p. 759; and Lewis J. Paper, *The Promise and the Performance* (New York: Crown Publishers, Inc., 1975), p. 294.

13. Bruce Miroff, *Pragmatic Illusions: The Presidential Politics of John F. Kennedy* (New York: David McKay Co. Inc. 1976), p. 110.

14. Jerome Levinson and Juan de Onis, *The Alliance That Lost its Way* (Chicago: Quadrangle, 1970), p. 50.

15. Ibid., p. 50, citing telephone conversation with Richard Goodwin.

16. Schlesinger, p. 191. The next several paragraphs are based on Schlesinger's account, pp. 191–94.

17. Quoted in Peter Schwab and J. Lee Shneidman, *John F. Kennedy* (New York: The New College and University Press, 1974), p. 103.

18. Schlesinger, p. 204.

19. *New York Times*, 15 March 1961.

20. Ibid., 12 April 1961.

21. Ibid., 20 July 1961.

22. Ibid., 13 August 1961.

23. Ibid., 20 August 1961.

24. Ibid., 23 August 1961.

25. *Public Papers of the Presidents of the United States: John F. Kennedy* (Washington: Government Printing Office, 1961), p. 565.

26. Paper, p. 177. The following paragraphs are based on Paper's account.

27. *Public Papers of the Presidents of the United States: John F. Kennedy* (Washington: Government Printing Office), pp. 90, 91.

28. *New York Times,* 12 March 1962.

29. Ibid., 18 March 1962.

30. Schlesinger, p. 197.

31. *New York Times,* 12 March 1962.

32. *New York Times,* 15 March 1962. All the quotes in this paragraph are from the same source.

33. *Public Papers* (1962), p. 221.

34. Ibid., p. 221.

35. Ibid., p. 222.

36. Ibid., p. 223.

37. Ibid., p. 231.

38. Ibid., p. 495.

39. *New York Times,* 2 August 1962.

40. The special status of the Alliance became something of a joke at the Agency for International Development (AID). For example, an AID official in Washington, considering a loan proposal under the program, explained: "We all know there are only three categories of loans in the Alliance for Progress: very high priority, hysterical, and if-we-don't-make-this-loan-the-Communists-will-take-over-the-country. On that scale, this loan has a very low priority." Levinson and de Onis, p. 112.

41. *New York Times,* 2 August 1962.

42. Ibid., and Levinson and de Onis, p. 114.

43. *New York Times,* 2 August 1962.

44. See *Public Papers* (1962), pp. 675, 676, 883, 884.

45. *Public Papers of the Presidents of the United States: John F. Kennedy* (Washington: Government Printing Office, 1963), p. 17.

46. Cablegram, Department of State, 16 October 1963, John F. Kennedy Library.

47. *New York Times,* 18 August 1963.

48. *Ibid.,* 17 November 1963.

49. *Ibid.,* 18 August 1963.

50. *New York Times,* 12 November 1963.

51. Schlesinger, p. 1001.

52. *New York Times,* 18 August 1963.

53. Sorensen, p. 537.

54. Quoted in *New York Times,* 18 August 1963.

55. Quoted in Miroff, p. 118.

56. *New York Times,* 12 November 1983.

57. Malcolm C. Smith, *John F. Kennedy's Thirteen Great Mistakes in the White House* (Smithtown: Suffolk House, 1980), p. 198.

58. *New York Times,* 18 August 1963.

59. Schlesinger, p. 204.

60. *Public Papers* (1961), p. 276.

61. Schlesinger, p. 761.

62. A December 1961 visit to the Dominican Republic led the following year to the first general election the people had known in generations. See Schlesinger, p. 772.

63. See *Public Papers* (1961–1963.)

64. *Public Papers* (1962), pp. 220–223.

65. Schlesinger, p. 768.

66. *Public Papers* (1963), pp. 621, 873.

67. Schlesinger, p. 767.

68. See *Public Papers* (1961), pp. 804–7.

69. *Public Papers* (1962), p. 525.

70. *Public Papers* (1963), pp. 269–72.

71. See Schlesinger, pp. 767–68; and Herbert S. Parmet, *The Presidency of John F. Kennedy* (New York: Dial Press, 1983), p. 223; and *New York Times,* 20 March 1963.

72. Paper, p. 177; and Foreign Service dispatch from São Paulo, Brazil, 23 April 1962, John F. Kennedy Library.

73. Memorandum from Andrew E. Rice to Chester Bowles, 28 March 1962; and John F. Kennedy Library, p. 18.

74. Telegram to the secretary of state from La Paz, Bolivia, 15 March 1962, John F. Kennedy Library.

75. Juscelino Kubitschek de Oliveira, "Report on the Alliance for Progress," John F. Kennedy Library, p. 24. Kubitschek de Oliveira also stated that Congress's allotment of funds was insufficient to the task, and that there were too many "formal and technical requirements for the approval of projects . . ."; *Ibid.,* pp. 16, 24.

76. Alberto Lleras Camargo, "Report on the Alliance for Progress," John F. Kennedy Library, p. 15.

77. Schlesinger, p. 764.

78. *New York Times,* 12 March 1962.

79. Lleras Camargo, p. 7.

80. Rice, memorandum to Bowles, p. 118.

81. Levinson and de Onis, citing 20 August 1968 interview with Teodoro Moscosco, p. 111.

82. Schlesinger, p. 1001.

83. Lleras, p. 7.

84. Memorandum from Arthur M. Schlesinger, Jr., to John F. Kennedy, 27 June 1961, John F. Kennedy Library.

85. Ibid.

86. Foreign Service dispatch from São Paulo, Brazil, 23 April 1962, John F. Kennedy Library.

87. Staff report, "Survey of the Alliance," 16 June 1962–12 July 1962, p. 33.

88. Memorandum from Arthur M. Schlesinger, Jr., to Ralph Dungan, 15 October 1962, John F. Kennedy Library.

89. Quoted in Paper, p. 293.

90. Other reasons mentioned by Goodwin were "impossible personnel procedures, a structure which discourages individual initiative and responsibility, a careerist mentality, and an inability to recognize mediocrity when it is seen." Quoted in ibid.

91. For example, in remarks to the embassy staff in Caracas, Venezuela, on 16 December 1961, and in an address to the Foreign Service in July 1962. See Public Papers (1961), p. 804; ibid. (1962), p. 532. In addition, Kennedy occasionally called "lowly State Department desk officials" himself asking for information or giving instructions. Levinson and de Onis, p. 110.

92. Letter from Alexander Nimick, Jr., to T. Graydon Upon, 9 February 1962, John F. Kennedy Library.

93. Rice memorandum to Bowles, p. 10.

94. For example, he urged "more education"; "increased emphasis to working with students and labor"; recruitment of "domestic allies" in "attempts at persuasion and pressure"; and "reaching the military forces" in Latin America by "developing *in our military* personnel in Latin America a keener understanding of and dedication to the Alliance." *Ibid.,* pp. 10–12.

95. Staff report, p. 33.

96. For example, it proposed learning more about "key opinion groups," impressing upon Latin American governments "the importance of public relations," learning more about what meaning is given to "Alliance words, symbols and projects by the various elements of the Latin public," and "direct influencing of the public by senior officials of our missions." Ibid., p. 33.

97. To support this assertion, the *Times* added that the new chief of the State Department's Bureau for Inter-American Affairs "is a respected economist who happens to lack any Latin American experience," *New York Times,* 18 March 1962.

98. Ibid., 11 November 1963.

99. Miroff, p. 132.

100. Ibid., p. 132, and Sorensen, p. 535.

101. Schlesinger memorandum to Dungan.

102. Miroff, p. 123. Miroff has an extended and very useful analysis of the failed Alliance, pp. 117–42.

103. Passman is quoted in the *Congressional Quarterly Almanac, 1961* (Washington: Congressional Quarterly, Inc., 1962), p. 312.

104. Miroff, p. 118.

6

Lyndon Johnson's Involvement in Vietnam

The American covenant called on us to help show the way for the liberation of man. And that today is our goal. . . . Change has brought a new meaning to that old mission. We can never again stand aside, prideful in isolation. If American lives must end, and American treasure be spilled, in countries that we barely know, then that is the price that change has demanded of conviction and of our enduring covenant.

—Inaugural Address, January 20, 1965

BACKGROUND

Lyndon Johnson presents a difficult challenge for anyone who wants to understand his presidency. His associates, as well as historians who are more objective, all agree that he was an unusually complex man, but to say that reveals little. What is so striking about his career is that it was filled with irony. He preferred domestic politics to world affairs, yet his presidency was dominated by his conduct of the Vietnam War. He preached reason and consensus, but his foreign policy created bitter divisions. He invoked the prophet Isaiah to ask the country, "Come now, let us reason together," and then accused his opponents of subversion or worse. And when he left office under attack for his escalation of the war in Southeast Asia, many of his critics nevertheless praised his talents as an architect of domestic policy.

Johnson wanted to be a great president. But unlike his predecessor John F. Kennedy, LBJ's ambition was not to be dominant as a world leader. Rather, he wanted to be the most effective domestic policy president in the twentieth century. Because of his long experience in Congress, his methods were those of a legislative leader. Perhaps as a consequence, when he transferred his ends and means to the White House, he endured tragic failure as well as remarkable success. He won support for a broad array of legislative initiatives; but he also became an architect of war, and that fact ultimately drove him from office.

LBJ's dream was to build a Great Society in the United States. That vision implied aggressive governmental action to promote civil rights and provide a wide range of programs to assist the poor and underprivileged. But while his heart was at home, he had to deal with the reality of American involvement abroad. In fact, he genuinely believed that the United States was obligated to save South Vietnam from conquest by the communist North. Not only had that been the policy of Presidents Eisenhower and Kennedy, but as we see in the above Inaugural quote, it also coincided with Johnson's view of America's role in the world. Moreover, LBJ also reasoned that either withdrawal from the conflict, or a larger war, would interfere with and finally obliterate his domestic policy initiatives.

What Johnson feared most was a divisive national debate on Vietnam. Such a controversy would draw both attention and resources away from his Great Society programs. He therefore chose a middle road. He conducted a limited war, one requiring the minimum effort necessary to hold off a victory by the North Vietnamese. A conflict of this kind did not require a significant disruption of American life. Reserve forces did not have to be mobilized nor the economy retooled. And although the military draft inevitably called young men away from home to fight, even it was designed so as to minimally intrude. Men could defer military service for a variety of reasons, and a tour of duty in Vietnam was limited to only one year.

It was a compromise approach to foreign affairs. But, then, Lyndon Johnson was a master of compromise. His political career had been built on using his skill at reconciling opposing groups to increase his personal power. He had survived in Texas politics by balancing the liberal and conservative factions of the state's Democratic party. And as Senate majority leader in the 1950s, he was able to serve as a bridge between conservative Southern Democrats and their more liberal counterparts from the Midwest and Northeast.

As a result, he was able to transform the majority leader's position from a minor office to one of considerable national influence.[1] He ran the Senate as his personal domain, deferring to senior members as necessary but coordinating an elaborate "Johnson network" of members and staff through legislative sessions that were remarkable for the volume of laws passed under his leadership. With Republican Dwight Eisenhower in the White House, LBJ became the most powerful Democrat in the nation.

Johnson coveted political power. David Halberstam has written that he "was the elemental man, a man of endless, restless ambition. Nothing was ever completed, each accomplishment was a challenge to reach for more. . . . He was a man of stunning force, drive and intelligence, and of equally stunning insecurity."[2] Throughout his career, LBJ sought greater power to achieve greater things. "He did not dream small dreams. Nor did he pursue small challenges."[3]

Despite his influence, Johnson was not satisfied with his post as majority leader. As a disciple of Franklin Roosevelt, he saw the presidency as the one office that offered the opportunity for true national leadership. So he sought the White House in 1960, but lost his party's nomination to John Kennedy. Thereupon, he reluctantly agreed to accept the vice-presidential nomination. While the two men were rivals, the Catholic New Englander Kennedy needed the Texan to balance his ticket, and LBJ did not want to be seen as nothing more than JFK's man in the Senate.

As vice president, Johnson felt frustrated as a close observer of power that he could see but not touch. As a Southerner, he did not fit in with JFK's Eastern-oriented circle of the "best and the brightest" and was relegated to the traditional ceremonial duties of the nation's second officer. Indeed, faced with the prospect of possibly eight years in this role, he hinted to friends that he might retire from politics in 1964. When JFK was assassinated, Johnson was suddenly thrust into the presidency. Now he had the power that he wanted, but only as heir to a martyred leader.

President Johnson's leadership style can be characterized by three key elements: (1) mastery of detail, (2) hard work, and (3) personalization of politics. Like King Louis XIV of France, LBJ apparently believed that "genius lies in the taking of infinite pains." In domestic affairs, this penchant for detail helped him win support for his major initiative, the War on Poverty.[4] It was apparent as well in his approach to international problems, ranging from nuclear arms to the famine in India (1965–1967) to the war in Vietnam. For example, Johnson's memoirs relate with pride his efforts to deal with India's food shortage.

> Throughout this period [the first few months of the crisis] I made sure that the grain that was absolutely essential was shipped and arrived on time. . . . I became an authority on the climate of India. I knew where the rain fell and where it failed to fall in India. I became an expert in the ton-by-ton movement of grain from the wheat fields of Kansas to ports like Calcutta—how many tons and how long the operation took. I described myself as "a kind of county agricultural agent with international clients." One high-ranking State Department official called me "the first Populist ever to arrive on the international scene."[5]

Hard work was the second element of Johnson's leadership style. It flowed naturally from his energy and attention to detail. His daily calendar provides the best indicator of his long hours. He literally worked two shifts in a single day, napping for an hour or so in between. In all, LBJ worked about eighteen hours a day. He seemed convinced that such exertion would enable him to triumph over obstacles and opponents. He would master the famine crisis, choose bombing targets in Vietnam, greet dignitaries, and still have time to visit the White House Situation Room (the president's center for communications and control of American forces around the world) in the middle of the night. Moreover, he demanded similar efforts from his staff.

As a result of his high degree of personal involvement, LBJ's White House revolved entirely around him. His first press secretary, George Reedy, would later compare it to a royal court. Reedy implied that Johnson behaved like a fearsome monarch, surrounded by sycophants who would tell him only what he wanted to hear. Everything in the White House was "designed for one purpose and one purpose only—to serve the material needs and desires of a single man."[6] This royal analogy seems apt, for Johnson personalized politics. The soldiers in Vietnam were "my boys" and government officers were "my people." Once, when escorting LBJ to the presidential helicopter, a young air force corporal told him, "This is your helicopter, sir." Johnson replied, "They're all my helicopters, son."[7]

Johnson employed a version of Kennedy's collegial model for decision making. Such a system eschewed the traditional hierarchy among advisers and kept the president in firm control of his subordinates. But LBJ adapted the system to suit his own personality. He organized foreign policy–making around himself and those he could trust. He used small, informal meetings to consider his policy options. Whereas JFK had stressed teamwork and shared responsibility among his aides, Johnson insisted on loyalty and hard work in his personal service. He told one aide, "I don't want loyalty. I want *loyalty.*"[8]

LBJ thought carefully about the links between foreign and domestic policy. Indeed, many of his policies abroad resembled his policies at home, such as in the Indian famine. He was proudest of those programs that extended the Great Society beyond American shores. He followed through on JFK's Alliance for Progress, built up the Peace Corps, and convinced Congress to increase economic assistance to developing nations. He even envisioned bringing the Great Society to Vietnam. In a speech at Johns Hopkins University in 1965, he outlined his plan for a "billion-dollar American investment in the Mekong River delta."[9]

Johnson fashioned his presidency from his dreams and the legacy of Kennedy's New Frontier. That meant invoking the memory of JFK in support of his own domestic initiatives. But it also meant continuing Kennedy's policies abroad. Even after winning the presidency in his own right in the 1964 election, LBJ maintained what he understood to be the policies of JFK. He pursued a nuclear arms agreement with the Soviet Union. He continued Kennedy's efforts to provide American aid to developing nations. He advanced initiatives to promote international economic stability and growth. And he assumed Kennedy's policy of containing communist influence around the world. It was this last policy, global containment, that included an American presence in Vietnam.

LBJ pursued Kennedy's policies for two reasons.[10] First, since he had been JFK's rival for the 1960 presidential nomination, LBJ was regarded by many of the late president's supporters as a usurper in the Oval Office. To dispel that image, Johnson believed it essential that he demonstrate his fidelity to the legacy of his predecessor. This message was clearly communicated in his first message to Congress after succeeding to the Oval Office. Kennedy had proclaimed his policy goals by exhorting, "Let us begin"; Johnson echoed that spirit by urging, "Let us continue." The second reason for keeping the Kennedy flame alive was that JFK's agenda in fact reflected his party's program. In the early 1960s, the Democratic party stood for civil rights, social programs, Third World development, and the containment of communism. Johnson felt comfortable with that platform and his policy goals were shaped with it in mind.[11]

An example is in the area of nuclear arms control. In 1962, JFK signed the Partial Test-Ban Treaty. Under this agreement, the United States and Soviet Union halted testing of nuclear devices above ground and in the atmosphere. The next logical step was to negotiate further limits on the spread and growth of nuclear weapons.

Early in 1964, Johnson wrote to Soviet premier Nikita Khrushchev about the need to continue discussions about nuclear issues. He particularly alluded to two problem areas: The first was the need to restrain growth in the size of American and Soviet nuclear arsenals. Talks were initiated and in 1968 they became more formal. These Strategic Arms Limitation Talks (SALT) were directed toward preventing a runaway nuclear arms race between the two superpowers.[12] Richard Nixon would later build on these discussions to produce the first SALT agreement with the Soviet Union in 1972.

The second issue concerned nuclear proliferation. Talks aimed at curbing this problem were more immediately productive. In 1968, the United States and Soviet Union drafted a Non-Proliferation Treaty (NPT) that bound all signatories to check the spread of nuclear weapons beyond the existing "nuclear club." In other words, parties to the agreement would not provide nonnuclear states with nuclear weapons or the technology for building them. While France and China were important exceptions, most states possessing nuclear arms joined the agreement.

But for all his efforts on behalf of peace, LBJ is best remembered as an architect of war. The war in Southeast Asia not only dominated American foreign policy during the Johnson years, but it came to overshadow his entire presidency. Despite his protests to the contrary, the conflict became "Lyndon Johnson's war," from general strategy to the president's selection of specific bombing targets in North Vietnam. As Larry Berman describes life in the Johnson White House, the president was torn between fears of what might go wrong and a desperate search for signs of progress in the field.[13]

The Vietnam War reveals much about Lyndon Johnson and his concept of leadership. He prosecuted the war as much from fear as from a determination to direct national policy.[14] He was afraid of being the president who "lost" Vietnam, even if the conflict was controversial and kept him away from domestic issues. As he told a confidante after leaving office: "I knew from the start that I was bound to be crucified either way I moved. If I left the woman I really loved—the Great Society—in order to get involved with that bitch of a war on the other side of the world, then I would lose everything at home."[15] In fact, LBJ's failure to resolve that dilemma cost him the presidency.

NATIONAL LEADERSHIP: PRESENTING THE CASE AT HOME

When Lyndon Johnson assumed the presidency, the United States's presence in Vietnam was almost a decade old. Over sixteen thousand American military personnel were stationed there as part of an American commitment that dated from the Eisenhower administration.

Nor was LBJ a stranger to the issue of Southeast Asia. As Senate majority leader in the 1950s, he had been involved in debate over the region, particularly in President Eisenhower's consideration of American intervention when France withdrew from its former colonies in Indochina. Moreover, as vice president, Johnson had toured Asia for the Kennedy administration in 1961, including a stop in Saigon, the capital of South Vietnam.

After this trip, Johnson's view of the situation in Vietnam was uncertain. On the one hand, he shared Kennedy's anticommunism and was concerned about the possibility of a North Vietnamese (communist) victory. But on the other hand, he was not a forceful advocate for American involvement in the distant conflict. He reported to JFK that the United States would soon face an important choice: "Whether we commit major American forces to the area or cut our losses and withdraw should our other efforts fail."[16]

While LBJ generally supported President Kennedy's increase of American troops in Vietnam, after his trip to the area he was not consulted on America's

Southeast Asian policy. Since he was not a member of JFK's inner circle, his views were not sought by the "best and the brightest" who shaped foreign policy. Thus, when LBJ became president, he was more aware of our role in the region than most Americans, but he was not an authority on the subject, nor had he had much direct experience with the issue of American involvement.

In the early days of his presidency, Johnson gave Vietnam little attention. On November 26, 1963, he approved National Security Action Memorandum 273, thereby formally endorsing our existing policy in Southeast Asia. But he was preoccupied with developing his Great Society programs.

During his first year in office, the situation in Vietnam deteriorated. Shortly before JFK's assassination, the United States had backed a coup d'etat against South Vietnamese president Ngo Dinh Diem. Diem was a corrupt politician who persecuted his country's Buddhists. The Kennedy administration believed that Diem's conduct of his office was alienating the South Vietnamese population and weakening its resistance to the North. He was assassinated and replaced by the first of a line of military rulers. (South Vietnam would not have another civilian government until 1967.) LBJ was advised that the new government was unstable and that it would need more aggressive American support to stave off a communist victory.

Johnson's response was designed to provide him with maximum flexibility. He increased the United States' participation in the conflict, albeit covertly. He authorized secret naval attacks against North Vietnamese coastal installations. (At the same time, the navy began a series of intelligence-gathering patrols using American destroyers.) He further instructed the Joint Chiefs of Staff to prepare contingency plans for increased military pressure against the North, and, finally, LBJ conducted deliberations within the administration on the possibility of bombing North Vietnam and obtaining a congressional resolution that would justify such an action.[17]

President Johnson would soon have an opportunity to make his case publicly. On August 2, 1964, the USS *Maddox* was fired upon while returning from a patrol in the Gulf of Tonkin. Johnson ordered another destroyer, the USS *C. Turner Joy*, to assist the *Maddox*. Two days later, both ships were reportedly attacked.

Today there is considerable uncertainty about the second "attack"; indeed, it is not even clear that it ever occurred. Nevertheless, Johnson exploited the incident to win overwhelming support for a congressional resolution that gave him the freedom to escalate the war as he saw fit. For the president the incident was, in any case, a convenient device to win the backing of the legislature for his policy in Vietnam. Only years later did he finally admit, "For all I [knew], our Navy was shooting at whales out there."[18]

In a televised speech to the nation, Johnson justified what was commonly referred to as the Gulf of Tonkin Resolution as a "limited and fitting" response to the attacks on United States ships. He emphasized that "we Americans know, although others appear to forget, the risks of spreading conflict. We still seek no wider war." Yet the resolution did bestow sweeping power on the president:

> . . . The Congress approves and supports the determination of the President, as Commander in Chief, to take all necessary measures to repel any armed attack against the forces of the United States and to prevent further aggression. . . . The

United States is, therefore, prepared, as the President determines, to take all necessary steps, including the use of armed force. . . .[19]

To be sure, this broad language was balanced by administration assurances that the resolution was not a "blank check." In the Senate's debate on the proposal, Johnson's position was represented by Senator William Fulbright, chairman of the Foreign Relations Committee and a widely respected expert on world affairs. When the senator was asked "whether there is anything in the resolution which would authorize or recommend or approve the landing of large American armies in Vietnam or China," he responded, "There is nothing in the resolution, as I read it, that contemplates it. . . . However, the language of the resolution would not prevent it."[20] When Senator Jacob Javits expressed concern that passage of the proposal would make it possible for the president to ignore Congress in the future, Fulbright answered, "We have had positive assurances from the Secretary of State about the very matter the Senator is discussing."[21]

LBJ thus achieved the early congressional endorsement he sought by presenting it as a limited American commitment to Southeast Asia, not a virtual declaration of war. In the summer of 1964, the Gulf of Tonkin Resolution provided President Johnson with justification for U.S. involvement. Later, when he further expanded American participation in the conflict, he would use the resolution to conduct the war as he saw fit.

The administration's brief flurry of interest in Vietnam was overshadowed by the 1964 presidential campaign. The war was an issue in the electoral contest, but not really a major one. In particular, Johnson's campaign gave voters no reason to anticipate the extended American involvement in Vietnam that lay ahead. In fact, throughout the 1964 presidential campaign, LBJ portrayed himself as the "peace candidate"—in contrast to his opponent, Senator Barry Goldwater, who had a reputation for being "trigger happy." Indeed, Goldwater had made a number of statements suggesting the possibility of using nuclear weapons to advance American foreign policy interests. Maintaining that "victory is our goal,"[22] the Republican candidate portrayed the Democratic president as too cautious in his use of force.

With an opponent like Goldwater, LBJ had no difficulty in staking out a popular position: peace in Southeast Asia. In September, Johnson told a campaign rally in Oklahoma, "There are those that say you ought to go north and drop bombs, to try to wipe out the supply lines, and they think that would escalate the war. We don't want our American boys to do the fighting for Asian boys. We don't want to get involved in a nation with 700 million people [China] and get tied down in a land war in Asia."[23]

A now-famous television campaign commercial starkly illustrated Johnson's message. The film showed a child, a young girl, picking daisies, counting the petals as she plucked them one by one. Her small voice was soon drowned out by the harsh sound of a missile launch countdown. Momentarily, the missile was fired, exploding on screen into a telltale mushroom cloud. The commercial ended with LBJ's voice admonishing the peoples of the world to learn to live with one another or face destruction.[24]

In most of the president's campaign appearances, Vietnam received only minor attention. Indeed, in some of LBJ's most important speeches, such as his acceptance address before the Democratic National Convention, the conflict in Southeast Asia was not mentioned at all.[25] Instead, Johnson hammered on his domestic goals and his simple desire for world peace.

Peace in fact was the elemental theme whenever Johnson discussed international relations. In a typical remark made in Boise, Idaho, he told his audience, "So you will select the leader to find peace in the world, and the leader to find peace at home, and the leader to develop prosperity to our people."[26] In sum, LBJ presented himself as the candidate of love and the Great Society, not war.

On the relatively few occasions when Vietnam was addressed, certain basic themes recurred. The first was the American obligation to assist South Vietnam. LBJ was fond of quoting from a letter President Eisenhower had sent to President Diem in 1954 in which he promised: "If you want to help yourself, we will give you advice and support."[27] Thus he would remain loyal to American allies in the area, even if, years later, no clear success had been won.

Johnson's second theme was restraint in the face of attacks by North Vietnam.[28] As he told one audience, "It is not any problem to start a war. That is the easiest thing in the world. I know some folks that I think could start one mighty easy. But it is a pretty difficult thing for all of us to prevent one, and that is what we are trying to do."[29]

Finally, LBJ maintained that the war was for "Asian boys." He repeated variations on the theme: "We don't want our American boys to do the fighting for Asian boys." This sentence in fact became a refrain. The United States under President Johnson was not going to get involved in a land war in Asia.

In the fall of 1964, the president was thus sending American voters a mixed message. He was determined to stand by American obligations in Southeast Asia. But, at the same time, he was the candidate of peace and restraint. In his memoirs, he captured the essence of his appeal to voters: "A good many people compared my position in 1964 with that of . . . Barry Goldwater, and decided that I was the 'peace' candidate and he was the 'war' candidate. They were not willing to hear anything they did not want to hear."[30] In short, either because LBJ's message was deceptive, or because the American people heard only what they wanted to hear, they were simply not prepared for what lay ahead.

Nineteen sixty-five was the turning point, the year LBJ committed the United States to the war in Southeast Asia. Immediately after the 1964 presidential election, the president's aides informed him that the South Vietnamese government was on the brink of collapse. To prevent such an outcome, the commander in chief ordered American planes to begin bombing North Vietnam. This action (Operation Rolling Thunder) put into effect a plan the Pentagon had actually drafted months before and set into motion a policy of bombing the enemy that would continue for three years. In February, Vietcong forces (communist guerrillas in South Vietnam, part of the internal opposition to the Saigon government) attacked a United States air base at Da Nang, whereupon the president dispatched two battalions of marines to protect it from further encroachment. These soldiers would be the first American combat troops—

not military "advisers"—in South Vietnam. While their original mission was defensive, soon they would be engaging in offensive operations against the Vietcong. Communist forces continued to advance throughout the spring of 1965. Finally, in July, the president made the decision to commit an additional 125,000 American troops to the defense of South Vietnam. By year's end, the United States presence there amounted to nearly 200,000 men.

Despite Johnson's campaign promises, the conflict had become an American war, and from 1965 until he left office, LBJ ran the war more or less by himself. He kept tight control over all information and decision making pertaining to the conflict.

One very important mechanism of presidential control was the so-called Tuesday Cabinet. This was the weekly lunchtime gathering of Johnson's key advisers on Southeast Asia. Included were Secretary of State Dean Rusk, Secretary of Defense Robert McNamara, Assistant for National Security Affairs Walt Rostow, the president's press secretary (first Bill Moyers and then George Christian), the chairman of the Joint Chiefs of Staff, the director of the CIA (first John McCone and then, from 1966, Richard Helms), and select others whom LBJ would invite on an individual basis. Here, among an assembly in which "the only men present were the ones whose advice the President most wanted to hear,"[31] Johnson made decisions on the conduct of the war.

Nor were all members of this inner circle equally influential in shaping Vietnam policy. After the president, Robert McNamara was the principal architect of the war. He argued for escalation in 1965 and planned the bombing program used for most of the Johnson years. Armed with a tremendous array of statistics on the conflict, he provided LBJ with much of the information he needed to manage American military action in Southeast Asia. McNamara's data were supplemented by the intelligence estimates of the CIA, which exerted its influence by its assessments of what would and would not work on the ground in Vietnam. The CIA was an important source of information on enemy resources and was used to implement many political aspects of Johnson's war. Secretary of State Dean Rusk largely deferred to McNamara in administration deliberations. His role was confined to the search for diplomatic options, defending American involvement in Vietnam before Congress and the world, and moderating the military's pressure for a more aggressive bombing strategy.

Virtually everyone excluded from this small group were less well-informed about the extent and direction of American policy in Southeast Asia. Moreover, LBJ hid much of the real cost of the war in various positions in the defense budget, so Congress was kept in the dark about the price of the conflict.

Greater American involvement was not, however, matched by a change in presidential rhetoric. LBJ continued to echo the familiar themes of the 1964 campaign. Clearly he was determined to manage the war, not initiate a debate about it. Even as the war expanded, Johnson emphasized its limits. Even as he suspected it would drag on, he held out hopes for success in the near future. And even as he came increasingly to rely on the use of force, he talked of the quest for peace.

Because the president's goal was public and congressional acquiescence in his conduct of the war, he continued to present his policies in ways that were most likely to make them palatable. His 1965 speech at Johns Hopkins University, promising development of the Mekong Delta, was typical. America's Vietnam policy was still framed in terms of the search for peace:

> We fight because we must fight if we are to live in a world where every country can shape its own destiny. And only in such a world will our own freedom be finally secure. This kind of world will never be built by bombs or bullets. Yet the infirmities of man are such that force must often precede reason, and the waste of war, the works of peace.[32]

Speeches such as this one generally served their purpose; editorial, congressional, and public reactions were mostly positive. The *New York Times* praised a Vietnam policy "in which the nation can take pride."[33] The *Washington Post* and other leading newspapers followed suit.[34]

On Capitol Hill, the Johns Hopkins address seemed to satisfy even some critics of the war. Senators George McGovern and Frank Church, early and outspoken critics of American involvement, praised the president's vision of the war. Church canceled his plan to deliver an attack on the war on the floor of the Senate, while McGovern withdrew from a public presentation against Johnson's foreign policy. Senate Majority Leader Mike Mansfield, an old friend of the president's and an authority on Asia, agreed. He had been counseling LBJ against overcommitment. But he saw this speech as a demonstration of "President Johnson's resolve and his deep concern for the welfare of all people."[35]

The American people were also responsive. A poll taken in the summer of 1965 showed that 70 percent of those questioned supported the president's policy in Southeast Asia. Letters and telegrams to the White House confirmed the majority view: they were heavily in favor of the administration's position.[36]

Yet despite signs of support such as these, consensus on Vietnam in fact eluded the president. While he had a relatively high level of support for his conduct of the war, LBJ soon came under mounting attacks for his overall policy. In fact, the warm reception for the Johns Hopkins speech would soon give way to increasingly bitter criticism of Johnson and the American role in Southeast Asia, precipitated by larger draft calls, rising casualty rates, and a growing sense of stalemate in the war. Thus, from 1965 until the spring of 1968, when Johnson announced that he would not run for a second term, the level of support for the administration's foreign policy continued to wane.

Criticism came from two completely different directions. On the one hand were *doves* who questioned American intervention in Southeast Asia at any level. They were found mostly in Congress and on college campuses—and soon they would take their objections to the streets. On the other hand were *hawks* who wanted Johnson to use force as necessary to achieve unequivocal victory over the communist North. Republicans and a number of Southern Democrats were hawkish. But so were many ordinary Americans. In November 1965, 55 percent of those responding to a national survey favored a more intensive war effort. A year later, 53 percent still wanted further escalation.[37]

Because Johnson feared attack by both camps, he continued to chart a middle course between them. When he did enlarge troop commitments in July 1965, the president tried to reassure both sides. The public was told that he had "ordered to Vietnam the Airmobile Division and certain other forces which will raise our fighting strength from 75,000 to 125,000 men almost immediately."[38] For the benefit of the hawks, LBJ added that "additional forces will be needed later, and they will be sent as requested."[39] For the benefit of the doves, Johnson ruled out summoning the National Guard and Reserves. Moreover, he insisted that the nation could afford both the war and the Great Society. There would be no "war economy," no delay in social programs, and no increased taxes to finance the war.

Taking the middle road made it impossible for LBJ to develop a hard-core following in either camp. He was ultimately unable to exercise leadership with regard to the very groups whose support he most needed. In Congress, Johnson clearly felt the pinch of being caught between the hawks and the doves. The voices of antiwar senators grew louder and they gained increasing attention in the media. In 1966, the highly influential Senator Fulbright turned against the war, in particular because a growing body of evidence showed that LBJ had misled Congress about the Gulf of Tonkin incident. Fulbright also disagreed with Johnson's iron-fisted control over Vietnam policy. In 1966, he held well-publicized hearings to investigate the president's conduct of the war, as well as his apparent duplicity.

By 1967 and 1968, Senators Eugene McCarthy and Robert Kennedy expanded the attack to the national level by opposing LBJ's policies in the Democratic presidential primaries. Kennedy's criticism of the war was particularly troubling. Opposition to the war by JFK's brother weakened the president's claim to the legacy of his predecessor.

At the same time, congressional hawks, while willing to support Johnson, continually urged him to strive for victory. LBJ had to ask for their forebearance while pursuing a course they considered far too timid. He soon found himself in the awkward position of being a liberal Democratic president forced to rely on Republicans and Democratic conservatives for support. He now needed the help of Goldwater and others whose aggressive foreign policy views he had once scorned. Of course, the very act of accepting that help made it that much harder to persuade antiwar critics of his peaceful intentions.

LBJ also found it increasingly difficult to communicate with the press. He tried to cultivate those journalists considered "friendly" to the administration by favoring them with special interviews and invitations to White House social functions. "Hostile" reporters, on the other hand, had trouble even gaining access to the president and other members of the administration. On some occasions Johnson would woo and cajole the press; on others, he resorted to intimidation. In her book on the subject, Kathleen Turner refers to the president's "dual war": one was abroad, in Vietnam; the other was at home, the campaign to win media support.[40]

In the end, LBJ would lose both. Despite his best efforts, the major national news organizations turned against the war. The "prestige press" in the United States, including publications such as the *New York Times,* the *Washington Post, Newsweek,* and *Time,* all took strong antiwar editorial positions, which were also reflected in their reporting, with *Life* magazine publishing vivid photographs of scenes from the bloody conflict. The three television networks took similar stands and made the Vietnam conflict a "living room war." Americans were treated to graphic films of the fighting each evening on the news. The public was presented with an endless stream of stories on the number of American casualties in the conflict, on corruption in the South Vietnamese government, and on the seemingly hopeless prospect of winning a war a long way from home against resourceful and highly motivated guerrilla forces.

One important source of Johnson's press problems was the so-called *credibility gap*. This gap was the perceived distance between what the administration reported as truth and what the truth really was. Charges of a credibility gap were many and varied, and ranged from underestimates of enemy troop strength and American casualty rates to deception in the Gulf of Tonkin incident. Some focused on LBJ's use of misinformation to promote his own ends; others centered on his tendency to tell outright lies. For example, CBS News correspondent Dan Rather learned of the administration's plans to develop an electronic antiinfiltration barrier for use in Vietnam. On the president's orders, Johnson's press secretary told Rather that his story was wrong and it was never shown. Within days, the administration announced plans to develop the barrier, leaving Rather with the feeling he had been duped by the president. By the time of the next presidential election, critics doubted even Johnson's vaguest claims to desire peace in Southeast Asia.

Journalists were particularly furious at the credibility gap. They itemized Johnson's false statements and the occasions on which the administration provided misinformation. Columnist Walter Lippmann, highly influential in his time, took the president on both in print and in public speeches. He accused LBJ of a "180-degree turn away" from the peaceful campaign promises of 1964."[41]

A growing antiwar protest movement put further pressure on the president. It began with relatively mild expressions of dissent in 1964, led by prominent intellectuals who questioned whether the United States had sufficient interests in Southeast Asia to justify its intervention there. When, a short time later, student leaders at a number of elite American universities engaged in demonstrations and civil disobedience against Vietnam policy, several institutions of higher learning became hotbeds of antiwar sentiment. Some of this opposition subsided after the Johns Hopkins speech, but as more and more young men were drafted in 1966 and 1967, student protests became even louder and more frequent. Indeed, radical organizations opposing the war and American intervention in the affairs of other nations, such as the Students for a Democratic Society (SDS), became fixtures of college life.

Johnson felt considerable pressure from the antiwar protesters. They taunted him with chants such as: "Hey, Hey, LBJ, how many kids did you kill today?" They received extensive coverage on the evening news. And they threatened to disrupt national life in order to stop American involvement in Southeast Asia. To be sure, the man who had dreamed of the Great Society and who had fashioned sweeping domestic reforms in civil rights and welfare considered the demonstrators spoiled children of the elite. But because the early protests were strongest at top campuses such as Harvard, Berkeley, and Columbia, they were impossible for the president to ignore. Yet he never understood how to reach his youthful opponents. He was therefore unable to counter charges that he was responsible for senseless killing.

Nevertheless, throughout this period, Johnsonn was able to resist much of the pressure put on him by the antiwar movment, the prestige press, and doves in government because the public continued to support the war.[42] The public also approved Johnson's performance in office. During 1966, popular support for the president hovered at around 50 percent. In 1967, it declined, but it generally remained above 40 percent.[43] Armed with this information, LBJ, while feeling pressured, nevertheless was able to withstand his adversaries.*

Perhaps the most painful wounds to President Johnson were those inflicted by members of his own administration. Because of his tendency to personalize politics and his insistence on the loyalty of his subordinates, the president was particularly troubled by the departure of several of his key aides. By 1967, a number of Kennedy's men had quit. Each one had been closely identified with American policy in Southeast Asia: McGeorge Bundy, special assistant for national security affairs; Roger Hilsman, director of the State Department Bureau of Intelligence and Research; and Robert Kennedy, the late president's brother and attorney general (who had become an antiwar senator). Early in 1967, Johnson's press secretary and confidante, Bill Moyers, also resigned, primarily because he could not support Johnson's conduct of the war. Later that year, Secretary of Defense Robert McNamara left office as well. Even he had come to doubt the wisdom of American involvement in a land war in Southeast Asia.

The carefully managed war effort was starting to unravel. The bombing program was under attack, doves calling it inhumane, hawks calling it inadequate. And when American troop levels in Vietnam reached nearly 500,000 in 1967, public protests escalated as well. The president was under increasing pressure either to pull out, or to pursue a strategy for all-out victory.

Johnson now found it nearly impossible to justify his conduct of the war. There had been no demonstrable progress in the fighting, despite increasingly common talk of a "light at the end of the tunnel" (the phrase originated at the U.S. embassy in Saigon but became current throughout the administration). Moreover, the credibility gap had taken a heavy toll. Opinion leaders, such as Fulbright and Kennedy in the Senate, Walter Cronkite of CBS News, and student radicals no longer believed Johnson's claims to a presidency of peace.

Late in 1967, President Johnson made one more major attempt to present his case for the war. At a speech in San Antonio, he stressed the need to remain steadfast: "I would rather stand in Vietnam, in our time, and by meeting this danger now, and facing up to it, thereby reduce the danger for our children and for our grandchildren."[44] He further insisted that progress had been made:

> There is progress in the war itself, steady progress considering the war that we are fighting; rather dramatic progress considering the situation that actually prevailed when we sent our troops there in 1965; when we intervened to prevent the dismemberment of the country by the Vietcong and the North Vietnamese.[45]

*LBJ's approval ratings in 1964 (75 percent) and 1965 (66 percent) had been higher. Moreover, his two predecessors had also had more support. But Johnson could resist his critics so long as half the American people supported him, and, more importantly, the war. Finally, his approval ratings even in 1966 and 1967 were as good as or better than those received by Presidents Ford, Carter, and Reagan (first term) for most of their time in office.

Johnson's case was not, however, a compelling one. The political attacks on him continued unabated.

In 1968, the Johnson presidency came to an end. The Tet offensive exploded any administration claims of progress: North Vietnamese forces pressed into South Vietnam and even threatened Saigon. While, in the end, they were repelled by American forces, the operation was a major political embarrassment for the administration. Since Tet revealed the enemy to be far more powerful than LBJ or his advisers had ever acknowledged, nothing the president could say would eliminate the shock of the communist attack.

Finally, after years of supporting the president, public opinion turned against the war. Johnson was now openly opposed for the leadership of his own party. Senator Eugene McCarthy, running as a "peace candidate," challenged LBJ in the New Hampshire presidential primary. The president came in first, with 49.5 percent of the vote (as a write-in candidate). But McCarthy polled 42.4 percent, which was widely considered humiliating to President Johnson. Soon thereafter LBJ announced that he would not seek reelection. Instead, the president said that he would devote the remainder of his time in office to the search for peace in Vietnam.

WORLD LEADERSHIP: IMPLEMENTING THE POLICY ABROAD

LBJ's strategic approach to the war abroad was similar to his strategic approach to politics at home. It combined compromise with arrogance. The president believed that, by using measured force to achieve his goals, he would deny North Vietnam a victory and thereby compel it to come to the bargaining table. He would, in short, offer a deal to entice the enemy to give in. At the same time, however, he refused to listen to anyone who challenged the war and his conduct of it.

But while Johnson's strategy may have worked for a time in Washington, it was doomed thousands of miles from home. The conflict could not be resolved by the sort of consensus politics LBJ was familiar with. As the voluminous literature on the war attests, by neither withdrawing nor engaging in a full-scale war, the president chose precisely the wrong course.[46] Had the United States pulled out, unification of the two Vietnams would simply have happened sooner (it happened anyway in 1975). Moreover, the United States would have been spared the tragedy of thousands of dead and wounded. On the other hand, an expanded war might well have achieved a military solution quite quickly.

As the months dragged on, only Johnson and some of his closest advisers continued to defend the centrist. As one observer put it, LBJ's strategy was "like playing the middle hand in a game of high-low poker." He had placed himself in a no-win situation. As he told his wife in 1965, "I can't get out. I can't finish with what I have got. So what the Hell can I do?"[47]

The military effort was an example of how poorly the middle road served. For example, Johnson mandated that bombs could not be dropped within a thirty-mile radius of Hanoi, and he prohibited the American military from pursuing communist forces into Laos, Cambodia, and North Vietnam—

despite his commanders' claims that such actions were necessary. Moreover, he regularly authorized troop-level increases that were less than those recommended by his military advisers.

In 1965, Secretary of Defense McNamara told Johnson that 600,000 United States troops would be needed in Vietnam in the next two years. Even that many soldiers, McNamara warned, "will not guarantee success." However, Johnson never authorized more than 549,500, and that number was reached only after many more months had passed. In 1967, General William Westmoreland, the American commander in Vietnam, requested almost 200,000 additional troops. But the president sent only 55,000.

At the same time, he stubbornly refused to consider the possibility of withdrawal. LBJ thus pursued a course that his subordinates told him *might* succeed. Because he never made clear-cut victory the aim of the war—such a goal might touch off the domestic debate Johnson feared—he did only the minimum necessary not to lose. Of course, that inevitably meant raising the level of American involvement. After the escalation of 1965, American military advisers were supplanted by United States combat troops that did not operate even under the pretense that the war was for "Asian boys." U.S. troops did not accompany South Vietnamese forces; they fought on their own.

But American ground troops were essentially restricted to playing a defensive role in South Vietnam. They were prohibited from conducting offensive forays into enemy strongholds in the north or in the neutral countries of Laos and Cambodia. Because Johnson feared that further escalation might bring China or the Soviet Union into the conflict, direct action against North Vietnam was essentially limited to the bombing program, which was carried out according to LBJ's instructions. *Carrots* (unilateral bombing pauses every so often during the period 1965–1968) and *sticks* (incremental increases in bombing) were offered alternatively to bring the enemy to the bargaining table.

Johnson further decided to have the United States "go it alone" in its conduct of the war. He made only perfunctory efforts to win support from America's allies, to use the United Nations as a forum for negotiations, to enlist the Soviet Union and China in an effort to resolve the conflict, or even to approach the enemy through diplomacy.

In any case, allied support for American policy was tepid at best. The Johnson administration made half-hearted attempts to persuade other nations to join the fight, but with little success. South Korea sent two divisions to fight in Vietnam, but they were funded by the United States. Only Australia sent and paid for combat forces in support of American efforts. As Gelb and Betts observed in their book on the war: "While the administration pointed proudly to vast numbers of nations giving assistance to South Vietnam, almost all of them made no more than token gestures: a medical team here, engineers there, a few hospitals and police advisers, a shipment of blankets, and so on."[48] Great Britain endorsed United States policy in Southeast Asia as long as peace was the obstensible goal. But it did not genuinely share the American commitment. Nor did LBJ seem to care that the allies held back; as long as they did not openly oppose his war, he chose to count them on his side.

Several nations did play a role in various diplomatic overtures to North Vietnam. Each channel of diplomacy was given its own code name and the appearance of progress. Initiatives were undertaken through Poland (MARI-GOLD), Romania (PACKERS), Sweden (ASPEN), Norway (OHIO), Italy (KILLY), and France (PENNSYLVANIA).[49]

In fact, none of these diplomatic efforts bore fruit. The North Vietnamese were not willing to negotiate with the United States as long as the bombing continued, and LBJ was unwilling to halt the bombing. Moreover, the president insisted that communist infiltration of the South had to stop in order for talks to begin, while the North insisted that negotiations had to come first.

To a considerable extent the failure of diplomacy was the consequence of President Johnson's lack of interest. He was committed to his policy, convinced that the bombing strategy would work, and unwilling to "lose" Vietnam through negotiation. He was willing to support diplomatic initiatives only as long as he did not have to change course and the enemy made the first concessions. In fact, as Gelb and Betts suggest, LBJ may have been more interested in the appearance of progress than in any real progress: he wanted to be able to claim that he explored every chance for peace, when in reality he was unwilling to alter his strategy of limited war and carrot-and-stick bombing.[50]

As to other international actors, Johnson kept them at bay. Because of what were reputed to be "secret treaties" between the communist superpowers and Hanoi, he feared that the Soviet Union and China might be drawn into the fighting. In truth, LBJ was persuaded that, as long as he did not take actions that would activate these treaties (such as bombing Hanoi), he could keep the Soviet Union and China out of the war. In 1967, he even attempted to use the Soviets as a conduit for communication with North Vietnam, but this initiative was no more successful than any of the others.

A number of neutral states condemned American policy in Southeast Asia, but Johnson felt free to ignore them. The United Nations was also a forum for denunciations of United States imperialism in Vietnam, but these pronouncements too had precious little effect on American policy. Typically, the president would respond to his attackers by reiterating his desire for peace talks.

At one point, LBJ did in fact attempt to contact the enemy directly. In 1967, during a "peace offensive" in which bombing was temporarily halted, he wrote a letter to North Vietnamese president Ho Chi Minh. As usual, he tried to bargain: he would cease hostilities if the North would stop infiltrating the South. Ho's reply summarized North Vietnam's position and vividly illustrates why Johnson's attempt to compromise was doomed:

> ... The U.S. Government has unleashed the war of aggression in Vietnam. It must cease this aggression. That is the only way to the restoration of peace. ... *The Vietnamese people will never submit to force; they will never accept talks under the threat of bombing. Our cause is absolutely just. It is hoped that the U.S. Government will act in accordance with reason.* [Italics ours][51]

In the face of such a determined adversary, neither Johnson's carefully managed war, nor his use of American-style politicking, worked. As early as 1965, Press Secretary Bill Moyers had pinpointed this problem. After delivering his Johns Hopkins address offering to develop the Mekong Delta, LBJ confidently predicted that "Old Ho can't turn that down." But here was an adversary who could resist the old political professional. As Moyers saw it, "If Ho Chi Minh had been George Meany [president of the AFL-CIO], Lyndon Johnson would have had a deal."[52] Instead, what the president got was stalemate and ultimately that meant failure.

JOHNSON AS WORLD LEADER

Lyndon Johnson did not create the conflict in Vietnam. As he liked to remind anyone who would listen, he had inherited it from Eisenhower and Kennedy. But it became his war when he insisted on taking total control and fighting a land war in Southeast Asia according to his own conceptions. No longer did the United States merely provide assistance to the South Vietnamese government; now the U.S. was itself a belligerent.

Johnson took on the war for what were essentially domestic reasons. He was afraid to be labeled the president who "lost Vietnam" because the national debate that might ensue might well bring a halt to his plans for a Great Society. It seemed easier, therefore, to engage in a limited war than to face the bleak alternatives. The result of his action, however, was that large-scale American intervention led to a turning point in U.S. foreign policy.

Johnson's difficulties in Southeast Asia point to a problem Robert Divine identified in the post–World War II American presidency more generally: "We have tended to choose Presidents experienced and skilled only in domestic politics. . . . Yet once in office, we expect these executives to deal with complex foreign situations and to exhibit great skill in diplomacy."[53] In many ways, LBJ was the consummate domestic politician. He understood Congress, its rhythms and its methods, and was able to marshal a coalition in support of his clearly social and economic goals. But it was precisely those objectives that drove him to fight an unwinnable war. He did not invoke a communist enemy to distract attention from internal problems. Rather, he attempted to hold the world at bay while he forged ahead with his ambitious plans at home.[54] Committed to his course, he ignored the advice of many senior statesmen—Clark Clifford (Truman aide and future Defense secretary), Richard Russell (LBJ's mentor in the Senate), and George Ball (under secretary of state)—and proceeded with escalation.[55]

Because of his domestic goals, LBJ refrained from using many of the more conventional means for winning congressional support for the war— amenities, bargaining, or services—because he did not want to draw too much attention to the conflict. Instead, he presented his Vietnam policy as a sort of fait accompli, then relied on his office and appeals to both anticommunism and the desire for peace to win support for his actions.

At the same time, the president refused to undertake a campaign to win public support for an all-out war:

> Oh, I could see it coming all right. History provided too many cases when the sound of a bugle put an immediate end to the hopes and dreams of the best reformers: the Spanish-American war drowned the populist spirit; World War I

ended Woodrow Wilson's New Freedom; World War II brought the New Deal to a close. Once the war began, then all those conservatives in Congress would use it as a weapon against the Great Society.[56]

The second pressure on President Johnson was the irreversible passage of time. The Great Society could be realized only if LBJ acted quickly, capitalizing on the apparent martyrdom of Kennedy and preempting the trouble ahead in Vietnam. The president's intimate knowledge of Congress convinced him that if he delayed his initiatives because of the problems in Southeast Asia, he would never have another chance at domestic reform. As he told his aide, Harry McPherson, "You've only got one year."[57] After that, he believed, a president inevitably lost congressional support and political momentum, so any chance at sweeping reform would be lost.

LBJ thus committed himself to a war he did not want, hoping to somehow keep it from public view. He drew on the tendency of Congress and the public to defer to the president on matters of foreign policy. He tried to manage his way out of trouble in Vietnam, rather than withdraw or press for total victory. But in taking this approach, he failed to exercise one of the fundamental obligations of leadership: to choose. He did not want to lose his dream at home, but neither did he want to pay the price for a clear resolution of the conflict abroad. But to refuse to make that choice meant that LBJ crippled himself. Instead of exercising foreign policy leadership, he tried to hide his policy. Instead of applying his considerable political skills to building support for the war, he asked Congress and the American public to trust him to make the right decisions. Instead of building a coalition in Congress, despite the pleas of many of his friends there, he feared the "sound of the trumpet" and refused. Finally, even many of the war's advocates grew frustrated and argued that the United States could win only if the president would "do more."

Moreover, LBJ angered the members of Congress by the way he insisted on maintaining absolute control over the conflict. They bristled at his unilateral war making. Many came to oppose American involvement. After Richard Nixon continued this sort of presidential war, still more voted for the War Powers Resolution that was designed to restrain executive power.

Johnson never made a public case for the war. In the 1964 campaign, his theme was peace and restraint. He seemed to believe that if he persisted in expressing his desire for peace, the nation would accept whatever sacrifices he demanded of them. But as commentator Norman Podhoretz has observed, LBJ failed to provide a "convincing moral justification" for American intervention,[58] so he was unable to justify the casualties or explain to student demonstrators why his actions were necessary. LBJ lost what one adviser bluntly called the "propaganda battle" for public opinion.[59]

Instead, he concentrated his efforts on warning of the consequences of American withdrawal. He argued that if the United States pulled back, it would no longer be trusted to defend its friends against aggression. But he failed apparently to consider the costs of stalemate. Critics came to describe the war as a quagmire in which the United States was stuck. That quagmire damaged the reputation of the nation as a leader of the noncommunist world and weakened Johnson's claim to effectiveness as president. If the best that he could deliver was a draw, then what did that say about the capacity of the United States to protect its friends around the world?

He had no answer to that question. Because LBJ would not make a strong case for American intervention in Southeast Asia, he had to justify it by results. But progress was difficult to measure in a guerrilla conflict without fixed battlefronts. As Larry Berman documents effectively in his book on Johnson's conduct of the war, the administration tallied statistics of casualties ("body counts") and damage to enemy operations, trying to assemble what National Security Aide Rostow called "sound evidence of progress in Vietnam."[60] In the end, however, the president could only plea for the nation to persevere while he took care of everything. But this "trust me, it's working" approach was only as good as LBJ's ability to deliver substantive results.

He did not deliver as promised. He tried to conceal that fact by duplicitous statements and actions. Journalists and members of Congress, and even some of his subordinates, accused him of a credibility gap. The president was concerned, as are all presidents, about image management: he wanted to always give the appearance of slow but steady progress in Vietnam. But the lengths to which he would go to preserve this image alienated those whose support he needed most. He had come to the presidency in 1963 with a reservoir of goodwill and then intensified his support in the 1964 electoral landslide. But the growing credibility gap squandered his political resources needlessly. It meant that as time passed he was sustained only by a shrinking group of hawks in Congress (many of whom were Republicans) and an ill-informed public.

LBJ was able to hold out against the protesters and the media and antiwar legislators as long as the general public acquiesced in his conduct of foreign policy. But the American people did so because Johnson deceived them about the war. He kept the public in the dark about the nature, extent, and cost of the conflict.[61] He emphasized its limits and spoke of "demonstrable progress" in the effort to throw off the North Vietnamese invaders. When the Tet offensive came, however, his "trust me" domestic strategy collapsed completely.

Instead of exercising world leadership, instead of marshaling followers abroad, Johnson decided to go it alone. Just as he would not appeal for support at home, he hardly even tried to win the support of America's allies and adversaries. To do so would mean risking either a larger war (a sort of "grand alliance" to save Vietnam) or rejection of American policy. LBJ would not take such a chance. The result was that the president could point to token efforts by American allies to assist in the war effort but to nothing of substance (except the Australian commitment). He could list a number of diplomatic initiatives through Poland, France, and other nations, but these were generally sterile. The conflict was truly Lyndon Johnson's war.

LBJ's involvement in Vietnam was his major overture as a world leader and his greatest failure. Leadership is composed of three elements: the leader, the followers, and the situation. Johnson's previous reputation as an effective leader was built on his control over the Senate's operations, his ability to negotiate compromises, and his capacity to outmaneuver opponents. In the White House, this approach worked to some degree in winning passage of Great Society programs. But it did not work in the case of Southeast Asia.

Because of LBJ's leadership style, he was sure that mastery of every detail and greater personal effort were the keys to finding his way out of trouble. To be sure, he knew more about the specifics of the war than almost any other issue. As his former assistant, Harry McPherson recalled: "He said he was sure he wanted to be called every time something happened in the Vietnam War era. . . . He really wanted to know the particulars."[62] Indeed, his appetite for information was legendary. He kept three televisions in the Oval Office in order to watch each network's evening news, and he had a news service teletype installed virtually adjacent to his desk.

But knowledge of facts is no substitute for leadership. President Johnson knew the details of bomb targets and troop strength, but his finely calibrated carrot-and-stick approach was ineffective in the face of a highly motivated adversary. Nor did his mastery of detail help to develop a national consensus on the war or force the North Vietnamese to the bargaining table.

Instead of engaging would-be followers at home and abroad, the president's "stunning insecurity" drove him to try to control events lest they overtake him. One important device for maintaining that command was the Tuesday Cabinet. But that council illuminates a number of problems in an informal system of presidential decision making:[63] First, the group lacked a structured agenda. The issues raised and discussed at meetings were not backed by adequate staff work to provide background or define options. Therefore the group lacked the information necessary for it to serve as useful advisory body. Participants could do little more than react to the issues at hand. Second, the group was unable to provide coordination for the diverse military, economic, and political elements of Vietnam policy. Johnson used the meetings to circumvent the National Security Council, but the Tuesday Cabinet was no substitute for that institution. Because no minutes were kept, none of the president's decisions were formally recorded. Moreover, because attendance at the Tuesday lunches was by presidential invitation only, Johnson used the occasions to exclude those officials whose advice he simply did not want to hear. As George Reedy commented of discussions around Johnson, "they were really monologues in which one man got a reflection of what he sent out."[64] The Tuesday Cabinet was thus a highly personal instrument to support Johnson and to ensure his absolute control over the American participation in the war.

Johnson's followers never really had the chance to respond to a leader's cues. The people and their representatives gave him considerable leeway to conduct the war when they thought he was sincere. In 1964, they voted for the man they thought was the "peace candidate." But after the election, when LBJ changed course, he never bothered to rally support for his escalation of the conflict. Moreover, he squandered the public's trust by the way he managed the conflict, by concealing the extent and cost of American involvement, and by his insistence on exercising absolute control. Consequently, when the shock of Tet exposed his lies, the people voted for a new "peace candidate": Senator Eugene McCarthy.

As for the situation in Vietnam, it was intractable to American-style bargaining. To be sure, LBJ was not the last to learn this lesson. Richard Nixon came to the presidency believing that the war would be negotiated to a conclusion by the autumn of 1969.[65] When he resigned in 1974, it was still raging. Clearly America now faced an adversary that resisted both compromise and accommodation. Guerrilla warriors opposing a government win so long as they are not defeated. Thus, the Vietcong and North Vietnamese continued to fight so long as they did not lose.

Lyndon Johnson authored his own problems in Vietnam. He had been an extraordinarily effective leader at home, winning passage of the 1965 Civil Rights Act as well as a string of Great Society programs. But those had been policies to which he was passionately committed. In contrast, LBJ's Vietnam policy reflected his fears rather than his ambitions. For all the dangers it entailed, he chose it because to him it was better than the alternatives. But it is hard to lead on the basis of a lesser of evils. So Johnson managed the policy, but he failed to provide leadership.

Notes

1. See Rowland Evans and Robert Novak, *Lyndon B. Johnson: The Exercise of Power* (New York: Signet, 1966), pp. 61–209.

2. David Halberstam, *The Best and the Brightest* (Greenwich, Conn.: Fawcett, 1972), p. 522.

3. Ibid. The literature on Johnson generally supports this portrait, although early portraits of him were adulatory. For a survey, see Robert Divine, "The Johnson Literature," in *The Johnson Years, Volume I: Foreign Policy, the Great Society, and the White House*, ed. Robert Divine (Austin, Tex.: University of Texas Press, 1987), pp. 3–23. Revealing portraits of LBJ are to be found in Robert Caro, *The Years of Lyndon Johnson, Volume I: The Path to Power* (New York: Vintage, 1981) and Doris Kearns, *Lyndon Johnson and the American Dream* (New York: Signet, 1976). The best book on Johnson's career in Washington (through 1965) is Evans and Novak, op. cit. The best memoir from the Johnson administration is Harry McPherson, *A Political Education* (Boston: Little, Brown, 1972).

4. See Kellerman, *The Political Presidency*, chapter 7.

5. Lyndon B. Johnson, *The Vantage Point: Perspectives of the Presidency, 1963–1969* (New York: Holt, Rinehart and Winston, 1971), pp. 225–226.

6. George Reedy, *The Twilight of the Presidency* (New York: Mentor, 1970), p. 4.

7. Quoted in Halberstam, p. 526.

8. Ibid., p. 526.

9. *Public Papers of the Presidents* (April 7, 1965), pp. 394–98.

10. Kearns, pp. 159–60. This point is made throughout the literature on LBJ, but Kearns's discussion is representative.

11. On the domestic policy consensus, see James L. Sundquist, *Politics and Policy: The Eisenhower, Kennedy, and Johnson Years* (Washington: Brookings Institution, 1968). On the consensus supporting containment, see Leslie H. Gelb with Richard Betts, *The Irony of Vietnam: The System Worked* (Washington: Brookings Institution, 1979).

12. Walt W. Rostow, *The Diffusion of Power* (New York: Macmillan, 1972), chapter 34.

13. See Larry Berman, *Lyndon Johnson's War* (New York: Norton, 1984).

14. Kearns, p. 283.

15. Ibid., p. 283.

16. Johnson, p. 54. For background on American involvement in Vietnam at the time, see William J. Rust, *Kennedy in Vietnam* (New York: Scribner, 1985); Halberstam; Gelb and Betts; Frances Fitzgerald, *Fire in the Lake* (Boston: Little, Brown, 1972); Chester Cooper, *The Lost Crusade* (New York: Dodd, Mead, 1970); George M. Kahin and John W. Lewis, *The United States in Vietnam* (New York: Dial Press, 1969); George C. Herring, *America's Longest War*

(New York: Knopf, 1979); or one of the editions of the Pentagon Papers (a collection of internal Defense Department studies on American intervention in Southeast Asia). There are three editions of the Pentagon Papers: Neil Sheehan et al., *The Pentagon Papers as Published by the New York Times* (New York: 1971); U.S. Senate, Committee on Government Operations, Subcommittee on Buildings and Grounds, *The Pentagon Papers,* Senator Gravel Edition, 4 vols. (Boston: Little, Brown, 1971); and U.S. House of Representatives, *United States–Vietnam Relations 1945–1967: A Study Prepared by the Department of Defense,* 12 vols. (Washington: Government Printing Office, 1971).

17. BDM Corporation, "The Strategic Lessons Learned in Vietnam," vol. 3, sect. 3, p. 37. Cited in Larry Berman, *Planning a Tragedy: The Americanization of the War in Vietnam* (New York: Norton, 1982), p. 32. Berman's book offers an intensive study of LBJ's decision to escalate in 1965. His sequel, *Lyndon Johnson's War,* provides an in-depth examination of the president's conduct of the war, with an emphasis on how Johnson searched for signs of progress.

18. Quoted in Joseph C. Goulden, *Truth is the First Casualty: The Gulf of Tonkin Affair—Illusion and Reality* (Chicago: Rand McNally, 1969), p. 160.

19. Reprinted in John Galloway, *The Gulf of Tonkin Resolution* (Rutherford, N.J.: Fairleigh Dickinson University Press, 1970), pp. 169–70.

20. Reprinted in ibid.

21. Quoted in ibid., p. 71.

22. Barry Goldwater, "Victory in Asia," reprinted in *Vietnam: Anthology and Guide to a Television History,* ed. Stephen Cohen (New York: Knopf, 1983), p. 97.

23. *Public Papers of the President* (September 25, 1964), p. 1123.

24. The commercial was broadcast only once, due to complaints from the Goldwater campaign. Nevertheless, it achieved wide attention and its unmistakable message was not forgotten.

25. Vietnam was also ignored in Johnson's speech at Cadillac Square in Detroit on Labor Day, the traditional place and occasion for beginning a Democratic candidate's presidential campaign.

26. *Public Papers* (October 12, 1964), p. 1325.

27. *Public Papers* (October 1, 1964), p. 1181.

28. See ibid., p. 1181.

29. *Public Papers* (August 12, 1964), p. 953.

30. Johnson, p. 68.

31. Rostow, p. 360.

32. *Public Papers* (April 7, 1965), pp. 394–98.

33. Quoted in Kathleen J. Turner, *Lyndon Johnson's Dual War* (Chicago: University of Chicago Press, 1985), p. 129.

34. Ibid.

35. Ibid., p. 130.

36. Ibid., p. 130.

37. Rostow, p. 480. See also Richard K. Betts, "Misadventure Revisited," *The Wilson Quarterly* (Summer 1983).

38. Quoted in Gelb, p. 129.

39. Ibid., p. 129.

40. See Turner, op. cit.

41. Ibid., p. 177.

42. Rostow, p. 479.

43. Ibid., p. 479.

44. "San Antonio Address," 29 September 1967, reprinted in Cohen, pp. 156–59. For a discussion of the speech within the context of LBJ's search for "signs of optimism," see Berman, *Lyndon Johnson's War,* pp. 83–84.

45. Ibid., p. 157.

46. The literature analyzing the war from this perspective is extensive. For a representative work advocating withdrawal, see Howard Zinn, *Vietnam: The Logic of Withdrawal* (Boston: Little, Brown, 1967). A representative work on the other side is Dave Richard Palmer, *Summons*

of the Trumpet (San Rafael, Calif.: Presidio Press, 1978). The literature analyzing American strategy within the confines set by LBJ is represented by Guenter Lewy, *America in Vietnam* (New York: 1978).

47. Lady Bird Johnson, *A White House Diary* (New York: Holt, Rinehart and Winston, 1970), p. 248. For a thorough examination of Johnson's problems in this regard, see Berman, *Lyndon Johnson's War*, chapter 8.

48. Gelb with Betts, p. 161. On the Australian effort, see Frank Frost, *Australia's War in Vietnam* (Sydney: Allen and Unwin, 1987) or Peter King, ed., *Australia's Vietnam* (Sydney: Allen and Unwin, 1983).

49. Ibid., pp. 162–63. See also David Kraslow and Stuart H. Loory, *The Secret Search for Peace in Vietnam* (New York: Oxford University Press, 1968), which concerns MARIGOLD.

50. Gelb, pp. 162–67. Johnson's management of war strategy, particularly his control over bombing, is examined in Berman, *Lyndon Johnson's War*, especially pp. 39–42, and in Ralph Stavins, Richard Barnet, and Marcus G. Raskin, *Washington Plans an Aggressive War* (New York: Random House, 1971), pp. 150–195.

51. "Ho Chi Minh's Reply to Lyndon Johnson," 15 February 1967, reprinted in *America in Vietnam: A Documentary History,* ed. with commentary by William Appleman Williams, Thomas McCormick, Lloyd Gardner, and Walter Lafeber (Garden City, N.Y.: Doubleday, 1985), pp. 261–62.

52. Quoted in John P. Burke and Fred I. Greenstein, "Presidential Personality and National Security Leadership: A Comparative Analysis of Vietnam Decision Making" (mimeographed, Princeton University, 1988).

53. Robert A. Divine, *Eisenhower and the Cold War* (New York: Oxford University Press, 1981), p. vii.

54. Kearns, p. 264. For a consideration of whether LBJ's perceptions of the political situation were accurate, see Fred I. Greenstein and John P. Burke, "The Dynamics of Presidential Reality Testing: Evidence from Two Vietnam Decisions" (presented at an annual meeting of the International Society of Political Psychology, Tel Aviv, Israel, June 1989).

55. See David M. Barrett, "Political and Personal Intimates as Advisers: The Mythology of Lyndon Johnson, His Advisers, and the 1965 Decision to Enter the Vietnam War" (presented at an annual meeting of the Midwest Political Science Association, Chicago, Illinois, April 1988), p. 25. Barrett's points are summarized in idem., "Six Who Told Johnson to Get Out of Vietnam," *New York Times,* 8 April 1989, p. 27.

56. Quoted in Kearns, pp. 263–64.

57. Quoted in Kernell and Popkin, pp. 96–97.

58. Norman Podhoretz, *Why We Were in Vietnam* (New York: Harper & Row, 1983).

59. Abe Fortas, quoted in Berman, *Lyndon Johnson's War*, p. 87.

60. Quoted in ibid., p. 84.

61. See Sheehan et al., *The Pentagon Papers,* particularly pp. xiii and 521; Halberstam, pp. 752–53; Kearns, pp. 292–93 and 312 (in which it is made clear by Charles Schulz, LBJ's budget director, that the president was concealing the cost of the war).

62. Quoted in Kernell and Popkin, p. 59.

63. Discussed in Henry Graff, *The Tuesday Cabinet* (Englewood Cliffs, N.J.: Prentice-Hall, 1970). See also I. M. Destler, *Presidents, Bureaucrats, and Foreign Policy* (Princeton: Princeton University Press, 1974), pp. 109–18; Townsend Hoopes, *The Limits of Intervention* (New York: David McKay, 1983), p.7; and James C. Thompson, Jr., "How Could Vietnam Happen?" *Atlantic* (April 1968). For a useful discussion of Johnson's organization of national security policy making, in the context of modern presidents, see Phillip G. Henderson, *Managing the Presidency: The Eisenhower Legacy—from Kennedy to Reagan* (Boulder, Colo.: Westview Press, 1988).

64. Arthur Schlesinger, Jr., *The Imperial Presidency* (New York: New American Library, 1974), p. 185.

65. H. R. Haldeman, quoted in Kernell and Popkin, p. 94.

7

Richard Nixon's Overtures to the Communist Superpowers

The greatest honor history can bestow is the title of peacemaker. This honor now beckons America—the chance to help lead the world at last out of the valley of turmoil and onto the high ground of peace that man has dreamed of since the dawn of civilization . . . . This is our summons to greatness.

—First Inaugural, January 20, 1969

BACKGROUND

The 1968 election brought to the presidency a new "peace candidate," one pledged to ending the war in Vietnam and promoting the larger cause of negotiation and compromise in world affairs. Richard Nixon made peace the theme of his campaign, of his inaugural address, and of his foreign policy. His record as president demonstrated both the opportunities and the frustrations awaiting the statesman who proclaims such a goal.

Nixon was no stranger to either experience. He came to the White House at the culmination of a political career that had included both remarkable successes and dramatic setbacks. He had first achieved attention as a young member of Congress in the 1940s, relentlessly pursuing diplomat Alger Hiss in a famous case involving allegations of communist spying. Nixon's success in assembling sufficient evidence to convict Hiss of perjury won him a reputation as a tough anticommunist and helped him gain election to the Senate. He was also known as a devoted Republican partisan.[1]

Those two qualities appealed to presidential candidate Dwight Eisenhower in 1952, particularly since Ike needed a vice-presidential running mate who could strengthen his ties to the Republican party (especially its conservative wing). Thus, at age thirty-nine, and in politics for less than a decade, Richard Nixon became vice president.

Overshadowed by a widely popular president, Nixon set about developing his own particular set of credentials. He was never close to the president, but he was able to make use of his time in office to build his standing in the party and, at the national level, to become an expert on foreign affairs.[2] Over time he became a national figure in his own right and in the 1960 election was the standard bearer of the Republican party. Narrowly defeated by John Kennedy in the 1960 presidential election, RN returned to his native California to run for governor in 1962. At this point, his career went into eclipse. He lost the race badly and became embittered about politics. Meeting with reporters after the election, Nixon vowed that he was now giving his "last press conference" and retiring from public life. He told his astonished audience, "You won't have Nixon to kick around anymore."

He moved his family to New York and began a highly successful practice as a corporate lawyer. At the same time, however, he continued to nurture his reputation as an authority on world politics. He spoke frequently on foreign policy and in 1967 he published an essay on "Asia after Vietnam" in the prestigious journal *Foreign Affairs*.[3] These moves signaled either a return to politics or an emerging role as a Republican elder on international relations.

In 1968, Nixon came out of political retirement and undertook an aggressive campaign to become the Republican nominee for president. Running on his carefully crafted reputation as a world affairs expert and promising that he had a "secret plan" to end the war in Vietnam, Nixon defeated Vice President Hubert Humphrey in a close contest.

Throughout the years between 1962 and 1968, RN had remained a highly visible, yet elusive figure. By nature secretive, brooding, and aloof, he sustained himself through the ups and downs of his professional life by a fierce determination to succeed. Interestingly, both victory and defeat made him suspicious of others. He was sure that the press, the bureaucracy, and the "liberal establishment" were all out to get him. Like LBJ, he preferred to trust a few close aides whose devotion to him was unquestioned.[4]

One former assistant, who remains loyal to his former boss, described the dimensions of Nixon's character:

> One part of Richard Nixon is exceptionally considerate, exceptionally caring, sentimental, generous of spirit, kind. Another part is coldly calculating, devious, craftily manipulative. A third part is angry, vindictive, ill-tempered, mean-spirited. . . . Those of us who have worked with Nixon over the years often refer to his "light side" and his "dark side."[5]

Both sides would be apparent in his conduct of the presidency. During the 1968 campaign, his staff tried to downplay his "dark side" by portraying him as a "new Nixon," one full of kindness and generosity. But the essential man had not changed. He remained, as two close observers of his administration described him, "a complicated, enigmatic man—sometimes super-pragmatic, sometimes doctrinaire, sometimes decisive and sometimes vacillating, but always alone and often lonely."[6]

Richard Nixon's priority as president was in foreign affairs. Here he believed he could demonstrate the full measure of his worth. In contrast to Lyndon Johnson, but like John Kennedy, Nixon saw politics at home as far less interesting or important than politics abroad. In 1967, he summarized his attitude: "I've always thought this country could run itself domestically without a President. All you need is a competent Cabinet to run the country at home. You need a President for foreign policy. No Secretary of State is really important; the President makes foreign policy."[7]

Nixon's goals and his leadership style were closely related. He wanted to be the architect of what he called a "structure of peace," a set of political arrangements that would promote progress in a post–cold war era.[8] To that end, he employed the skills and methods he had developed since his entry into public life. First, Nixon concentrated on developing a grand strategy for foreign policy. Consistent with his view that "the President makes foreign policy," he tried to shape the international political order. To help him in this effort, he enlisted Henry Kissinger as his assistant for national security affairs. A respected, albeit controversial, scholar of international politics, Kissinger became the president's close ally and confidante.[9] Together they developed specific plans for implementing Nixon's structure of peace. These included: conclusion of the Vietnam War, support for American allies as regional powers around the globe, better relations with the Soviet Union, and probing the possibility of reestablishing communication with the People's Republic of China.

Second, like LBJ, Nixon believed in the importance of hard work. But he did not share LBJ's passion for detail. He was content to leave such matters to Kissinger (first as national security adviser and, in the second term, as secretary of state), who made himself invaluable to Nixon because of his mastery of the fine points of foreign policy. Kissinger has described the president's approach to the negotiation of a strategic arms agreement with the Soviet Union:

> Nixon took a keen interest in the strategy for SALT and in what channels it should be negotiated. But the details of the various plans bored him. . . . I therefore scheduled over Nixon's impatient protests a series of NSC meetings where options were presented to a glassy-eyed and irritable President so that directives could be issued with some plausibility on his authority.[10]

Third, President Nixon preferred to work alone, with a veil of secrecy surrounding his efforts. In particular, he did not trust the State Department to assist him in his plans for reshaping foreign policy. Since his earliest days in politics, Nixon had been suspicious of the department's career staff. At best, he feared that the careerists would resist his ideas as new and because they did not originate with them. At worst, he worried that the bureaucracy at State would actively undermine his plans.

Nixon and Kissinger worked well together. Both were interested in developing policy and both were impatient with the foreign affairs bureaucracy. They therefore drew all major foreign policy decision making into the White House. Moreover, a number of the most important international negotiations were run directly from Kissinger's office, circumventing the State Department altogether.

To advance the president's goals and accommodate his style, Kissinger created a hierarchical system of foreign policy–making that revived the National Security Council as an important instrument of government. The NSC had been little used under Presidents Kennedy or Johnson, because they favored informal groups such as JFK's ExComm (used in the Cuban missile crisis) and LBJ's Tuesday Cabinet. Now the NSC would become the center of action. Kissinger established a group of interdepartmental committees and panels that could integrate foreign policy through the NSC. He chaired each committee and his staff serviced it. This arrangement made the assistant for national security affairs the president's chief foreign policy agent. It concomitantly made Kissinger the most powerful national security assistant in the history of American presidential administrations.[11]

Under this system, the national security adviser had a broad mandate to shape and direct the process of foreign policy—making. President Nixon's secretary of state, William Rogers, played only a minor role in the administration. Indeed, he had no background in foreign affairs and was, in all likelihood, appointed to the post so the State Department would be deprived of strong leadership. Not surprisingly, the department was overshadowed by the NSC System (as Nixon and Kissinger called their policy organization). But, ironically, Kissinger did draw upon the human resources of the State Department: he filled the National Security Council staff with a number of Foreign Service officers. Under this arrangement, he was able to draw on the department's expertise without accepting its traditional organization and bureaucratic interests. The NSC's chief experts on Latin America (Viron P. Vaky), China (John Holdridge), and Asia (Richard Sneider) were all originally at State, as was Lawrence Eagleburger, an important Kissinger aide.[12]

With the NSC System in place, President Nixon was able to devote himself to international relations. He used Kissinger's NSC staff to survey American policy around the globe and proceeded to issue annual "State of the World" messages to Congress that were meant to parallel the standard presidential messages on the State of the Union and on the economy.[13]

To build his structure of peace, Nixon first had to deliver on his plan to end the war in Southeast Asia. He initially attempted to devise a negotiated settlement to the war. He came to the presidency fully believing that the North Vietnamese government was interested in a deal, and, indeed, he expected to have an agreement to bring the war to a close by the fall of 1969.[14] During the transition period after the 1968 election, Nixon sent a message to Hanoi indicating his desire to begin serious discussions aimed at a diplomatic end to the fighting. His proposal was promptly rebuffed.

The president then adopted a different approach. With a campaign pledge, public opinion, civil unrest, and Congress all pressuring him to end the war, Nixon and his advisers developed what became, in effect, a policy of unilateral American withdrawal from Vietnam. This scheme involved a long series of graduated troop reductions over the course of several years, along with continued attempts to negotiate a truce in Southeast Asia. The new policy was described as *Vietnamization,* that is, it turned responsibility for the conflict back over to the South Vietnamese. Nixon hoped that this strategy would disentangle the United States from the conflict without leaving the South Vietnamese completely at the mercy of the North. At the same time, the president hoped to weaken the enemy by expanding the war through secret attacks on Vietcong strongholds in Cambodia and Laos. But manifestly the main purpose of Vietnamization was to give priority to bringing American soldiers back home.

By 1972, the United States was still heavily involved in Southeast Asia and still determined to withdraw. Vietnamization appeared to strengthen the position of the Saigon government, until a communist offensive in April put new pressure on the South. Nixon responded with renewed bombing of

North Vietnam and the mining of Haiphong harbor. Finally, in December 1972, a cease-fire agreement that had secretly been negotiated in Paris by Kissinger was announced.

By the end of Nixon's first term in office, the war appeared to be winding to a conclusion. But it would still be raging when he left office in 1974. The president's weakened political position, a consequence of the Watergate scandal, stimulated North Vietnamese intransigence and prolonged the conflict.[15]

Despite this ultimate failure, Nixon was determined to carry on with his plan for building a structure of peace. Looking beyond Vietnam, in 1969 he announced a new principle to guide American policy on regional conflicts around the world. This policy was to be consistent with the new realities of the United States' interest in world affairs: on the one hand, the U.S. wanted to remain a leading actor on the international scene, but on the other, the American people were much more leery now of foreign entanglements. The compromise policy, announced in a speech on the island of Guam in November, became known as the "Nixon Doctrine."[16]

The Nixon Doctrine contained three key elements:

1. the United States would keep all of its treaty commitments
2. the American nuclear shield would continue to protect allies and other vital interests from nuclear attack
3. in other types of conflict the United States would provide assistance but would "look to the nation directly threatened to assume the primary responsibility of providing the manpower for its defense."[17]

In other words, the Nixon Doctrine was Vietnamization writ large: the United States would assist other nations with weapons, money, technology, and supplies but would not commit forces.

The Nixon Doctrine addressed important aspects of American foreign policy. But it did not address the president's primary concern, which was the relationship between the United States and the world's other superpowers. Here is where Richard Nixon's most significant effort at reshaping foreign policy would lie: in his approach to the two giant communist states, China and the Soviet Union. And it is here that he would also achieve his most tangible successes. In 1972, his efforts vis-à-vis both countries bore fruit. In February he visited the People's Republic of China (PRC), the first president ever to do so. Ending twenty years of American hostility toward China's communist government, Nixon's visit was important largely because it opened the possibility of a closer relationship between the two nations in the future. And in May of 1972, the president and Soviet leader Leonid Brezhnev signed the SALT I agreement, which consisted of an Anti-Ballistic Missile (ABM) Treaty (limiting such systems) and an Interim Agreement on Offensive Weapons. Both were subsequently approved by the Senate by large margins.

Nixon's overtures to the communist superpowers, as well as the ultimate outcome of his efforts, reveal much about him and his concept of leadership. They help to demonstrate what a determined president can do in order to achieve the goals he has set for himself, as well as the risks involved in attempting dramatic shifts in national policy.

NATIONAL LEADERSHIP: PRESENTING THE CASE AT HOME

Richard Nixon believed that he had an opportunity to influence the course of international politics in his time. He was sure that effective presidential leadership could lay the foundation for progress in U.S.-Soviet relations, as well as alter the American policy toward China that had existed since 1949. He believed that both moves would help to stabilize world politics and allow the United States to balance between the two communist giants.

Improving relations with the Soviet Union was the most complicated aspect of the president's grand strategy. Its centerpiece was the negotiation of an arms-control agreement (or SALT, from the Strategic Arms Limitation Talks begun under President Johnson). Nixon believed he could use it to enlist Soviet assistance in settling other international problems, such as continuing strife in the Middle East. An arms treaty would involve not only delicate negotiations with Moscow but would also require effective politicking at home to win its acceptance by the United States Senate.

The president began building domestic support for SALT long before he had an agreement with the Soviet Union. He had to deal with three key groups in winning its acceptance: the state department, the armed forces, and the Senate. The State Department presented Nixon with a dilemma. On the one hand, it was in charge of the "official" negotiations taking place in Vienna and Helsinki. These talks had gotten underway even before Nixon took office. To cancel them would only stimulate criticism at a time when several voices in the press and many members of Congress were calling for arms control. But on the other hand, the president did not trust the State Department bureaucracy. He was convinced it would interfere with his plans.[18]

Nixon decided to allow these negotiations to continue under the direction of Ambassador Gerard Smith. Unbeknownst to Smith and his colleagues, however, Kissinger (and, at times, the president) conducted a series of top-secret meetings at the White House with Soviet ambassador Anatoly Dobrynin. The official talks in Europe were in some ways useful, but manifestly they were used by the president to conceal the real negotiations operating through the Kissinger-Dobrynin Channel. Indeed, shortly before SALT I was signed in 1972 (SALT II was the agreement signed by Jimmy Carter in 1979), Kissinger was obliged to inform Ambassador Smith that the major issues of the agreement had been settled in secret in Washington.[19]

The military could not be so easily circumvented. In order to win Senate passage for an arms-control treaty, Nixon would have to win the approval of the armed forces. Their objection to an agreement could convince many Republican and conservative Democratic senators to vote against any deal with Moscow.

The president sought the Pentagon's acquiescence by agreeing to a buildup of particular weapons systems. This approach lessened military resistance to limits on other kinds of weapons, provided additional funds for the armed forces, and allowed the president to portray arms control as part of a general improvement in the nation's security. While negotiating on arms control with the Soviets, the administration simultaneously pressed for the development of an antiballistic missile (ABM) defense system, the Trident submarine, the Minuteman III missile, and multiple independently targeted reentry vehicle (MIRV) technology. The Pentagon had eagerly sought each of these programs and lent its support to the pursuit of a SALT deal.[20]

But the president almost lost the military at a crucial moment, during the United States–Soviet summit in Moscow in May 1972. The *New York Times* had obtained information that showed the SALT agreement would tolerate a numerical inequality of missiles favoring the Soviet Union.[21] (A difference in technology undercut those differences, plus Nixon and Kissinger were using SALT I to prevent an even wider gap between Soviet and American forces.) The Joint Chiefs of Staff threatened to withdraw their support. But Nixon was determined to see it through: "The hell with the political consequences; we are going to make an agreement on our terms regardless of the political consequences if the Pentagon won't go along."[22] In the end, he in fact did worry about the consequences and won the military's acquiescence only by a promise to further accelerate strategic programs not covered by the agreement (which he had planned to do anyway).[23]

With regard to the Senate, Nixon's leadership efforts during the period 1969–1972 involved action on several fronts.[24] He looked to the buildup of the ABM, Trident, MIRV, and other weapons, along with the approval of the Joint Chiefs of Staff, to assist him in winning over skeptical but influential senators such as Henry Jackson. Moreover, he drew upon support from a group of senators eager for an arms-control agreement. Senators William Fulbright, John Sherman Cooper, Mike Mansfield, and Hubert Humphrey all urged the president to reach an agreement. While less than delighted by promises for weapons development intended to win over hawks, they were not about to vote against an arms accord with the Soviet Union. Finally, the administration provided senators with rather *pro forma* briefings on the progress of arms talks.

By appealing to both hawks and doves, the president thus assembled a coalition that would be receptive to SALT I. At the same time, his natural inclination to work in secret meant that he paid little attention to consultation with senators about the emerging agreement. Only on the very day that the SALT I agreement was signed in Moscow were aides to key senators invited to a White House briefing on the accord. Since the order of the day was to win votes in the Senate, the president and his staff were finally more forthcoming about sharing information.[25]

President Nixon made other efforts to win support for SALT I. He had actually signed two pacts with the Soviet Union: the ABM Treaty and the Interim Agreement on Offensive Weapons. Only the first required Senate ratification. The second was essentially a policy statement on United States and Soviet nuclear arsenals and a commitment to conclude a more comprehensive agreement in the future. But in order to ease passage of the ABM Treaty and legitimate the Interim Agreement, the president also submitted the second pact to approval by Congress.

Immediately upon his return from Moscow on June 1, Nixon personally led the drive to win the votes he needed. Less than an hour after landing at Andrews Air Force Base outside Washington, he appeared before a joint session of Congress to speak about his success at the summit. Two weeks later, he and Kissinger briefed 120 members of Congress at the White House. Rather than a peremptory meeting, the president and his chief foreign policy adviser now presented a long and detailed case for adoption of the two agreements.

Over the course of the next two months, administration officials testified before Senate committees on behalf of SALT. At the same time, Secretary of Defense Melvin Laird lobbied Congress for money for the Trident submarine, the B-1 bomber, and the strategic cruise missile.[26] Clearly, the president was continuing his two-pronged strategy of pressing for both SALT I *and* new weapons.

On August 2, the Senate approved a defense procurement bill that included funds for weapons development. The next day, it also approved the ABM Treaty portion of SALT I. But the Interim Agreement on Offensive Weapons appeared to be in trouble, since a number of senators said they would offer amendments to the legislation approving the pact when it reached the Senate floor.

Henry Jackson led the critics, charging that the Interim Agreement gave the Soviet Union an advantage in nuclear throw weight. He and his colleagues supported an advisory amendment to the bill approving the pact that called for numerical equality between superpower nuclear arsenals in all future agreements. The Jackson Amendment also called for a vigorous program of research and development in support of "a prudent defense posture."[27] Finally, it stated that any Soviet action or weapon deployment that threatened the American deterrent capability would be grounds for canceling the treaty.

While the amendment did not bind the administration, it did present a challenge to the president. It implicitly charged him with risking American security in order to make a deal with Moscow. But what was more important was the fact that the amendment threatened Nixon's deal. An impasse between the White House and Jackson's supporters might kill the Interim Agreement.[28] Therefore, the president sought to compromise. In exchange for dropping the section of the amendment setting conditions for canceling the Interim Agreement, Nixon offered to accept the Jackson Amendment.

Finally, on September 14 the Senate endorsed the Interim Agreement. The two halves of SALT I had been accepted by twin votes of 88 to 2. Richard Nixon thus achieved his goal of negotiating the first treaty between the United States and the Soviet Union limiting the number of strategic weapons and winning its ratification by the Senate.

The other element of the president's grand design was less complex but politically more sensitive. Ever since Mao Zedong's accession to power in 1949, the United States had done its best to ignore Red China. The United States recognized the exile government on Taiwan as the only legitimate government in China and used its influence to keep the People's Republic (PRC) out of the United Nations. American and Chinese representatives even avoided each other at diplomatic functions in capitals where both countries had missions.

This official position was backed by political pressure within the United States. Conservatives put particular stress on American support for the Taiwan regime. In the late 1940s and 1950s, Republicans accused the Truman administration of "losing" China to communism. This charge had been an effective weapon for influencing America's China policy throughout the cold war period. Indeed, one faction in the political debate over foreign policy was known as the China Lobby; the name referred to members of Congress and political activists who advocated continued opposition to the PRC.

Early in his political career, Richard Nixon had been associated with the China Lobby. This affiliation was consistent with his overall anticommunist views. But as early as 1954, he began to express interest in examining American opportunities for engaging the communist Chinese government. As vice president, he had proposed in a National Security Council meeting that the United States explore the possibility of dividing the communist superpowers.[29] Ever interested in strategy and geopolitics, Nixon moved away from the conventional anticommunist view of the PRC.

This shift was evident in his 1967 article in *Foreign Affairs,* "Asia after Vietnam." Writing in a journal read by the foreign policy establishment, Nixon suggested the need for a change in the American approach to China:

> Any American policy toward Asia must come urgently to grips with the reality of China. . . . Taking the long view, we simply cannot afford to leave China forever outside the family of nations, there to nurture its fantasies, cherish its hates and threaten its neighbors. There is no place on this small planet for a billion of its potentially most able people to live in angry isolation.[30]

A year later, after receiving the 1968 Republican nomination for president, Nixon affirmed this position. He told an interviewer: "We must not forget China. We must always seek opportunities to talk with her, as with the USSR. . . . We must not only watch for changes. We must seek to make changes."[31] Although his comments did not receive much attention because the campaign was consumed with issues of Vietnam and domestic unrest, they indicated Nixon's interest in altering existing policy.

Once in office, President Nixon began exploring possibilities of a new relationship with the PRC. While a variety of diplomatic channels were being explored, subtle messages were being delivered at home of a shift in official United States policy toward China. The administration had to undertake a careful balancing act: it wanted to signal its changing attitude toward the PRC, but it had to be careful not to stimulate active resistance to its initiatives by what remained of the China Lobby.

Nixon's approach to the domestic politics of China policy was characteristic. On the one hand, administration spokesmen began talking about the need to reevaluate American policy toward the PRC. Efforts were made to quietly gauge possible public reactions to an opening to China. Subtle policy initiatives were also undertaken, from minor changes in rules regarding American trade with China to a shift in the assignment of United States ships in the Taiwan Strait. On the other hand, nearly all contacts and talks with China itself were kept secret, so as not to alert the forces of domestic opposition.

Two speeches were part of Nixon's dual strategy: The first, by Secretary of State William Rogers in Australia on August 8, 1969, declared the United States' interest in improving relations with China. But the second was the subject of even more scrutiny, for it was delivered in New York City by Under Secretary of State Elliot Richardson. Speaking before the American Political

Science Association on September 5, Richardson proclaimed: "In the case of Communist China, longrun improvement in our relations is in our own national interest."[32] Richardson's remarks appeared in the *New York Times*. Later, when contact between the United States and China became a public matter, his speech would be recalled as a precursor of what followed.

Another aspect of this public campaign was the appointment of a presidential commission for the observance of the twenty-fifth anniversary of the United Nations in 1970. This group of prominent citizens, chaired by Henry Cabot Lodge (former senator, United States representative to the UN, and Nixon's running mate in the 1960 election), was obstensibly charged with assessing the overall mission and operations of the United Nations and America's role in that body.[33] But the commission was also assigned the particular task of weighing potential reaction to the admission of the PRC to the United Nations. Indeed, as one member of the commission has indicated, the president was more interested in that assignment than in any other aspect of the group's work.[34]

The commission held public hearings around the nation, with the question of PRC admission to the UN as a major issue at each one. It found that there was continuing support for the government on Taiwan, but there was also public sympathy with the idea of ending China's position on the periphery of world affairs. The commission's report to the president concluded that "exposure of the Peking government to the open forum of the UN, to world public opinion, to the free press, and to the way of the free world, may result in more harmony among the nations of the world community."[35]

Through these efforts, the Nixon administration was laying the groundwork for a shift in American policy toward the PRC. The president was assessing public attitudes and hinting at the forthcoming change in Sino-American relations.[36]

Nixon prepared carefully for the change. At one point, he was even assisted by the Chinese, who were engaged in their own efforts to evaluate American interest in potential contact. In 1971, at the World Table Tennis Championship, members of the United States team were befriended by athletes from the PRC. By the end of the competition, the Chinese invited the Americans to visit Beijing for exhibition games. The visit, widely hailed as "Ping-pong diplomacy," was warmly welcomed by the American media and public. Domestic reaction was not lost on the White House.

The State Department had played a role in this affair, as it did in most aspects of the opening to China. The president involved the department in his public campaign and even in certain diplomatic developments with Beijing. But the actual negotiations to agree upon and arrange a meeting between the president and the Chinese leaders were run out of the White House. Nixon believed that only strict secrecy would allow him to act before adherents of the China Lobby, in and out of government, could oppose contact with the PRC. Not only were there some members of Congress opposed to any warming of relations, but even Vice President Spiro Agnew had publicly criticized the idea of improving American relations with China.[37]

In 1971, the time of hinting and probing ended. On July 15, President Nixon announced to the American people and to the world that he had dispatched his assistant for national security affairs to China. Henry Kissinger was sent to Beijing to arrange a visit by the president the following year and to begin the process of "normalization" of relations between the two nations. Despite the quiet preparation and hints, the news came as a shock to nearly everyone. This stern anticommunist president, who had accused Truman of "losing China," and who was engaged in a war against Chinese-assisted North Vietnam, was going to sit down with Mao Zedong.

The initial shock soon gave way to wide support for the president's move, although a number of conservatives roundly criticized Nixon for a willingness even to talk to Chinese communists. By this point, however, there was nothing that critics could do to stop the planned trip.

In February 1972, President Nixon traveled to China for a week-long visit. Attentive to the need to continue building domestic support for his initiative, Nixon brought along a bevy of journalists. Television cameras covered the event in detail, from banquets in Beijing's Forbidden City (the former Imperial Palace) to Richard Nixon's walk along the Great Wall of China. These images made clear for all to see that Nixon had revolutionized American foreign policy. A few diehards continued to condemn the president's action, but they were a minority. Even among conservatives, there was praise for the visit. Indeed, as two close observers of Nixon have noted: "In fact, Nixon's eight days in China . . . had dazzled a nation—Republicans and Democrats, conservatives and liberals, young and old. As communications satellite technology beamed the pictures from China every night, America watched in fascination."[38]

At the end of Nixon's journey, the two governments issued a joint statement. The Shanghai Communiqué, as it was called, noted differences between the two nations on the Vietnam War and on the delicate question of Taiwan. The two sides took positions that allowed the Nixon administration to justify talking to Beijing, while supporting its traditional ally on Taiwan. The United States stated that "all Chinese on both sides of the Taiwan Strait maintain there is but one China, and that Taiwan is a part of China."[39] Not surprisingly, despite the careful wording of the communiqué, some commentators in the United States criticized the president for capitulating to Beijing on Taiwan. But the language of the statement was vague enough for the president to respond that he had not ceded any part of the American alliance with Taiwan. All he had done was to stop acting as if one billion Chinese did not exist.

Just as the nation's reaction to Nixon's trip was overwhelmingly positive, renewed relations between the two nations were warmly received. Even conservative spokesmen such as Senator Barry Goldwater and California governor Ronald Reagan endorsed the president's achievement, and the bipartisan leadership of Congress did likewise.[40] In sum, Nixon had returned home in triumph.

WORLD LEADERSHIP: IMPLEMENTING THE POLICY ABROAD

In attempting to play the role of world leader, Richard Nixon had to deal with several international actors. He had to consider China and the Soviet Union separately, and in relation to one another. Nixon also had to contend with Europe and the United Nations, because they would play roles in implementing his plans. Moreover, he needed the cooperation and assistance of several individual states (such as Pakistan) to act as intermediaries in negotiations with China. Therefore, the story of Nixon's world leadership is one of delicate talks with the two communist superpowers; triangular diplomacy between Washington, Beijing, and Moscow; and efforts to persuade America's allies and the UN to accommodate his grand design.

The president approached Moscow with caution. While he was interested in an overall improvement in relations, he believed that progress in arms talks was a necessary prerequisite.[41] During the transition period after the 1968 election, Nixon and Kissinger constructed a "conceptual framework" for policy toward the Soviet Union. It was composed of three principles:

1. *concreteness*—that negotiations between the United States and the Soviet Union would deal with specific causes of tension
2. *restraint*—that relations between the superpowers would improve only if each side restrained itself, which meant that Soviet adventurism (in the Third World or elsewhere) would be penalized
3. *linkage*—progress in negotiations would be linked to advances in other areas of Soviet-American relations (for example, in the Middle East).[42]

Nixon believed that Moscow was interested in moving toward an arms agreement, so he was determined to use that ambition to press for an overall relaxing of cold war tensions. Later, this relaxation came to be known as "détente.") Therefore, his policy was to pursue SALT negotiations while at the same time exploring other issues for negotiation (and pressuring Moscow through continuation of the American arms buildup).

SALT was the key. By making progress here, Nixon could demonstrate his statesmanship and pursue his goal of a structure of peace. He was determined to take full presidential control of arms negotiations, such as when he inaugurated the Channel on February 17, 1969. In addition, he supplemented talks in the Channel with correspondence to Soviet premier Aleksey Kosygin and (after August 1971) General Secretary Leonid Brezhnev. These incentives, plus the threat of new weapons development, were intended to push Moscow to come to terms.[43]

Nixon's carrot-and-stick approach proceeded through the next two years with slow progress toward a SALT agreement, but in 1971 talks became deadlocked over the issue of which weapons an arms agreement would cover. The United States wanted an agreement to apply to both offensive and defensive weapons, while the Soviet Union wanted only a pact limiting antiballistic missiles (ABM). To break the impasse, Nixon and Kissinger intensified their secret negotiations and ultimately threatened to break off negotiations. In May, a compromise was reached and the president was able to announce a U.S.-Soviet agreement to restrict ABM systems and to discuss limits on offensive weapons systems (such as ICBMs, nuclear bombers, and submarines).[44]

Still, a final accord had not yet been reached. Pressure was building for a summit meeting between Nixon and Soviet general secretary Brezhnev in order to conclude an agreement and discuss a wide range of other issues in superpower relations. Determined to maintain White House control over diplomacy, the president resisted attempts by the State Department to assume responsibility for summit preparations. In April 1972, he dispatched Kissinger to Moscow for a secret meeting in the Kremlin to plan for a summit meeting to be held later that year.

Differences over SALT, which would be the centerpiece of the forthcoming summit, were by now considerably reduced. Kissinger's secret trip to Moscow produced a clarification of the ABM Treaty, a general compromise on the nature of the Interim Agreement on Offensive Weapons, and an agenda for the presidential visit in May.

The visit seemed to be jeopardized, however, by administrative action in Southeast Asia. In response to a North Vietnamese offensive against the South, in April 1972 the United States laid mines in the North's Haiphong harbor. Once this was made public, nearly all observers declared that it would surely abort the summit. Since the Soviet Union was one of North Vietnam's chief allies, it was presumed that the mining would not go on with impunity. But Nixon and Kissinger had information that Moscow wanted the summit to proceed even in the face of this attack on its ally. Since the Soviet government badly wanted a deal on SALT, it was willing to overlook the American action.[45]

The summit provided a good opportunity for Richard Nixon to play the role of world leader. Here he was in Moscow, personally bargaining with the Soviets over the most pressing issues of the day. The main item of business was, of course, the arms agreements. The final negotiations were conducted at the top: Nixon and Kissinger worked directly with Brezhnev and other high Soviet officials to hammer out the last details of a deal.

Nixon balanced his interest in a SALT agreement with his concern for domestic reaction in the United States. He did not want to be seen as conceding too much to the Soviet Union and thereby face a potential revolt by the military over the limits on superpower arsenals contained in the Interim Agreement. He also had to consider the effect of SALT on the triangular politics of American-Soviet-Chinese relations. The president had to reassure the PRC that détente and arms agreements did not constitute a Soviet-American condominium designed to dominate world politics. After their border war with the Soviet Union, the Chinese were especially fearful of a shift in the balance of power against them. During both Kissinger's secret trip in 1971 and the president's visit in 1972, the United States had to emphasize to the Chinese that while it would continue to deal with Moscow, it would inform Beijing of any agreements that might affect Chinese interests. Such assurances were necessary in order for one part of the grand design not to damage the other.

On May 23, 1972, the two SALT agreements were signed in a formal ceremony in Moscow. The summit provided the president with an opportunity to meet directly with Soviet leaders and to initiate a new phase in superpower relations. He proudly declared the SALT accords to be "the first step toward a new era of mutually agreed restraint and arms limitations between the two principal nuclear powers."[46]

Nixon's dream of reopening American relations with China involved more than merely testing domestic reaction and surprising the China Lobby. It meant dealing with extremely cautious PRC leadership, which wanted to talk to Washington but not have it appear that it was making concessions in order to reenter the community of nations.

In 1969, the new administration began exploring the possibility of improving relations between the United States and China. Internal studies were initiated, such as the one authorized by Kissinger in the Under Secretaries Committee of the NSC. Then, in March, reports of clashes between Soviet and Chinese border troops at the Ussuri River provided the president with an occasion to send signals of shifting American policy toward the PRC.

The Ussuri River clashes not only indicated the gravity of the split between the two communist superpowers, but they also threatened a Sino-Soviet war. Indeed, in August, a midlevel State Department official was asked by a Soviet diplomat about the potential American reaction to a Soviet attack on Chinese nuclear facilities. Kissinger brought this issue to Nixon, who at an NSC meeting on August 14 declared that the United States would not allow China to be "smashed."[47]

This policy was quietly signaled in Under Secretary of State Richardson's speech in September to the American Political Science Association. His address, which was important later for the domestic signal it sent, was immediately relevant as a warning against Soviet attack and a message to China about new American attitudes.

The Richardson speech was accompanied by yet another signal. Under White House direction, the State Department quietly announced the easing of restrictions on trade with and travel to the PRC. These subtle messages were not lost on Chinese leaders, who used a Pakistani official to inform Kissinger that they were looking for a more concrete indication of American intentions about better relations.

In response, the president authorized a change in the United States naval patrols of the Taiwan Strait. Two destroyers permanently stationed in the strait since the 1950s were reassigned, in a move that still left Taiwan heavily defended but extracted a symbolic thorn from the side of the PRC. At the same time, Nixon passed a message to Beijing through the president of Pakistan that the reassignment was indeed the action that China had requested.[48]

From that fitful beginning, a diplomatic minuet began. Over the course of the next year, American and Chinese officials made a number of contacts, usually at diplomatic functions. On December 3, 1969, Ambassador Walter Stoessel (the American representative in Poland) literally chased the Chinese chargé d'affaires through a reception in Warsaw until he cornered him at the bottom of a flight of stairs. He expressed an American willingness to talk, but the PRC representative had no instructions and said nothing. A week later, Stoessel was invited to the Chinese Embassy, the first American official to be received by the PRC since 1949.[49]

Other contacts were made over the months, usually of the same informal type. The White House was probing Chinese interest in talking, while trying at the same time to keep its efforts as quiet as possible. American and Chinese authorities also communicated directly through personal notes in order to maintain absolute secrecy.[50] Other roundabout signals were sent, such as a change in United States policy regarding the use of passports for travel to the PRC.

Early in 1970, official diplomatic meetings were held in Warsaw between American and Chinese representatives. Coincidentally, both sides suggested that the talks be elevated in importance and moved either to Washington or Beijing.[51] The president made clear to Kissinger that he wanted a special presidential envoy to travel to China, in the hope of accelerating the tempo of the minuet.[52] But there was little real movement that year, only more signaling. In October, Nixon once again used President Yahya Khan of Pakistan to make overtures to Beijing.

Finally, in 1971, there was substantial progress. Early in that year, Washington sent a message through Romania indicating that the administration wanted to send an envoy and expressing the president's desire to visit China. There was no direct reply, but Ping-Pong diplomacy broke out that April. Here was Beijing's answer. Nixon responded by further easing trade restrictions.

On April 27, the White House tried to create further movement by sending a message through the French government suggesting direct talks in Paris. While his proposal was en route to Beijing, a note arrived in Washington via Pakistan. It carried an invitation for a United States envoy to visit China. In order to maintain presidential control over events, Nixon rejected the idea of sending the secretary of state and instead decided to dispatch Kissinger.[53] Soon, the American public and the world were astonished to learn that the president's national security advisor was on his way to Beijing in order to arrange a presidential visit the next year.

Nixon's visit to China did not produce any particular substantive achievements. What it did do, however, was to bring an end to the American policy of officially ignoring the PRC. It was no small achievement. As one observer of American foreign policy has put it, Nixon's opening to China "has fundamentally affected the conduct of international relations since that time."[54]

Nixon's China policy complicated relations with the Soviet Union. On December 22, Kissinger informed Dobrynin that the United States sought to improve its relations with China, that doing so was not aimed against the Soviet Union, and that America would take no sides in the Sino-Soviet dispute.[55] Three years later, at the Moscow summit, an exchange between Brezhnev and Nixon reaffirmed the "Soviets' raw nerve about China."[56] The president simply held to the line that U.S. relations with China were a fact and did not in any way threaten Moscow.

Thus, Nixon was able to successfully negotiate the tortuous passages of the triangular relationship. He had moved United States foreign policy into a new era and thereby ushered in a fundamental shift in international relations.

But the president's grand design affected actors beyond the three superpowers. To exercise world leadership, he also had to deal with America's allies and with the United Nations.

The European allies' attitudes toward SALT, and the general improvement in U.S.-Soviet relations, reflected the ambivalence of once-great European states now caught between two superpowers. As Kissinger notes in his memoirs: "For over three years, at every meeting with every European leader, they had pressed us toward negotiation with the Soviets. . . . Tactfully—but also publicly—they had let it be known that we were too slow in improving our relations with Moscow and that we were running needless risks of war."[57] Thus, during the three years of negotiations on SALT, Nixon kept the leaders of Britain, France, and West Germany quietly informed on the general progress of talks with the Soviet Union. But the larger European reaction to the new relationship between Moscow and Washington surprised the White House. All along, the allies had supported the president's policy of détente, that is, an easing of tensions between the United States and the Soviet Union. But now the concern in Europe was that détente might lead America to reevaluate its commitment to the defense of Europe.[58] Whereas the president expected wide praise from the continent, what was conveyed were mixed reviews and a sense of European anxiety about the future.

This uneasiness was compounded by the president's initiative toward China. Again, the European reaction was ambivalent. On the one hand, the allies had encouraged the United States to reevaluate its hostility toward the PRC, and thus they generally supported Nixon's policy shift. But when Nixon had achieved his dual triumph in Moscow and Beijing, many Europeans felt left out. The president faced a set of old allies who supported his policies but believed they were being ignored in favor of new friends.

Nixon's response was to promise new and greater attention to Europe. Kissinger held reassuring meetings with senior officials from Germany, Britain, and France. And, in 1973, the administration announced a Year of Europe, designed to highlight the United States' interest in, and support for, its traditional allies.

Other American allies had a somewhat different reaction to the president's grand design. Japan did not oppose better relations between Washington and Beijing, but its leaders had prided themselves on being ahead of the United States on approaching China. Indeed, Japan moved much more quickly than the Nixon administration to ease trade and travel restrictions to the PRC. But officials in Tokyo were embarrassed by the sudden announcement on July 15, 1971, that the president would visit Beijing. In fact, the news was received in Tokyo as a "Nixon shock."[59] In time, Tokyo accepted and supported the president's initiative. But the American failure to inform the Japanese government before its public announcement was, at best, "a serious error in manners" (Kissinger's characterization) or, at worst, a case of "mistreating our allies" (the charge of some critics).

The Republic of China (ROC) on Taiwan obviously opposed the president's initiative toward Beijing, but it could do nothing to stop it. Nor was there much that Nixon could do to make his China initiative more acceptable to the Taiwanese government. But what he did do, as the protector of the ROC, was to make clear the continuing American commitment to Taiwan, even as he altered the state of world politics. He refused to renounce the mutual defense treaty between Washington and the ROC. And he refused to formally recognize the PRC. The United States was now talking to Beijing, but formally it was still tied to Taiwan.

The Nixon administration also attempted to win support for its position in the United Nations. The Beijing-Taiwan split was an issue in that body, for it raised the question of who was the "real" representative of China. The prerevolutionary Republic of China had been a founder of the United Nations, and after the communist victory in 1949, the Taiwan government kept the Chinese membership in the body and a permanent seat on the Security Council. The PRC was excluded. But the admission of many new African and Asian countries to the UN shifted support toward PRC admission and expulsion of the ROC. In 1970, the State Department told the president that admission of the PRC to the UN was all but inevitable. A number of states (such as Canada) moved to improve their relations with Beijing, so it was only a matter of time before the communist regime would be allowed to join the assembly of nations. The Nixon administration was now in a delicate position: it wanted to make progress in its relations with Beijing, but it also wanted to protect its ally in the world diplomatic community.

First, the United States tried to block admission of the PRC (and expulsion of the ROC); later, it proposed a scheme of dual representation of both Chinas. But American efforts were unsuccessful. In October 1971, the General Assembly voted to expel the Taiwan government and assign its seat (including permanent membership on the Security Council) to the PRC.[60]

Thus, while Nixon was generally successful at implementing his grand design, there was a price to be paid. Taiwan was expelled from the most important international forum, and our allies were unnerved by the creation of a new triangular superpower relationship. Still, there can be no doubt that the benefits of Nixon's grand design outweighed the costs.

NIXON AS WORLD LEADER

In his memoirs, Kissinger wrote: "In retrospect all successful policies seem preordained."[61] He was being ironic, of course, since there is no reason for statesmen to assume that their goals can be achieved if only they exercise patience and skill.

When Richard Nixon attempted to implement the grand design he had charted with Kissinger, the context of domestic politics suggested that he had a chance for success; but he knew from his own experience the force of opposition to important elements of his plans. President Truman had been severely weakened by the charge that he had lost China and Lyndon Johnson feared the prospect of being labeled "soft" on communism. As an ardent anticommunist, Nixon understood that international tensions were not easily erased.

The state of international relations also complicated and threatened the president's efforts to improve American relations with the Soviet Union and China. While progress had been made on arms talks during the Kennedy and Johnson administrations, the condition of Soviet-American relations at the end of the 1960s was still that of a cold war. Only a few years before, the two superpowers had nearly come to nuclear war over the Cuban missile crisis. While China sent signals that it no longer wanted to be an outcast in world affairs, its leaders were reluctant to move quickly or to make concessions in order to gain acceptance. Moreover, both communist states also supported America's nemesis, North Vietnam, in the war in Southeast Asia.

China and the Soviet Union represented everything that Nixon had stood against during his career: both possessed considerable military power that was potentially threatening to the security of the United States, both were driven by an ideology Nixon had built his career on opposing, and both were governed by cliques and factions that battled each other in the thickets of bureaucratic politics.

Still, in a curious way each regime also suited the president in important ways: they were systems accustomed to operating behind a heavy veil of secrecy in the conduct of affairs; they were military superpowers that had interests extending beyond their own borders; and they were headed by leaders (Brezhnev in the Soviet Union, Mao Zedong in China) who fancied themselves global statesmen—as did Nixon.

Richard Nixon knew what he wanted to achieve and had long prided himself on being a strategic thinker. At the height of the cold war in the 1950s, while many American leaders were immobilized by the question "Who lost China?" Nixon was looking for ways to split the closely allied communist superpowers. In 1967, while the Vietnam War unraveled Lyndon Johnson's politics of consensus, Nixon proposed to look beyond the war to the future of Asia. Therefore, when he won the presidency, he was determined to be the architect of a new American foreign policy in a new world order.

To assist him in his plans, he enlisted Henry Kissinger. The team of Nixon and Kissinger was a close one: the two men complemented each other effectively, and each preferred to work in the secrecy and high politics of international diplomacy. Their grand design was not, however, for public consumption. Rather, Nixon and Kissinger were sure that it might succeed only if they could keep it hidden, to be slowly revealed through subtle actions, negotiations, and finally dramatic announcements. Indeed, the president believed strongly in the value of "bold strokes" in international affairs—such as the revelation of his trip to China—that could capture the public's imagination and focus international attention on his leadership.

It is not surprising then that the unfolding of Nixon's plans proceeded quietly during the first three years of his presidency, to be fulfilled in the triumphal fourth year. He wanted to prepare the public for a change in American foreign policy but not be too specific about when that change might occur. That is why he and administration representatives, such as Elliot Richardson, spoke in general and tentative terms about the president's goals. In his Inaugural Address and afterward, President Nixon spoke often of peace and his willingness to seek better relations with all nations. But specific changes in policy, especially those toward China, were executed quietly. Ping-Pong diplomacy was conducted almost as if the government had nothing to do with it.

In addition, the president worked to head off potential criticism. To win the support of the armed forces and conservatives in Congress, he pushed for weapons systems and defense modernization. He affirmed the American commitment to Taiwan while dealing with the PRC. And he drew on his own reputation and record as an anticommunist. Where Lyndon Johnson feared being "soft" on communism, Richard Nixon could afford to take risks in the name of peace and the national interest.

Thus, the president set the stage for his dramatic gestures—the trip to Beijing and the Moscow summit. The public was not so much educated as minimally prepared for what lay ahead. What Nixon learned was that he could expect domestic resistance to his policies but not enough opposition to defeat him.

When his plans were fulfilled, the president worked hard to gain their acceptance by Congress and the public. In the case of SALT I, Nixon drew on a general public desire for peace and an existing bloc of pro–arms-control senators for help. Then, he compromised with his critics in order to widen the coalition voting for his pacts. Those efforts, plus the arms buildup he pushed for at the same time as SALT I, allowed him to carry the day. In reopening American relations with China, Nixon built domestic support in two ways: First, he carefully weighed potential public reaction to such an opening, as it was made manifest at hearings of his commission on the UN, in the positive reaction to Ping-Pong diplomacy and responses to other administration signals. Then, he made his trip to the PRC a major television spectacular, winning accolades from all but a few observers.

In the realm of international politics, the president's plans were generally concealed until late in the game. Besides the superpower leaders with whom he dealt, Nixon informed the top leaders of few states. American allies knew about some progress in United States relations with China and the Soviet Union but never much about specific developments. Individual states such as Pakistan and Romania assisted in communicating with China, but their involvement was confined to the highest levels of each nation's government and they knew little about what transpired between the parties for whom they served as intermediaries. When he was able to announce his impending trip to China and the Moscow summit, the president therefore took both his domestic and international audiences by surprise. Nixon could move decisively and withstand any opposition.

President Nixon understood the potential power of his office, and he was willing to use it to achieve his foreign policy goals. He made the most of his ability to negotiate with foreign governments, an authority that is essentially unlimited by the Constitution. He needed no one's permission to communicate with the PRC, despite two decades of American policy to the contrary. Nor did he have to consult with the Senate on the emerging SALT I agreements, only to submit the ABM Treaty for approval once it was signed. Therefore, as 1972 took him first to Beijing and then to Moscow and then back to Washington, his critics were presented with a *fait accompli*, a "done deal." Because the American political system grants all power of foreign policy initiative to the president, his critics could only react to what he had done.

In framing and implementing his plans, he took advantage of his ability to bypass the bureaucracy and deputized Kissinger as his agent. Here again, he was determined to maintain control over policy and communicate directly with his adversaries, not to be bound by standard diplomatic procedures, even when it meant embarrassing his chief arms-control negotiator or his secretary of state. Thus, for all the State Department complaints about being left out of important developments in foreign policy, Nixon demonstrated the discretion that presidents have in their conduct of foreign affairs.

The president also chose to take advantage of the United States' position as a superpower and leader of the Free World. He did not need to seek the approval of American allies in shaping policy. While no president would want to risk wrecking American alliances in order to succeed, the chief executive can have the nation act unilaterally. No matter the concerns expressed in Europe, Nixon could sign the SALT I agreements with the Soviet Union. No matter the "shock" experienced by Japanese leaders upon learning of Nixon's trip to Beijing, he did not need their permission. No matter the objections of Taiwan to even talking to the PRC, the ROC could do nothing to punish the United States for its change of policy.

Not only did Nixon seize the power to shape American foreign policy, but his tactics also contributed to his success. His leadership style consisted of three elements: a grand design, hard work, and secrecy. Having an overarching plan gave the president a compass to guide him through the difficult negotiations with both China and the Soviet Union. Moreover, it enabled him to continue work on superpower contacts even while the Vietnam War dragged on much longer than he had anticipated.

The president's hard work assisted his efforts. While he relied heavily on Kissinger, Nixon was unwilling to leave everything in the hands of his security adviser. The president pushed for progress in all aspects of his grand design, and he was willing to take the necessary risks to see it through. He was sure that, in the end, he would be rewarded (at the polls and in the judgment of history) for what he accomplished. He was prepared to take on the Joint Chiefs on SALT I and won their support by compromise in weapons development. He was prepared to negotiate with Henry Jackson and win his support. He consistently pressed for progress with China, even when the PRC at times appeared to lose its interest in the United States. When he made his state visits to Beijing and Moscow, the president carefully studied the briefing books the NSC staff had given him so he could negotiate with his Soviet and Chinese counterparts with little or no assistance.

Secrecy was also important to Nixon's achievement. By guarding information, he could advance his plans and deliver results before potential opposition could galvanize. Using the Channel broke through bureaucratic resistance to an arms deal both in the United States and in the Soviet Union. Secret negotiations with China circumvented opposition and avoided the State Department's lingering fear of the power of the China Lobby. In the 1950s, a number of Foreign Service careers were ruined over the issue of "Who lost China?" It is fair to say that a more open approach to implementing Nixon's grand design would not have worked or would have taken much longer to achieve.

But that does not mean there were no costs associated with the way in which Richard Nixon conducted foreign policy. Nixon's circumvention of the State Department created problems just as it solved them. As Kissinger notes, Nixon was

> a President who neither trusted his Cabinet nor was willing to give them direct orders. Nixon feared leaks and shrank from imposing discipline. But he was determined to achieve his purposes; he thus encouraged procedures unlikely to be recommended in textbooks on public administration that, crablike, worked privily around existing structures. It was demoralizing for the bureaucracy, which, cut out of the process, reacted by accentuating the independence and self-will that had caused Nixon to bypass it in the first place.[62]

Nixon's methods also created problems with Congress, particularly in the areas of defense and arms control. His overall handling of Senate consultation during the negotiation of SALT I—perfunctory briefings of Congress—created a climate of skepticism about the president's pacts. The Jackson Amendment was born of that climate as much as of security considerations by the senators who supported it. Moreover, this climate contributed to congressional hostility toward the president in his second term, when the War Powers Resolution and other measures were passed to limit unilateral presidential control over foreign affairs.

President Nixon's successors would pay for his treatment of the Senate. When Jimmy Carter negotiated SALT II and then sent it to the Senate for ratification, he too encountered resistance from Henry Jackson and others who were wary of presidential domination on issues of arms control. When Carter brought the opening to China to its logical conclusion by recognizing the PRC (while canceling the defense treaty with Taiwan), Congress reacted sharply. Left out of decisions regarding China in the early 1970s, in 1979 it passed the Taiwan Relations Act, writing into domestic law security guarantees to the ROC that had previously existed by treaty. Carter was virtually forced to sign the bill.

Finally, Nixon's methods damaged relations with America's allies. Taiwan was left hanging as a result of the new structure of peace (which was probably inevitable), while Japan and Western Europe felt slighted (although they agreed with the president's policies). On the continent, there was a growing sense of the need for Europeans to go their own way in dealing with Moscow. America's alliances were not severed by Nixon's exercise of world leadership, but they were in fact bruised by it.

What, then, is Nixon's record as a world leader? The answer is complex. One the one hand, he led the U.S. to come to terms with the two other superpowers, an achievement that fundamentally changed the nature of international relations. But he left American allies uneasy and concerned about their future. He took risks to implement his grand design, but he would have failed in his efforts if the Soviet Union and China had not also eagerly wanted what he desired. Moreover, timing was crucial. A decade before, attempts to make peace with Red China would have been political suicide even for Richard Nixon. In the end, it was Nixon's ability to grasp and adapt to changing conditions that enabled him to effect change at the international level.

Notes

1. On Nixon's life and early political career, see Stephen E. Ambrose, *Nixon: The Education of a Politician 1913–1962* (New York: Simon and Schuster, 1987), or Nixon's own memoirs, *RN: The Autobiography of Richard Nixon* (New York: Grosset & Dunlap, 1978). An insightful look into Nixon's personality and world view is to be found in Garry Wills, *Nixon Agonistes* (New York: Mentor, 1970). A useful sketch of Nixon's life and political career can be found in Richard M. Pious, "Richard M. Nixon," in *The Presidents: A Reference History*, ed. Henry F. Graff (New York: Scribner, 1984), pp. 615–38.

2. Nixon regarded his 1958 Latin American trip as one of the most important events of his career. See Richard Nixon, *Six Crises* (Garden City, N.Y.: Doubleday, 1962), pp. 183–234.

3. Richard Nixon, "Asia after Vietnam," *Foreign Affairs* 46 (October 1967): pp. 111–25.

4. William Safire, *Before the Fall: An Inside Look at the Pre-Watergate White House* (New York: Da Capo, 1975), p. 602, describes Richard Nixon as a "loner: a keeper of his own counsel, a sharer of his thought with a tightening circle of friends." (Safire's book is the best memoir of the Nixon presidency and includes considerable material on both the "light" and "dark" sides of RN's personality.) All portraits of Nixon by his former associates are remarkably consistent. They contrast his brighter and darker sides, his pettiness and cruelty, as well as his magnanimity and sentimentality.

5. Raymond Price, *With Nixon* (New York: Viking, 1977), p. 29.

6. Rowland Evans and Robert D. Novak, *Nixon in the White House* (New York: Vintage, 1972).

7. Quoted in ibid.

8. From comments on H. R. Haldeman in Samuel Kernell and Samuel L. Popkin, *Chief of Staff: Twenty-five Years of Managing the Presidency* (Berkeley, Calif.: Univ. of California Press, 1986), p. 94.

9. Bernard Kalb and Marvin Kalb, *Kissinger* (Boston: Little, Brown, 1974), pp. 6, 22–26. The best discussion of Kissinger's pregovernment thinking and career is in Stephen Graubard, *Kissinger: Portrait of a Mind* (New York: Norton, 1973). An analysis of Kissinger's world view can be found in Peter W. Dickson, *Kissinger and the Meaning of History* (New York: Cambridge Univ. Press, 1978).

10. Henry A. Kissinger, *White House Years* (Boston: Little, Brown, 1979), p. 118.

11. Kalb and Kalb, pp. 78–79. For further discussion and analysis of the NSC System, see John P. Leacacos, "Kissinger's Apparat," *Foreign Policy* 5 (Winter 1971–72): pp. 3–27; Safire, chapter 5; Joseph G. Bock, *The White House Staff and the National Security Assistant* (New York: Greenwood Press, 1987), pp. 83–101; and Seymour Hersh, *The Price of Power* (New York: Summit Books, 1983), pp. 25–36.

12. Kalb and Kalb, p. 84.

13. "The State of the World: First Annual Report by President Nixon Transmitted to Congress February 18, 1970," in *Documents on American Foreign Relations 1970*, ed. Elaine P. Adams and William P. Lineberry (New York: New York University Press, 1973), pp. 6–15.

14. From comments by H. R. Haldeman in Kernell and Popkin, p. 94.

15. Hersh, p. 610. See also Amos Yoder, *The Conduct of American Foreign Policy Since World War II* (New York: Pergamon Press, 1986), p. 112.

16. William P. Lineberry, *The United States in World Affairs 1970* (New York: New York University Press, 1972), p. 25.

17. Quoted in *Nixon: The First Year of His Presidency* (Washington: Congressional Quarterly, Inc., 1970), p. 18.

18. John Newhouse, *Cold Dawn: The Story of SALT* (New York: Holt, Rinehart and Winston, 1973), p. 43.

19. Yoder, p. 122. For Smith's side of the story, see Gerard Smith, *Doubletalk* (Garden City, N.Y.: Doubleday, 1980), pp. 222–46.

20. For a detailed analysis of this strategy, with specific attention to MIRV, see Hersh, chapters 12 and 13, especially p. 155. See also Newhouse, pp. 159–62, and Kissinger, p. 126.

21. Yoder, p. 122.

22. Ibid., p. 122.

23. Kissinger, p. 1240.

24. For a thorough discussion of those efforts, see Alan Platt, *The U.S. Senate and Strategic Arms Policy: 1969–1977* (Boulder, Colo.: Westview Press, 1978).

25. See Ryan J. Barilleaux, *The President and Foreign Affairs: Evaluation, Performance, and Power* (New York: Praeger, 1985), pp. 89–92.

26. Ibid., p. 91.

27. The Jackson Amendment is reprinted in Roger Labrie, ed., *SALT Hand Book* (Washington: American Enterprise Institute, 1979), pp. 141–143.

28. *Nixon: The Fourth Year of His Presidency* (Washington: Congressional Quarterly, Inc., 1973), p. 13.

29. Yoder, p. 126.

30. Nixon, "Asia after Vietnam," p. 121.

31. Quoted in *U.S. News and World Report*, 16 September 1968, p. 48.

32. Quoted in Kissinger, p. 184.

33. Executive Order 11546, reprinted in President's Commission for the Observance of the Twenty-fifth Anniversary of the United Nations, *Report* (Washington: 1971), pp. 59–60.

34. Author interview with William D. Jackson, a member of the commission (Oxford, Ohio: February 15, 1989).

35. President's Commission, pp. 35–36.

36. Interview with William D. Jackson, who was chief author of the section of the report dealing with China.

37. Kissinger, p. 713.

38. Evans and Novak, p. 422.

39. "The Shanghai Communique: Joint Statement Issued at the Conclusion of President Nixon's Visit, Shanghai, February 27, 1972," in *American Foreign Relations 1972: A Documentary Record,* ed. Richard P. Stebbins and Elaine P. Adams (New York: New York Univ. Press, 1976), pp. 307–11.

40. Kissinger, p. 1093.

41. See Barilleaux, pp. 73–74.

42. Kissinger, pp. 128–29.

43. Ibid., p. 208.

44. Newhouse, pp. 203–19.

45. Comments by Alexander Haig and H. R. Haldeman, in Kernell and Popkin, pp. 49–51.

46. "President Nixon's Message to Congress, June 13, 1972," reprinted in *Nixon: The Fourth Year,* p. 97-A.

47. Kissinger, p. 183.

48. Ibid., p. 187. See also Hersh, p. 356.

49. Kalb and Kalb, pp. 228–29.

50. Yoder, p. 125.

51. Kalb and Kalb, p. 229. See also Kissinger, pp. 684–687.

52. Hersh, p. 694.

53. Kissinger, p. 717. See also Kalb and Kalb, pp. 238.

54. Yoder, p. 126.

55. Kissinger, pp. 192–93.

56. Ibid., p. 1226.

57. Ibid., p. 1273.

58. Views of this sort are summarized in John Newhouse, "Stuck Fast," *Foreign Affairs* 51 (January 1973): pp. 358–60.

59. Kissinger, p. 761.

60. Hersh, pp. 378–79.

61. Kissinger, p. 167.

62. Quoted in Barilleaux, p. 86.

8

Jimmy Carter's Mission in the Middle East

You can depend on the United States to be in the forefront of the search for world peace. . . . And you can also depend on the United States to . . . do its utmost to resolve international differences in the spirit of cooperation.
—The President's Remarks to People of Other Nations on Assuming Office, January 20, 1977

BACKGROUND

On paper Jimmy Carter had what it takes to be a great president. He was smart. He was dedicated to the public welfare. He worked very hard and was a man of high moral principle. Yet as the drama in which he starred unfolded, it became apparent rather quickly that the former governor of Georgia was not a natural as national leader.

President Carter's domestic program was too complicated and ambitious to be easily understood or shepherded through the political process. He personally resisted doing much of the wheeling, dealing, and horse-trading that the political elite, particularly members of Congress, expect from a president anxious to realize his political agenda. And his ability to communicate with, and thus enlist the support of, the American people was meager at best.

Nor did President Carter compensate for his deficiencies by selecting a team familiar with Washington and the political tactics that enhance executive relationships. His cadre of loyalists was dominated by the "Georgia Mafia," men who had served him as governor and engineered his presidential campaign but who had little experience at the national—not to speak of international—level.

To be sure, during his time in the White House, President Carter learned some lessons. Indeed, he demonstrated considerably more political skill during the second half of his presidency than he did during the first. But it remained clear all the while that this man was not at ease playing the political game. He was never popular with those in Washington on whom he inevitably would have to depend if he was to accomplish his political goals. As a congressman observed at the time: "He just doesn't have the traditional politician's need for the warm kind of personal bond you feel with people you work with a lot."[1] Moreover, because he eschewed personal politicking and did not communicate particularly well with the general public, Carter lost so much ground in his first year in office that it was difficult for him to recover.

By October 1977, only a scant 24 percent of the American people approved strongly of the president's performance.

Of Carter it may fairly be said that while he knew facts and figures, he did not have a visceral understanding of the domestic political process. In particular, he apparently believed that a combination of intelligence and good intentions was the requisite of effective leadership. What he failed to recognize for too much of his one-term presidency is that, by definition, leadership is an interactive process in which the leader and his would-be followers must engage in one or another kind of social exchange. This applies to presidental direction of the political elite, and it pertains as well to leadership of the body politic. What Carter never seemed fully to grasp, in other words, was that so far as domestic politics is concerned, making a good decision is not enough. Communication, education, mobilization, and persuasion—these, too, are necessary to the leadership process.

In the main, the attributes that President Carter had stood him in better stead in the foreign policy realm. He was a quick study who was able, despite his previous lack of exposure to international relations, to master their complexities. He had an intuitive sympathy for those from cultures other than his own. He was persuaded that hard work and perseverance on his part would yield results. He was in fact convincing and effective in the kinds of small decision-making groups that sometimes wield considerable power at the international level. And, in contrast to his domestic advisers, his foreign policy team was knowledgeable and experienced.

Carter brought to the presidency "a world view that might be called Wilsonian in the high value it placed on cooperation among nations to secure human rights, and to achieve peace."[2] In his Inaugural Address he made a firm commitment to the defense of human rights everywhere and proclaimed his ultimate goal to be the complete elimination of nuclear weapons. His campaign for human rights seemed to be marked by a particular sense of urgency. Said Carter early in his term: "I feel very deeply that when people are put in prison without trial, and tortured and deprived of basic human rights, that the President of the United States ought to have a right to express displeasure and do something about it."[3]

Tellingly, Carter was chastised for even this initiative, one that on the surface would appear to be uncontroversial. He was accused of having a human rights policy that smacked of "an excess of idealism." It is true, in any case, that in the short term the costs seemed to exceed the benefits—at least so far as the president was concerned. Carter's human rights policy, however bold and noble in its conception, initially damaged America's relationship with some of her oldest allies, caused resentment in the Soviet Union, and contributed to the downfall of America's staunchest ally in the Middle East, the shah of Iran.[4] (Years after the fact, Carter has been more widely applauded for his human rights policy. The point we are making here is that at the time he suffered slings and arrows for his good intentions.)

Moreover, little progress was made during the Carter years toward slowing the arms race. His administration continued to increase the American nuclear arsenal at about the same rate as had the Nixon and Ford administrations. In addition, although détente was now out of favor, Carter had developed no clear policy toward the Soviet Union. In fact, some of the more significant divisions within the administration had their origins in the different views of how the United States should conduct itself vis-à-vis the other superpower.

The chief protagonists in this continuing struggle were Secretary of State Cyrus Vance, who favored a moderate and conciliatory approach to the Soviets, and National Security Advisor Zbigniew Brzezinski, who from the start made powerful arguments for not trusting our cold war adversaries. Clearly this debate, which was representative of a split within the American foreign policy elite after Vietnam, was critical, for how American foreign policy experts viewed the Soviets shaped American foreign policy itself. The tensions between the two men were exacerbated by their different personal styles (Vance was measured and courtly, and Brzezinski fast and curt); by their different domains (Vance's was diplomacy and Brzezinski's national security); by their different vantage points (Vance's was that of the Department of State and Brzezinski's that of the White House); by the press, which, to quote Brzezinski, seized on disagreements between the two men "with a passion and a vengeance";[5] and by what were in fact genuine differences of opinion between them. Carter himself wavered between the two, generally following Vance's moderate lead early on but adopting Brzezinski's more jaundiced view later in his term—especially as events seemed to confirm Brzezinski's suspicions. Finally, in April 1980, in protest over Carter's abortive attempt to rescue American hostages in Iran, the secretary of state resigned and the national security advisor was left to dominate the foreign policy process.

Notwithstanding some of the problems that beset the Carter administration in foreign policy, there were some considerable successes. Among the more outstanding was the ratification of the Panama Canal Treaty, widely regarded as one of Jimmy Carter's most significant achievements as president. To achieve ratification even in the face of strong opposition in the Senate, Carter took a clear and courageous stand on behalf of a cause he felt to be of major consequence.

But in an administration that lacked a grand vision, that tended to compartmentalize international relations into specific issue areas, it was the Middle East that would finally be the stage on which Carter would enact his greatest triumph.[6] At least since the end of the Second World War, the eastern end of the Mediterranean, where Western civilization began, had been a theater of intense activity. Arabs and Jews, in particular, compelled by the circumstance of history to lay claim to the same land, were engaged in a relentess struggle for territory. Moreover, both the United States and the Soviet Union bore responsibility for imposing cold war attitudes on the adversaries, thereby further exacerbating regional tensions and accounting for bewildering shifts in alliances. As a consequence of superpower intervention, instability in the area increased even more, with both sides alternately enjoying successes and then suffering debilitating setbacks.

For the United States and Soviet Union the stakes have been enormous. The Arab world is important because the Arabs sit astride the Suez Canal and beside the Strait of Gibraltar, because they consider themselves the guardians of Islam and its great shrines, and because they number about 185 million.

Moreover, together the Iranians and Arabs control much of the world's oil reserves, which happen to lie in the Middle East.[7]

In contrast, Israel has none of these advantages. As Stephen Ambrose has noted, Israel has neither oil nor population nor major strategic importance. It is without easily defended borders and is surrounded by numerous enemies. Israel does, however, have an army with the highest morale of any in the world; a highly educated, intense, and hardworking people; a moral claim on the world's conscience; and the active support of the politically powerful American Jewish community.[8]

Since 1948, when Israel achieved statehood, it has been the presence of the Jewish state on territory that once was Palestine that has been the main source of the intense regional discord. Indeed, the conflict between the Arabs and Israelis is considered by many to be the most intractable problem besetting the diplomatic community. There have been four major wars in forty years, and in the intervening periods, continuing strife. Never, in all these years, has the outlook for peace in the region been anything other than grim.

For American policymakers, then, the Middle East has always been a "headache, sometimes a nightmare, as each president has tried, in his own way, to pursue an evenhanded policy, if only because he needed both Arab oil and Jewish campaign contributions."[9] But Richard Nixon, in concert with Henry Kissinger, who was his national security advisor and then later his secretary of state, was the first executive whose administration made peace in the Middle East a priority. Nixon and Kissinger were goaded into action for three reasons:

1. From a global perspective, by the 1970s the Middle East resembled nothing so much as the fractured and fractious Balkans at the turn of the century.[10] The U.S. thus feared that, as in the case of the Balkans, a local battle might eventually trigger a major war.
2. The 1973 Yom Kippur War, in which the Israelis—the only reliable American allies in the region—were surprised by Egyptian and Syrian armies, demonstrated that the Israelis were not invulnerable nor the Arabs predestined always to lose.
3. The 1973 Arab oil embargo further persuaded the Americans of the need to act because it showed the West (particularly the oil-poor Europeans) that the Arabs were quite capable of acting in concert when it came to employing their greatest resource as a political weapon.

As a consequence, even though the odds were overwhelmingly against a breakthrough in negotiations, Kissinger spent years engaged in what he called "step-by-step diplomacy," and what others quickly labeled "shuttle diplomacy" (because in his quest for results he so often shuttled from one Middle Eastern capitol to another). The plan was to start talks on the easier issues and proceed gradually to the hardest ones. The idea underlying the strategy was that by successfully resolving the less fractious problems, a momentum would be established whereby the more difficult ones would be simpler to address. It was further hoped that success would separate the moderate from the more militant regimes, strengthening the former and weakening the latter.

But the conflicts among the nations in the area were too bitter and entrenched, and the issues too many, for magic to happen. Kissinger's performance was brilliant and his dedication remarkable, but ultimately his yield was far less than he must have anticipated. For all his personal efforts during the Nixon and, later, Ford years, he had little of major consequence to report. To be sure, he did make a difference. He helped ease tensions after the 1973 war; he arranged for the disengagement of hostile forces on the Egyptian Sinai and Syrian Golan fronts; and in 1974, he persuaded the Arabs to lift the oil embargo. Moreover, it was during his tenure that Soviet influence in the area waned while America's waxed. But when Carter took office in January 1977, the Arabs and Israelis were still at each other's throats. As Ambrose concluded: ". . . At the end of Kissinger's term of office, permanent solutions still seemed completely out of reach. The Middle East overall remained, as it had been so often described by American presidents, a tinderbox, ready to set the world afire from a single spark."[11]

President Jimmy Carter's interest in the Middle East was unusually strong. Maybe it was because that region of the world, the Holy Land, is cradle to three of the world's great religions and Carter is a religious man. In his autobiography, *Why Not the Best?* Carter writes about how in the late 1960s he experienced a deep spiritual awakening that he was to describe later as being "born again."[12] Moreover, the president's wife, Rosalynn, his partner and confidante, is also pious. She testified in her memoirs that as a child she was taught to love God and "to live the kind of life He would have us live, to love one another . . . and to be good."[13]

Or maybe Carter's interest in the Middle East grew out of knowing the area firsthand. As governor of Georgia he journeyed to Israel in 1973 as a guest of Prime Minister Golda Meir. In his presidential memoirs Carter writes about this trip in some detail, warmly recalling the impressive sights, the illuminating conversations with political leaders, and "the chance to learn more about the land of the Bible." He added: "This visit to Israel made a great impression on me. Later, in preparation for my presidential campaign, I continued my studies of the complicated history of the area."[14]

Or maybe, finally, Carter's special affinity for this region of the world stemmed from his tendency to be a problem solver—and, as already noted, no problems in international relations have been more intractable than those that beset the Middle East. While confirming in his own memoirs that peace in the area was an "urgent priority" of the new administration, Zbigniew Brzezinski expanded on why the Carter administration cared so deeply. The president was persuaded that the stalemate in the area that prevailed when he took office would sooner or later have "disastrous consequences for world peace as well as for the United States itself."[15]

Whatever the precise reasons for Jimmy Carter's particular preoccupation with the Middle East, of the fact that he was preoccupied and indeed still is, there can be no doubt. As a close aide observed in a later 1978 interview: "There's not a single issue, domestic or foreign policy, that the President has spent more of his time and energy and resources on than his quest to bring peace to the Middle East."[16]

In his excellent volume on the Camp David peace process, William Quandt, who as a member of the National Security Council staff participated in the events he described, wrote that why Americans were prepared to devote so much time and energy to the Middle East was "still something of a mystery."[17] Yet it seems quite clear that the key to that mystery is Carter himself. The president's keen interest in the area explains the fact that foreign policy in the Carter administration, especially in the first two years, was dominated by an overriding concern with the Arab-Israeli conflict. Even more to the point, it accounts for Carter's own indispensable role in furthering the Middle East peace process and, ultimately, in securing the first agreement ever between Israel and an Arab state. The Camp David accords, which established a framework for peace between Israel and Egypt, and were the result of a thirteen-day negotiating marathon that took place at the presidental retreat for which they were named, must be considered the fruit of Carter's own personal diplomacy. It was the president himself who begged, badgered, and browbeat the Egyptian and Israeli leaders, Anwar Sadat and Menachem Begin, until they surfaced with an agreement in hand.

NATIONAL LEADERSHIP: PRESENTING THE CASE AT HOME

Henry Kissinger had so dominated Arab-Israeli diplomacy that what would happen after he left government service was unclear. Moreover, although Carter had voiced strong support for Israel during the campaign, he had not even outlined the direction he might take if he actually became president. In fact, there was general uncertainty about Jimmy Carter as a foreign policy leader. This was, after all, a man whose most important previous credential was that he served one term as governor of Georgia. He had no direct experience in foreign affairs, and he had never made a foreign policy decision for which he was in any way responsible. The lack of earlier indicators made what he would do in the realm of world politics particularly difficult to predict.[18]

Since the 1967 Middle East war, official U.S. policy toward the Arab-Israeli conflict was based on UN Resolution 242, which called on the Arabs to recognize Israel's "right to live in peace within secure and recognized boundaries free from threats or acts of force," and enjoined Israel to withdraw its armed forces from "territories occupied in the recent conflict." After the 1973 war, UN Resolution 338 had been adopted; it called on parties to the conflict to begin negotiations "under appropriate auspices aimed at establishing a just and durable peace in the Middle East."[19]

When Jimmy Carter took office, then, the key question on this subject was: Is it possible to have negotiations between the Arabs and Israelis based on the "territory for peace" formulas outlined just above? While still highly unstable, as we saw earlier events had in fact conspired to make the picture in the Middle East ever so slightly less bleak than it had been before. Kissinger had provided the U.S. with at least a modest track record as a negotiator between the warring parties, the price of oil had stabilized, and the Soviets were considerably less influential in the area than they had been previously.

Thus it was not unreasonable for Carter to take his personal interest in the Middle East and transform it into a linchpin of American foreign policy during the four years he was president.

It was fortunate for the new American president that with regard to the Middle East, at least, there was agreement between his top foreign policy advisers. Both Secretary of State Vance and National Security Adviser Brzezinski were proponents of an active American role in the search for peace in the area. To be sure, the differences in style between the two men were as evident in this regard as they were in all others. Vance, the conciliator, remained the chief negotiator on Arab-Israeli affairs through the Egyptian-Israeli peace treaty and was always far more involved in the details of peacemaking than was Brzezinski. For his part, Brzezinski, who was by nature more confrontational and who had a particular distaste for Israeli leader Menachem Begin, remained in the background, although he continued to support the president in his role as peacemaker.

It was also to Carter's immense advantage to have on his side during the Middle East peace process a working group at the State Department which was highly competent and enjoyed a rare degree of internal camaraderie. William Quandt, who was the key Mideast specialist at the National Security Council during Carter's term, and Harold Saunders, who became assistant secretary of state for the Near East in early 1978, were only the most outstanding of several officials without whose dedication and expertise Carter's initiatives might have foundered.

Carter and Vance first discussed the basic elements of the administration's approach to the Middle East even before they took office. At Carter's home in Plains, Georgia, in late 1976 they agreed that, while the U.S.'s firm commitment to Israel would not falter, in order to be fair and active mediators Carter and his team would have to pay serious attention to both sides of the dispute. However, such an evenhanded approach carried with it an element of political risk. As Vance explained in his memoirs, Carter "could be seen both at home and in Israel as tilting toward the Arabs and pressuring Israel to make dangerous territorial concessions."[20] They nevertheless agreed it was a risk they would take, and indeed it is fair to say that Carter's ultimate success as a negotiator depended on his being at least relatively impartial.

One of the first directives to be issued by Brzezinski was to order a review of Middle East policy. Similarly, Vance's first trip abroad was to the Mideast. Manifestly, Carter had communicated to the home team that this region of the world had top priority. What had not been decided, however, was just how the team would proceed. The initial game plan was rather vague: to strive for an agreement that would encompass the entire region, probably through a series of negotiations that would conclude with the convening of a peace conference at Geneva. How, in the deep morass that was Mideast politics, the administration would progress from point A to point B was never spelled out.

Perhaps because of the administration's own lack of certainty about what exactly to do, the American public was never very well informed about Carter's own great ambitions for peace in the Middle East, or about the fact that he had concluded that in order to make progress toward peace the U.S.

would have to be more evenhanded in its approach to the Arabs and Jews. To be sure, most Americans had a low level of interest in the Middle East and so whatever mistakes were made with regard to the public at large did not matter very much. But there was at least one group, the American Jewish community, to whom the particulars of U.S. policy in the Mideast mattered very much. Yet it was precisely these powerful pro-Israeli sympathizers who were never carefully primed for Carter's regional agenda.

In part the problem lay in the past. Neither Carter nor his aides from Georgia who were responsible for domestic affairs had any experience with the national Jewish community. And in part the problem lay in the present. First, despite what were initially favorable relations with Israel's supporters, the administration aroused their suspicions by its willingness to deal with moderate Arabs. Second, there were tactical mistakes. "Carter habitually revealed his intentions toward the Mideast prematurely, thereby squandering precious political capital and drawing sharp criticism before it was necessary to do so."[21]

What can only be described as a lack of political skill in this regard cost the president throughout his administration. Carter repeatedly sought the support of American Jewish leaders in pressing Menachem Begin to make concessions, but he failed to get it. American Jews also refused, publicly at least, to condemn policies pursued by Begin's government, even though they had their own misgivings. As one historian of the period has written: "The administration's heavy-handedness toward Israel drove them to support Jerusalem, right or wrong. Snafus, leaks, and misstatements constantly kept Israel's supporters aware that the administration was at odds with Jerusalem and with their own preferences for U.S. policy."[22]

Early in his administration Carter was notably unconcerned about the anxiety he had so promptly generated among Israel's supporters in America. (In fact, throughout his term he never seemed to understand that others could see a contradiction between his commitment to Palestinian rights and his support for Israel.) But when the attacks on his Mideast overtures continued, he began to recognize that his political problems went beyond the American Jewish community; they extended to the Congress. As Quandt writes: "Even to refer to Palestinian rights or to a Palestinian homeland could set off shock waves within the American Jewish Community. These would be instantly felt in Congress and relayed back to the White House."[23]

In essence, members of Congress had misgivings about Carter's even-handed approach to the Middle East for two reasons: First, some were genuinely reluctant to deviate even slightly from a foreign policy that the U.S. had practiced for what they considered good reasons for three decades. They saw Israel as an indispensable American ally, and thus supported the unquestioned commitment to the Jewish state that had long been a bedrock of American foreign policy. Second, Jewish interest groups, especially the American Israel Public Affairs Committee, had considerable influence in Washington. No member of Congress was oblivious to the Jewish vote, to the contributions Jews made to politicians' coffers, or to their considerable role im American public life generally.

As time went on Carter did in fact take more seriously the idea that his cherished Middle East initiatives would profit from work on the domestic front. He articulated his own personal concern about a safe future for Israel. For example, in July 1977 he told fifty Jewish leaders that he would "rather commit political suicide than hurt Israel."[24] He tried on occasion to publicize the extent to which his administration was working in tandem with the Israelis. In October 1977, for instance, a joint U.S.-Israeli statement was issued that reiterated that the basis for any peace talks was UN Resolutions 242 and 338. And he brought on board individuals charged with mollifying American Jews. In 1977, Mark Siegal, an aide to Carter's close adviser Hamilton Jordan, was named liason to the Jewish community. And in 1978, he summoned Edward Sanders, an attorney and active Jewish leader at the national level, to be an adviser on Middle East affairs to both Vance and himself. Despite limited power and access, Sanders secured the confidence of both the president and the American Jewish community; indeed, his eighteen months in office "marked a relatively quiet period in the administration's relations with American Jews."[25]

Clear from the start, in any case, was Carter's decision to make peace in the Middle East a priority. It was also apparent that despite the political costs of his evenhandedness, the president was not going to waver from his chosen course. Moreover, his team of foreign policy advisers followed suit. Throughout the period, their behavior is notable not only for thoughtful and intelligent strategizing but for perseverance as well.

One is particularly struck by the regular reassessments of policy that served both to indicate where mistakes were being made and to reconfirm those courses of action that seemed to be paying off. For instance, in the summer of Carter's first year in office, Vance and his advisers took stock. While the thrust of the administration's Mideast initiative was still a comprehensive settlement, there was a growing understanding of how complex regional politics really were. In particular, concern was voiced over the timing and pace of negotiations with Mideast leaders. At the end of the deliberations it was decided to avoid "gratuitous confrontations" with Israel while intensifying efforts to persuade the Arabs that concluding full peace with Israel was indispensable to an overall settlement.[26]

But it was in November 1977, after the historic vist to Jerusalem by Egyptian president Anwar Sadat, that the major reassessment of Mideast policy took place. In a memorandum to the president, Vance noted—with some understatement—that adjustments in America's policy in the region were now necessary.[27]

Sadat's Jerusalem journey was a turning point. While it took some months to appreciate that the trip would shift America's attention from the impossible (a comprehensive Mideast accord) to the possible (a bilateral agreement between Israel and Egypt), it is clear in retrospect that from this moment on the situation in the Middle East was irrevocably altered. Moreover, the administration recognized immediately that Sadat's visit to Jerusalem had, in Vance's words, "affected profoundly the political and negotiating climate."[28] While on the surface this was no great feat, for Sadat's journey to Israel was nothing if not a striking departure from conventional diplomatic practice, it is nevertheless noteworthy that Carter's foreign policy advisers were flexible enough to reevaluate the situation and to change course accordingly.

It became apparent rather quickly that Sadat's bold stroke would be to no avail unless the U.S. became more deeply and directly involved. In fact, both Begin and Sadat badly needed an American proposal to break the deadlock. For his part, Carter had become more aware of, and sensitive to, the risks involved. Political considerations weighed more heavily in 1978 than in 1977 (in large part because of midterm elections), and the president had learned how controversial anything he might say on the Middle East could become. He did not, however, pull back. In fact, as far as he was concerned, it was full speed ahead on the Middle East—to the point where he began to feel that his personal involvement with Sadat and Begin might be desirable. In short, the idea of the three-way summit was taking shape.

By May 1978, progress toward a meeting between Jimmy Carter, Anwar Sadat, and Menachem Begin was inexorable. At the time, however, the course of history was much less clear. The only thing that was apparent was that so far as the American president was concerned, the momentum toward negotiations had to be maintained. From that point on, the Americans entered a stage in which all their efforts were concentrated on capitalizing on Sadat's initiative a half year earlier.

In order to gain a fresh perspective, a top-secret planning group was formed under Secretary Vance. This time Vice President Mondale and Brzezinski were included, as were Hamilton Jordan and Press Secretary Jody Powell, so as to ensure that domestic political realities would be taken into account. Interestingly, the political imperatives were quite different now from what they had been a year earlier. Whereas in the past domestic advisers were urging caution with regard to Mideast policy, by spring 1978 the president's stock had fallen so low that aides like Jordan and Powell were urging Carter forward. Only a diplomatic triumph, they argued, could help the president on the eve of the fall congressional elections.

In late July, Carter committed himself to a trilateral summit, one that, for political reasons, he wanted to be "rather dramatic."[29] The decision was made to send Vance to the Middle East to invite both the Egyptian and Israeli leaders to a joint meeting at Camp David. On August 8, the official announcement was made: Carter, Sadat, and Begin would meet in the U.S. in a bold attempt to reach a Mideast agreement.

For weeks before the event, preparations for the summit were all-consuming. The president's foreign policy team was engrossed in plans, papers, and briefing books, and Carter himself was also doing the requisite homework. Quandt makes the interesting point that Carter and his advisers were taking different approaches. "For Vance and Brzezinski, the crucial test would be whether Carter could persuade Begin to make some concessions on the Palestinian question. . . . Carter, by contrast, no doubt drawing on his judgment about Sadat's real bottom line, was more intent on reaching an Egyptian-Israeli accord, with or without much of a link to the Palestinian issue."[30]

Just before the meetings began, Carter sat down and wrote two pages of notes in his own hand. They indicate confidence that the many months of careful planning and the dedication to the cause were about to bear fruit.

WORLD LEADERSHIP: IMPLEMENTING THE POLICY ABROAD

While President Carter's domestic campaign to achieve a Middle East peace was initially disorganized and uncertain, his ventures abroad were bold and creative right from the start. Almost immediately upon taking office he became personally involved in negotiations with Arab and Israeli leaders. It bears repeating that at this initial stage, in early 1977, neither Carter nor Vance nor Brzezinski had a clear idea of which course they would eventually follow. Rather, it was the president's deep commitment to making a difference in this area that drove them to plunge straight into the turbulent waters of Mideast politics.

Less than two months after assuming the presidency, Carter's first direct involvement in Arab-Israeli peacemaking took place. Israel's prime minister, Yitzhak Rabin, flew to Washington to pay a visit—which did not turn out particularly well. In his diary the president wrote: "I found [Rabin] very timid, very stubborn, and also somewhat ill at ease. . . . He didn't unbend at all, nor did he respond."[31]

Ironically, given the long history of cooperation between the U.S. and Israel, the president was better disposed, even before meeting them, toward Arab leaders. In public he said, "We have strong indications the Arab leaders want to reach a substantial agreement."[32] And in private he wrote: "I've never met any of the Arab leaders but am looking forward to seeing if they are more flexible than Rabin."[33] He would find out soon enough. One month after the meetings with Rabin, Carter had another visitor: Egypt's president Anwar Sadat.

Whether Carter's apparent predisposition toward Arab leaders was responsible, or whether feelings would have been the same anyway, cannot be determined. The fact is that despite the inevitable differences of opinion, the president was very much taken with his Egyptian counterpart. Carter was unusually warm and convivial as host, as well as generous in his remarks and in the amount of time allowed for private exchanges. In his memoirs Carter recalls: "It soon became apparent that [Sadat] was charming and frank, and also a very strong and courageous leader who would not shrink from making difficult political decisions."[34]

Few specifics came out of this first meeting between the two presidents, but it was clear to Carter that Sadat wanted peace and that he was, above all, a reasonable man. Moreover, of the fact that a special relationship was being forged between the two, there can be no doubt. Carter writes that there was "an easy and natural friendship" between himself and Sadat right from the start: "We trusted each other. Each of us began to learn about the other's family members, hometown, earlier life, and private plans and ambitions, as though we were tying ourselves together for a lifetime. Rosalynn and Sadat's wife, Jihan, sensed this special relationship and joined it easily."[35]

Carter's White House conversations with Mideast leaders were meanwhile being supplemented by contacts initiated by the secretary of state. In February, Vance made an eight-day trip to Israel, Egypt, Jordan, Saudi Arabia, and Syria. He concluded that four fundamental issues would have to be addressed even before getting to the peace table: the nature of the peace to be negotiated, the ultimate boundaries between Israel and its neighbors, the question of a Palestinian homeland, and the procedural questions of how to organize and conduct negotiations.[36]

But the real action, both substantively and in terms of departures from ordinary practice, was still centered on Carter. Meetings between him and top officials from the Middle East were proceeding apace. Syria's foreign minister paid the president a visit and shortly thereafter, a mere three weeks after Sadat left town, King Hussein of Jordan came to call. Carter liked him and was quickly persuaded that he too would be a reliable ally. Two weeks later the president met yet another regional leader, Syrian president Hafiz Assad. Carter made special arrangements to meet him in Geneva (following a NATO summit in London), which meant they convened on what was considered neutral turf. Once again, the two men got along remarkably well. Assad impressed Carter with his intelligence, confidence, and strength; for his part, the Syrian leader clearly welcomed the opportunity to talk to an American president as an equal. The initial meetings between President Carter and Arab leaders were concluded by the end of May. Crown Prince Fahd, Princes Saud and Mohammad, and other Saudi Arabian leaders had a series of what Carter called "interesting and productive" discussions with various members of the administration. In sum, within five months of becoming president, Carter had met with virtually every Arab leader who mattered. Moreover, the encounters were, without exception, cordial and constructive.

In contrast, his face-to-face talks with Israeli officials had been limited to the one rather unpleasant exchange with Rabin. There was, in the meantime, another Israeli leader to be reckoned with: the new prime minister Menachem Begin. Unlike most members of Israel's political elite, who were well-known in Washington for having worked closely with U.S. officials for many years, Begin was an unknown quantity. His political party was the unfamiliar, relatively rightist Likud; his reputation abroad still derived from his years as a fiery revolutionary who played a major part in Israel's war of independence; and his persona appeared to be an unusual combination of courtly manners and stubborn arrogance.

Despite the uncertainties, an invitation to the White House was extended immediately. To the administration's chagrin, however, even before he arrived in Washington, in July, most of the original impressions had been confirmed. In particular, Begin took a hard line. He was unalterably opposed to a Palestinian homeland of any kind, and he planned to continue increasing the number and size of Jewish settlements in the occupied territories.

Vance has written that the Carter-Begin talks were a "sharp contrast" to the president's April meetings with Sadat. "Although respectful and courteous toward each other, Begin and Carter did not seem to spark the same degree of mutual trust that Sadat and Carter so clearly felt."[37] To be sure, the talks between the two men were cordial enough for Carter to have noted in his diary that he thought of Begin as a "very good man." He felt compelled to add, however, based on what he knew about the man and on what he had witnessed in person, that "it will be difficult for him to change his position."[38]

While Carter had revealed during his first months in office that the peace effort in the area was crucial to him and would be central to his presidency, his sense of how to proceed remained vague. In fact, his statements on the subject often seemed contradictory. On one occasion, for example, he declared himself in favor of "defensible borders," a code phrase that implied Israel should not withdraw from territory it had captured in 1967. But when asked a short time later to explain what he meant, Carter alluded to a "substantial withdrawal of Israel's present control over territories" and some "minor adjustments in the 1967 borders."[39] Indeed, he rephrased his views so often during the early months that observers both at home and abroad were confused. Moreover, his willingness to allow subordinates to express their own views added to the uncertainty.[40] Small wonder that Egypt's foreign minister recalled later that although he and Sadat had carefully studied Carter's early moves in foreign policy, "We found the signals to be very mixed."[41]

By late August 1977, the picture was, indeed, mixed. On the plus side was the fact that people were talking. Moreover, American leadership of the peace process was accepted by all of the major players. On the other hand, how the Palestinians were to be included in the negotiations—a point on which the administration still held firm—was completely unclear. As Vance had determined in yet another trip to the region, Begin was extremely critical of the U.S. for offering to deal with the Palestinians on any terms whatsoever. (The Palestinian Liberation Organization [PLO] and its chairman, Yasir Arafat, were considered terrorists by the Israelis, to be excluded completely from any negotiations.) In other words, ostensibly all the participants were still focused on the idea of a comprehensive Mideast agreement. But the specifics of how such an agreement might be reached remained elusive.

In September and October there was another flurry of activity. Carter met personally with the foreign ministers of Israel, Egypt, Syria, and Jordan. Moreover, he moved to bring the Soviets into the picture (or to at least neutralize them) by having the United States and Soviet Union sign a joint statement in favor of a comprehensive Mideast settlement. But by engaging in what turned out to be a series of increasingly complex diplomatic moves, the administration did not enhance its position. "Not surprisingly some of these steps got tangled up with others, thus giving off signals to the Middle East parties of confusion and a loss of stamina on the part of the United States."[42]

Confusions and concerns notwithstanding, it appeared on the surface that the negotiations were inching toward a Geneva conference in which all of the interested parties would, in one way or another, participate. The idea underlying the Geneva proposal, which was now strongly supported by the U.S., was that it was to be the first in a long series of steps toward a broad Mideast accord. However, Sadat's unprecedented trip to Jerusalem changed the picture entirely.

During November 19 through 21, Sadat visited the Israeli capital and delivered a speech to the Knesset (Israel's parliament). The occasion is still regarded as among the most dramatic in modern diplomatic history. The precise impact of Sadat's gesture remains a matter of debate. That the Americans were stunned by the initiative, however, is not in doubt. After months in which it was the American president who had shaped the discussions, now the course of Mideast policy was altered irrevocably by the Egyptian president. Moreover, although Carter may have played a part in persuading Sadat to take some type of initiative—in a private communication dated a month earlier, Carter observed the time had "now come to move forward"—the decision to go to Jerusalem was entirely Sadat's own. (In fact, it ran counter to the advice of his own foreign minister.[43]) Sadat merely informed Carter the day before the announcement "that he was thinking of going."[44]

For their part, the Americans would have to regroup. As Vance wrote in his memoirs, although he and the president concluded after Sadat's historic journey that their "broad objective continued to be a Geneva conference and a comprehensive peace, it was clear . . . that the probable outcome of Sadat's initiative would be an initial peace agreement between Egypt and Israel."[45] In effect, then, Sadat derailed—for at least the foreseeable future—what had been up to that point the main thrust of Carter's Mideast policy: a comprehensive agreement.

It took about three months for the dust to settle after Sadat's trip to Israel. There was activity during this period, but more than anything else it was a time of trying to figure out how to make progress in the new negotiating environment. Brzezinski has observed that by early 1978, U.S. policy toward the Middle East had become less ambitious but more focused. "We were now resigned to the fact that a comprehensive settlement was years away at best. Instead, we were determined to make certain that Sadat's peace initiative was translated into a tangible accommodation between Egypt and Israel. . . ."[46] Brzezinski's expression of the wish to support Sadat turns out to be a running theme in all the key memoirs of the period. Vance confirmed that, as he saw it, the administration's "immediate task was to ensure that Sadat gained positive results from his initiative."[47] And Carter's diary entry of December 17 speaks of feeling "protective" toward Sadat, who would need all the protection the administration could offer.

It became apparent rather quickly that if left to their own devices, the Egyptian president and Israeli prime minister would accomplish nothing. Conversations between them continued, but instead of yielding results they in fact seemed to diminish the feelings of good will generated by the journey to Jerusalem. In turn, the Americans, Carter in particular, were becoming frustrated by the slow pace of the negotiations. During the first twelve months of his administration, the president had spent a great deal of time on the Middle East—1977 was referred to by Carter, Vance, and Brzezinski as "the year of the Middle East"—but so far they had precious little to show for it. As Carter later admitted, at one point he was close to losing patience with the endless quibbling. He was prepared, he wrote, to withdraw from the Middle East issue altogether: "It would be a great relief to me, and I certainly had my hands full with other responsibilities."[48]

Still, the investments of time, energy, and commitment were by now too great to pull back. Therefore, instead of withdrawing from the negotiations, Carter dedicated himself to fashioning an agreement between Egypt and Israel.

For two reasons his natural ally in this process was the Egyptian president: one reason was Begin, the other Sadat. Begin was proving to be a difficult and intransigent negotiating partner, whose general attitude Carter found increasingly "outrageous." Brzezinski recalls that, as far as the administration was concerned, "the Egyptian leader had gone out on a limb in order to promote peace in the region and that Begin was busily sawing the limb off."[49] President Carter's relationship with Sadat, on the other hand, continued to blossom. In February 1978, Sadat and his wife visited the Carters at Camp David. The two couples had more time to get acquainted and a genuine friendship between them was forged. The meeting also produced an alliance of sorts between the U.S. and Egypt, one in which both sides would aim to persuade the Israelis to moderate their negotiating positions.

From this point one, through months of continued tortuous negotiations, President Carter was the indispensable third party. He was in the thick of the action between Israel and Egypt. The nature of his interventions varied, of course, depending on the circumstances. But it was the fact of his personal participation—as opposed to that of his surrogates—that turned out to be crucial. To be sure, the president had had face-to-face meetings with leaders from the Middle East all along. But now that the peace process was centered on an accord between Egypt and Israel, the president's efforts could be more precisely targeted and, ultimately, productive.

An important shift in Carter's attitude toward Begin occurred during the first half of 1978. In effect, the president moved from doubting whether he could work with Begin at all, to a feeling that the Israeli leader might, ultimately, cooperate. During this period the two men met twice. (Carter also received an array of other Israeli officials.) After the first such visit, in March, Carter was gloomy, so much so in fact that he wondered if there was any chance of attaining even the relatively modest goal of an accord between Egypt and Israel. The second visit, two months later, was very brief but considerably more cordial. While Carter wrote in his diary after their discussions that he still worried Begin "would not take the necessary steps to bring peace to Israel,"[50] he also described their meeting on that occasion as a "positive experience."

Movement in May and June was slow to nonexistent, in part because the administration was sidetracked by a congressional battle over the proposed sale of military hardware to Egypt and Saudi Arabia. However, the secret planning group referred to earlier (with Vance, Mondale, Brzezinski, Jordan, and Powell) had started its regular deliberations, and when Mondale came back from yet another discouraging trip to the Middle East, the decision was quickly reached to have Vance meet with both the Egyptian and Israeli foreign ministers.

While no one has claimed that the discussions conducted by Vance on that occasion were in and of themselves of great moment, they nevertheless were important precursors to the Camp David summit. For the first time Israeli and Egyptian officials sat down and dined together, and discussions were held in which progress toward a solution was slowly made.

It was upon the secretary's return from this meeting that President Carter reached a momentous decision. As he recalls in his memoirs, after discussing the situation with his wife Rosalynn: "I finally decided it would be best, win or lose, to go all out. There was only one thing to do, as dismal and unpleasant as the prospect seemed—I would try to bring Sadat and Begin together for an extensive negotiating session with me."[51] In his own hand he wrote long, almost identical letters of invitation to the two leaders, and he had Vance fly to the Middle East to deliver them personally. Both men accepted on the spot.

The American team spent much of August involved in lengthy preparations for the summit. But for all the planning, it was clear to those concerned that there was no predicting what might happen. The risks of the personal diplomacy in which Carter was about to engage were in any case high. First, it was altogether possible that the situation in the Middle East might actually deteriorate as a result of the conference. Second, Carter's own reputation was at stake. His stock was low both at home and abroad; therefore, a failed summit might well render him a fatal political blow.

Three key decisions were made before the proceedings even began. To minimize outside interference, it was agreed that Jody Powell would be press spokesman for all the parties and that he would say nothing of substance until the meetings were over. Further, to facilitate a more congenial atmosphere, the wives of all three leaders were invited to the summit along with their husbands. Finally, it was determined that the conference would be held away from Washington, at Camp David, a lovely, rustic presidential retreat in the mountains of Maryland. The Carters would stay in their regular cabin, Aspen. The Sadats would be in Dogwood, the cottage they had enjoyed during an earlier stay. And the Begins would be in Birch, the other prominent cabin on the grounds.

But despite the bucolic overtones, President Carter was anxious. He has recalled that expectations were at a "fever pitch" and that his own feelings before the summit were akin to those of men going into battle. To counteract the tensions and to join three men who were ideologically, experientially, politically, and culturally terribly different, a religious note was introduced. Rosalynn Carter had written a "call to prayer" for the success of the Camp David meetings: ". . . Conscious of the grave issues which face us, we place our trust in the God of our fathers, from whom we seek wisdom and guidance. As we meet here at Camp David, we ask people of all faiths to pray with us that peace and justice may result from these deliberations."[52]

During the entire thirteen-day span of the Camp David talks, President Carter was the central figure. In fact, after the third day, until the Camp David accords were ready to be signed, Begin and Sadat had no face-to-face meetings or even direct contact by phone. Every exchange between the two protagonists was routed through the U.S. delegation. Naturally, this made Carter's role nothing less than key. He served as go-between and as a direct participant in all the proceedings.

To understand exactly why the Camp David process was so difficult, it is important to remember that before the talks began no one, not even Carter, had a precise agenda. Although it was generally agreed that the overall objective remained a comprehensive settlement to which the other parties in the Middle East would later sign on, what would motivate Begin and Sadat to take such a big step was never clear. As a result, much of the first week was spent fighting over issues that were ultimately irrelevant to the agreement. In addition, what were originally considered to be virtues, such as the isolation of Camp David and the close proximity of the participants, took a toll as the talks dragged on and tempers flared. By the start of the second week, sardonic jokes were being made about "prison" and the "concentration camp" atmosphere, and Carter had been reduced, at least in private, to calling Begin "a psycho."[53]

After ten days of discussions, it appeared that the talks had reached an impasse. "The Egyptians are adamant on their conditions, and Begin has not moved on a single major issue since we've been here," the president lamented. "All our people have decided we're wasting our time."[54] On day eleven of the summit, September 15, he summoned the American delegation to his cabin to discuss how they would deal with their failure.

The nadir was reached later that same morning. Vance burst into the room in which the president was working, his face ashen, to report that "Sadat is leaving. He and his aides are already packed."[55] Carter recalls it as "a terrible moment." Now even his hopes for a harmonious departure were gone. He asked his advisers to leave, went to the window with the view of the Catoctin Mountains, and began to pray. Thereafter he changed into more formal clothes and crossed the way to see Sadat.

The Egyptian leader said he was furious with the Israelis because they had no intention now or ever of signing an agreement. In response Carter told Sadat he simply had to stick with him for another day or two, after which, if there was no change, they would all depart together. The president also promised that none of the proposals would take effect unless all three nations agreed to the entire package. Carter wrote: "Sadat stood silently for a long time. Then he looked at me and said, 'If you give me this statement, I will stick with you to the end.' "

As Quandt has observed, Carter was now faced with a classic political problem: "If he held out for a strong agreement on both Sinai and the West Bank and Gaza, he risked not getting anything at all. The alternative would be to aim lower and to raise the chance of salvaging at least something. This is the point at which every politician must recall to himself the maxim 'Politics is the art of the possible.' "[56] In that spirit the preferred alternative was to get Sadat what he most wanted, the removal of Israeli settlements and airfields from Sinai, while allowing Begin to protect what mattered most to him, namely Israel's claim to control over the West Bank and Gaza. According to this scenario, the obvious solution was an agreement in which the reference to Israel's withdrawal from the West Bank and Gaza was dropped in exchange for its willingness to leave the Sinai completely.

While progress during the last days of the summit was more consistent, expectations still oscillated. Rosalynn Carter has recalled that the tension was "just too much" for her; she thought she would be sick.

Finally, on September 17, there was a breakthrough. Two landmark agreements were signed by Sadat and Begin and witnessed by Carter. The first was a statement of general principles pertaining to the West Bank and Gaza. The second was a detailed formula for an Egyptian-Israeli peace treaty. While the formal accord between Israel and Egypt (finally signed in March 1979) was flawed in ways that would prove costly, the historic accomplishment of Camp David was never in doubt. It produced the first peace agreement ever between Israel and an Arab state.

For Carter, success at Camp David meant a considerable change in his political fortunes. With few exceptions, the agreement between Israel and Egypt was seen as a triumph for him personally. Typical of the accolades was this one by Norman C. Miller, writing in the Wall Street Journal: "Now, all the talk about Mr. Carter being an ineffectual amateur has been swept away by his extraordinary achievement establishing a framework for peace between Israel and Egypt. It is difficult to imagine a greater act of inspired leadership than bringing those age-old enemies to the threshold of peace."[57] But the ultimate compliments were paid by the two protagonists. "Dear President Carter," Sadat said before the television cameras, "you have been most courageous when you took the gigantic step of convening this meeting." And Begin added, "The Camp David conference should be renamed. It was the Jimmy Carter conference."[58]

CARTER AS WORLD LEADER

We have suggested that of all the challenges Carter faced as president, he was temperamentally best suited to the conflict between the Arabs and Israelis. Indeed, at the beginning of this chapter we speculated on why this particular man was so drawn to this particular situation. The question is an important one because it is clear that in his zeal to bring peace to the Middle East, Jimmy Carter consumed considerable resources.

The Mideast claimed his time. As Carter testified in his diary, in addition to his direct interventions he spent countless hours digesting analyses of regional issues, pouring over maps of Israel and Jerusalem, and studying the history of the Palestinian question. Moreover, the Mideast limited his capacity to address other concerns. The president recalls in his memoirs: "Though many other issues claimed my attention, the Middle East question preyed on my mind."[59] Finally, the Mideast cost Carter politically. On the domestic front, he gained little while losing support during his first years in office, particularly in the Jewish community. And at the international level, until the deed was done—that is, until the Camp David accords were reached—he received virtually no recognition for what he was trying to accomplish. In short, the fact that President Carter's reputation as an effective leader was in decline for the better part of 1977 and 1978 can be explained in good part by what might be seen—in terms of shrewd presidential politics—as an overcommitment to the Middle East.

There is no evidence to suggest that the thrust to bring peace to this region of the world came from anyone other than the president himself. To be sure, Carter was building on initiatives undertaken by Henry Kissinger in the previous (Nixon and Ford) administrations. Still, his own key foreign policy advisers (Vance and Brzezinski) had no particular familiarity with or interest in the area, nor was there a crisis at the time that would explain why the Middle East had top priority. Clearly, the powerful vision of peace between the Arabs and the Jews was the president's own, as was the drive and tenacity that ultimately brought it to fruition.

To his credit, Carter assembled a foreign policy team that gave unstinting support to his quest for a resolution of the Arab-Israeli conflict. He had a particularly good lieutenant in Secretary of State Vance, who, under his authority, established working groups of unusual competence and dedication. The president did not, however, recruit a single senior official who could serve as effective liaison to the American Jewish community or, indeed, caution the administration to potential political fallout.

There can be little doubt that the president's deep concern with the Middle East cost him at home. Indeed, this particular initiative is emblematic of a number of others in which Carter "failed to calculate the political effects of his public words and actions," while appearing to be far more concerned about his "personal reputation for rectitude."[60] Of course, Carter was well-intentioned in his quest for a comprehensive peace in the area. On the other hand, he failed to understand how sensitive a subject the Arab-Israeli conflict was to at least one important constituency, American Jews. To them, his more balanced approach to Mideast politics—which he never managed to articulate clearly, consistently, and persuasively—was no more than a cause for suspicion.

There is evidence throughout 1977 and 1978 of Carter's failure to educate in this regard. After he'd been in office only a few months, the American Jewish community was already fearful of Carter's approach to Mideast politics, which, among other things, it found confusing. On the one hand, it recognized that the president had tried to address Jewish concerns and that he had been more than cordial to the new Israeli prime minister (Begin) at their first meeting. But on the other, it was uncomfortably aware that he had authorized sensitive efforts to woo the PLO and to involve the Soviets in Mideast talks—both of which were anathema to the Israeli government and to its supporters in the United States.[61]

Over time Carter did learn to be more cautious. Above all, he became more discreet and said less in public. But his relations with American Jews never really recovered from the early misunderstandings. During the 1978 congressional battle over the proposed sale of jets to Egypt and Saudi Arabia, there were some bitter exchanges. Brzezinski has written tellingly about this "particularly trying period," in which administration officials felt they were "genuinely contributing to Israeli security" while under "severe attack from the Jewish lobby."[62]

President Carter has also shed light on his problems with American Jews. He recalls becoming "increasingly concerned about criticisms of our peace initiatives from within the American Jewish community" early in his term, and he refers as well to a later time (mid-1978) when there were still "serious political problems among American Jews." In fact, these problems were so serious that major Democratic fund-raising banquets had to be postponed because so many "party members," that is Jews, had canceled their reservations to attend.[63] But even after he left the White House, Carter was unwilling to shoulder the blame. In his memoirs he wrote of a "private-public disparity" among the leaders of the organized Jewish community. He charged that in private they tended to be supportive of his various overtures, urging him "to explore every avenue that might lead to peace." However, according to Carter, their public demeanor was quite different. Then they would "condemn" the administration for being "evenhanded" in its concern for Palestinian rights along with Israeli security.[64]

We are making more than a passing reference to Carter's domestic problems over this foreign policy issue not only for what it says about his leadership with regard to the Middle East but also because it is, as we suggested above, emblematic of this president more generally. Carter's failure from the start to effectively lead American Jews deprived him of their unswerving loyalty even after his triumph at Camp David. Perhaps more significantly, it was just one more in a long series of situations in which the president's own good intentions suffered for want of his political skills.

Whatever his deficits though, it cannot be said that he once wavered from his chosen course. At one point in the months between Camp David and when the treaty was formally signed, Carter told Vance that he wanted him to press Israel hard—even if it would cost him Jewish support and, ultimately, his own reelection as president.[65]

While Carter's political skills at home fell short, his interpersonal relationships with leaders from the Middle East generally worked to his advantage. Oddly, whereas on the domestic front the president manifestly felt that politicking was somehow beneath him or, at the very least, personally distasteful, he had no such compunctions when embroiled in the turbulence of the Mideast. Without reservation he made a special point of forging personal ties with key leaders from the region, including top officials from Israel, Egypt, Syria, Jordan, and Saudi Arabia. Moreover, he was clever and determined enough not to let his personal preferences interfere with progress toward peace. He clearly did not much like Israel's leading player, Menachem Begin. But he did not let this deter him from enlisting Begin as a partner in negotiations. At the same time he used his natural affinity with Anwar Sadat to good advantage, drawing on the reservoir of goodwill between them when the discussions at Camp David were at their most difficult.

Carter also demonstrated a flexibility with regard to the Middle East peace process that went beyond that in evidence on other issues. From the beginning of his term in office, right through to the signing of the treaty between Israel and Egypt in March 1979, the president shifted as the occasion demanded. In particular, when he saw that his original dream of a comprehensive peace was unattainable, he gave it up. And when he recognized that Sadat's journey to Jerusalem had left such a deep imprint, he sanctioned a change in America's negotiating strategy.

To be sure, as we indicated earlier, Carter was helped immeasurably in the execution of his Mideast policies by a team that was as competent as it was dedicated. The men at State and the NSC labored hard and well. For this too, however, the president deserves credit. Just as executives are blamed for the transgressions of their deputies, so they must be commended if the appointees for whom they are responsible perform well.

What is apparent, in any case, is the extent to which President Carter was personally invested in the Middle East peace process. He demonstrated his intellectual curiosity by becoming something of student of the area. He displayed his political commitment by staking his reputation both at home and abroad on achieving some level of success in the negotiations. He evidenced his private concern by investing an inordinate amount of time and energy on this particular initiative. And he showed moral commitment by virtue of his willingness to take genuine political risks.

Carter's sense of missionary purpose with regard to the Middle East is, of course, nowhere as evident as in the thirteen days spent at Camp David, where he begged and bullied the suspicious and temperamental Begin and Sadat to reach some kind of an accord. While the high drama of this period is impossible to recapture in a few pages—books have been written on the subject—it is apparent from even a brief description that this was an extraordinary exercise. It was the president's novel idea to have a Mideast summit at his mountain retreat, and it was the president's relentless persistence that brought the conference to a successful conclusion.

Carter's formal role was that of a third party. That is, he was external to the dispute between Israel and Egypt, and interposed between them. It was a risky position for him, for the inclusion of a third party can actually increase the level of turbulence. On the other hand, third parties often do facilitate negotiations between adversaries who are unable to resolve their own conflicts, but who are, nonetheless, open to conciliation.[66]

Several different functions may be served by third parties. The following particularly pertain to the president at Camp David:

1. It was Carter who decided to hold the summit in a remote, and neutral, location, and who suggested that the participants completely avoid their respective constituencies until after their talks were over.
2. It was Carter who served as go-between for the two principals, who would never have been able to engage in a reasoned dialogue on their own.
3. It was Carter who insisted that the discussions continue until they bore fruit.
4. It was Carter who implied that U.S. military and economic assistance were dependent on Israeli and Egyptian cooperation.
5. It was Carter who shaped the agenda and, ultimately, the accords themselves.
6. Finally, it was Carter who made a strong effort to bestow upon Begin and Sadat the international esteem they so clearly craved. Moreover, he enabled both to emerge from the summit without loss of face.

Interestingly, Carter's performance as mediator in the Middle East bore a striking resemblance to that of the only other high-level regional activist in recent American history, Henry Kissinger. Both Kissinger and Carter maintained control of the agenda throughout the negotiating process. Both used their strong, warm relationship with Sadat to reach a particular goal. Both implied costs to Israel should it block agreement. Both removed the most intractable issues—for example, the future of Jerusalem—from the bargaining table. Both resorted to "creative ambiguity" when reconciliation of differences between the disputants proved impossible. Both invoked the U.S. as a guarantor of the observance of treaties, thereby reducing the risks of concessions. And, finally, both rewarded flexibility and induced concessions through promises. For his part, between Camp David and the actual signing of the peace treaty several months later, President Carter pledged $3 billion to Israel and $2 billion to Egypt. The two signatories had become the largest recipients of American aid.[67]

The Camp David accords were less than an unmitigated success. Above all, the provisions for Palestinian representation were rejected, and today, ten years later, the Palestinian-Israeli deadlock persists. Jimmy Carter's Mideast policies did, however, result in a major breakthrough: Egypt and Israel made peace. While not "warm," it has nevertheless endured.[68]

In the end, then, Carter's accomplishment is vivid testimony to the fact that with the requisite amount of presidential will and skill, the executive is in a position to play a leading role at the international level. To a degree, at least, Carter acted outside conventional policy-making channels at home (Congress and the American people were by and large ignored in the Mideast peace initiative); similarly, he circumvented key actors in world and Mideast politics, such as the Soviet Union and the United Nations. Rather, the president followed his own compass in order to reach a goal that he considered both morally correct and in the best postwar American tradition of spreading peace (and freedom) around the globe.

In the process Carter pulled out all the stops. He invoked his *authority* as president of the United States—superpower and leader of the Free World. He used his *power* by drawing on material resources to reward both Israel and Egypt for their good behavior. And he exercised personal *influence,* particularly in his exchanges with Anwar Sadat and Menachem Begin. Thus, while President Carter could not have done it alone—in particular, Sadat's journey to Israel was an essential precursor—the fact is that in the Camp David peace process per se, Carter's role as peacemaker was no less than key.

At the same time, it must be said that the president's success as a regional mediator came at a price. For over two years it sapped valuable personal and political resources that could have been invested elsewhere. One might reasonably argue, then, that Carter's tilt to the Middle East was politically disadvantageous. His stock at home would almost certainly have been higher had his energies been more narrowly channeled into domestic affairs. But to argue this is to miss the point. For the fact is that Carter was never fully comfortable politicking in Washington, whereas he was in his element in the politics of the Middle East. To this particular president bringing peace to that region was a mission of the utmost importance. And it was, in the end, a mission at least partly accomplished.[69]

Notes

1. Barbara Kellerman, *The Political Presidency: Practice of Leadership* (New York: Oxford University Press, 1984), p. 217. For more on Carter's problems on the home front, see "Jimmy Carter and the Energy Package," pp. 185–219.

2. Erwin C. Hargrove, "Jimmy Carter: The Politics of Public Goals," in *Leadership in the Modern Presidency,* ed. Fred I. Greenstein (Cambridge, Mass.: Harvard University Press, 1988), p. 245.

3. Zbigniew Brzezinski, *Power and Principle: Memoirs of the National Security Adviser, 1977–1981* (New York: Farrar Straus Giroux, 1983), p. 83.

4. For a harsh assessment of American foreign policy under Carter, see Stephen E. Ambrose, *Rise to Globalism: American Foreign Policy Since 1938* (New York: Penguin, 1984), pp. 390 ff.

5. Brzezinski, p. 38. For more on the way in which Carter organized his foreign policy–making system, see Erwin C. Hargrove, *Jimmy Carter as President: Leadership and the Politics of the Public Good* (Baton Rouge: Louisiana State University Press, 1988), pp. 113–20.

6. Ambrose, p. 341. The following paragraphs are based on Ambrose's rendering, pp. 341 ff.

7. Ambrose, p. 344.

8. Ibid.

9. Ambrose, p. 346.

10. John Spanier, *American Foreign Policy Since World War II* (New York: Holt, Rinehart, & Winston, 1985), p. 237. The following paragraphs are based on Spanier, pp. 237–39.

11. Ambrose, pp. 237–39.

12. For more on Carter's "born again" experience, see Betty Glad, *Jimmy Carter: In Search of the Great White House* (New York: Norton, 1980), p. 108 ff.

13. Rosalynn Carter, *First Lady from Plains* (Boston: Houghton Mifflin, 1984), p. 10.

14. Jimmy Carter, *Keeping Faith: Memoirs of a President* (New York: Bantam, 1982), pp. 273, 274.

15. Brzezinski, p. 83.

16. Hamilton Jorden quoted in Steven L. Spiegel, *The Other Arab Israeli Conflict: Making America's Middle East Policy, from Truman to Reagan* (Chicago: University of Chicago Press, 1985), p. 328. For evidence of Carter's continuing interest in the Middle East, see the book he wrote after leaving office, *The Blood of Abraham* (Boston: Houghton Mifflin, 1985).

17. William B. Quandt, *Camp David: Peacemaking and Politics* (Washington: Brookings, 1986), p. 4. Quandt's is the best single source on the Camp David peace progress and, indeed, on Carter's Mideast policies generally.

18. Spiegel, p. 315.

19. Quandt, p. 33.

20. Cyrus Vance, *Hard Choices: Critical Years in America's Foreign Policy* (New York: Simon & Shuster, 1983), p. 163.

21. Spiegel, p. 316.

22. Ibid., p. 317.

23. Quandt, p. 322.

24. In Spiegel, p. 326.

25. Ibid., p. 327.

26. Vance, p. 185.

27. Quandt, p. 149.

28. Vance, p. 196.

29. Brzezinski, p. 250.

30. Quandt, p. 207.

31. Jimmy Carter, p. 280.

32. Quandt, p. 50.

33. Jimmy Carter, p. 280.

34. Ibid., p. 282.

35. Ibid., p. 284.

36. Vance, p. 168.

37. Ibid. p. 180.

38. Jimmy Carter, p. 290.

39. Spiegel, p. 331.

40. Ibid., p. 325.

41. Ismail Fahmy, *Negotiating for Peace in the Middle East* (Baltimore: Johns Hopkins University Press, 1983), p. 188.

42. Quandt, P. 130.

43. Fahmy, chapter 14.

44. Vance's phrase, p. 195.

45. Ibid.

46. Brzezinski, p. 235.

47. Vance, p. 195.

48. Jimmy Carter, p. 312.

49. Brzezinski, p. 243.

50. Jimmy Carter, p. 313.

51. Ibid., p. 316.

52. Rosalynn Carter, p. 246.

53. Brzezinski, pg. 262.

54. Rosalynn Carter, p. 261.

55. The account of this incident is from, Jimmy Carter, pp. 391–93. Brzezinski's tougher version may be found in his book, pp. 392–93.

56. Quandt, p. 235.

57. *Wall Street Journal,* 20 September 1978.

58. Quoted by Rosalynn Carter, p. 268.

59. Jimmy Carter, p. 289.

60. Hargrove in Greenstein, p. 254.

61. Quandt, p. 132.

62. Brzezinski, p. 249.

63. Jimmy Carter, pp. 288, 313.

64. Ibid., p. 286.

65. Brzezinski, pp. 272, 278.

66. Jeffrey Z. Rubin, ed., *Dynamics of Third Party Intervention: Kissinger in the Middle East* (New York: Praeger, 1981). See chapter 1 for the theoretical basis of the discussion in this and the next paragraphs. Also see Harold H. Saunders, *The Other Walls: The Politics of the Arab-Israeli Peace Process* (Washington: American Enterprise Institute, 1985).

67. The points I make in this regard are in Janice Gross Stein, "Kissinger and Carter: An Analysis of the Structures, Strategies and Tactics of Mediation in the Arab-Israel Conflict" (Paper prepared for the Annual Meeting of the International Society of Political Psychology, 1984).

68. William B. Quandt, "Ten Years after Camp David, Now What?" *New York Times,* 17 September 1988.

69. For a useful general discussion of Carter as leader, in particular his own conceptions of leadership, see Hargrove, *Jimmy Carter as President,* pp. 13–32.

9

Ronald Reagan's Campaign for Military Superiority

As to the enemies of freedom, to those who are potential adversaries, they will be reminded that peace is the highest aspiration of the American people. . . . When action is required to preserve our national security, we will act. We will maintain sufficient strength to prevail if need be, knowing that if we do so we have the best chance of never having to use that strength.

—First Inaugural Address, January 20, 1981

BACKGROUND

Ronald Reagan came to the presidency proclaiming the arrival of a revolution. His goal was nothing less than to reverse decades of public policy that he maintained had unwisely expanded the power of the government at home and weakened America's position in the world. While no one but his most devoted followers expected him to succeed, the nation was captivated by the boldness of his claims and the confidence with which he made them.

Many observers were surprised that Reagan had won the presidency at all. Politics, after all, was his second career. For most of his adult life, Ronald Reagan had been an actor.[1] But he had long shown an interest in politics. While in Hollywood, he was active in Democratic party politics and served as president of the Screen Actors Guild. When acting jobs were scarce, he found employment as spokesman for the General Electric corporation. He spent a number of years working as a sort of goodwill ambassador for GE, touring its plants around the nation making speeches that over time grew increasingly political.

Those talks were all variations on what came to be known among Reagan's intimates as "the Speech," a set piece on certain core themes that Ronald Reagan stood for and preached to his audiences. He railed against the growth of the federal government and alleged bureaucratic waste. He protested high taxes and overregulation of business. And he accused the "liberal establishment" of being "soft on communism" and of selling out United States' interests in order to negotiate with the Soviet Union. Reagan's themes became too controversial for his employers, but they made him a popular after-dinner speaker among business and conservative audiences.[2]

What made him so appealing was not only that message, but the personality of the messenger. Ronald Reagan was well-liked, even among those who disagreed with his opinions. He was highly personable, with a gift for small talk. He projected an easy manner, a good sense of humor, and great warmth. He was unfailingly optimistic about the chances of righting all the wrongs he diagnosed in American politics, and he saw the world in black-and-white terms that gave him confidence in his ideas and evoked loyalty among those who shared his views.

In 1964, Ronald Reagan entered national politics. Two years before, he had switched parties to become a Republican. Now he spoke on behalf of Barry Goldwater, Lyndon Johnson's opponent in the presidential election that year. Reagan delivered a half-hour version of the Speech to be shown on television. While the film, "A Time for Choosing," received little attention from the major news organizations, it was hailed by conservatives and re-broadcast in a number of cities during the campaign. It brought in $1 million for Republican candidates, more money than had even been raised by a political speech to that time.[3] With the defeat of Goldwater, Ronald Reagan rapidly became one of the most popular spokesmen for conservatives in America and a politician himself. In 1966, he defeated the Democratic incumbent to become chief executive of California. While continuing to talk his tough conservative line, Governor Reagan frequently compromised with the Democratic legislature. In 1968 and 1976, he made unsuccessful runs for the Republican presidential nomination. It was now clear that he had presidential ambitions and was emerging as one of his party's leaders.

Nineteen eighty would be Ronald Reagan's year. He swept the Republican nomination and took on a weakened incumbent president. Jimmy Carter tried to paint his opponent as too militant and too conservative, but he was already wounded by high inflation, the embarrassing Iranian hostage crisis, and the inability of the United States to bring pressure to halt the Soviet invasion of Afghanistan. Reagan, on the other hand, promised not only economic recovery but to restore respect for the United States around the world. Whereas President Carter had tried unsuccessfully to bring Americans to understand and accept limits on national power and prosperity, Reagan promised that U.S. resources were unlimited and that the nation could still reign supreme in the world. In foreign affairs, he portrayed himself as a strident anticommunist and spoke of his skepticism about any accommodation with the Soviet Union.

Reagan viewed Soviet-American rivalry as the central feature of the international arena. During the campaign, he told the *Wall Street Journal* that "the Soviet Union underlies all the unrest that is going on [around the globe]. If they weren't engaged in this game of dominoes, there wouldn't be any hot spots in the world."[4] What the world needed was a reassertion of the United States' rightful place in international affairs: "We did not seek leadership of the Free World, but there is no one else who can provide it, and without our leadership there will be no peace in the world."[5] As president, he would restore the nation to its place as number one in world politics through rearmament, challenges to the Soviet Union, firmness in the face of attacks by terrorists and Third World mobs, and a strong stand for freedom. He told cheering audiences that "we don't care whether we are liked by the rest of the world—we want to be respected."

The ideas underlying the "Reagan Revolution" had once made Governor Reagan appear too extreme to win national office. That fact, plus his career as an actor, left many observers to regard him as an ideologue and not as seriously as a politician. But by the late 1970s, with Jimmy Carter's presidency in trouble and growing public uneasiness about America's position in the world, the message of his "revolution" took on a new appeal.

It was also made more acceptable by Reagan's magnetic personality. In contrast to a somber and visibly tired incumbent, the challenger exuded strength, optimism, and warmth. In a televised debate between the candidates, Reagan disarmed Carter by discrediting the president's attacks against his stands on issues. Responding with a nonplussed "There you go again," Reagan acted as if he could not believe that his opponent was accusing him of being an extremist. Throughout the 1980 campaign, he joked about his age (sixty-nine), his acting career, and even his reputation as a right-wing hardliner. He quipped to reporters that being president would be easy: "You know, after you've canceled Social Security and started the war, what else is there for you to do?"[6] Candidate Reagan mixed resolve to make changes with a sense of trustworthiness, enabling him to draw support from a broad range of voters. He defeated Carter by a wide margin and on his coattails brought in the first Republican-controlled Senate in twenty-five years.

Now he faced the task of governing. He had already revealed his approach to that responsibility as chief executive of California. His operating style consisted of three key elements:

1. an emphasis on the use of rhetoric
2. a willingness to compromise on substance in order to advance larger goals
3. extensive delegation of power to subordinates.

The primary element of Ronald Reagan's leadership style was its emphasis on the use of rhetoric. Reagan was particularly drawn to strong words to rally supporters or attack policies he opposed. As Wilson Carey McWilliams has noted: "In speech, Reagan is almost invariably firm and decisive, certain of his values and direction, and inclined to strong language and striking expression."[7] His political career had been launched by a speech and was driven by his power as a public speaker. As an actor and an after-dinner speaker, he had developed a style that was both polished and simple. It enabled him to excel before nearly any audience and to use television effectively.

But there was more to Reagan's approach than an effective speaking style. The words were an important part of his presidency. William K. Muir, Jr., a close observer of Ronald Reagan as candidate and as president, has argued that "the key to the Reagan administration is its rhetorical character."[8] Therefore, a description of his tenure in office must focus on the spoken word. Reagan is the best example of Roderick Hart's observation about the contemporary presidency that "public speech no longer attends the processes of governance—it *is* governance."[9] He was not only a more accomplished speaker than most other American politicians, but he believed in the power of rhetoric to move an audience. Reagan paid more attention to rhetoric than any president since John Kennedy. As his speechwriter, Tony Dolan, put it:

> People say that the president is The Great Communicator. He's not. He's the Great Rhetorician. He uses words. He uses logic. There is substance in every paragraph. His arguments flow from one point to the next. . . . He has a philosophy. . . . As I said, the Reagan speechwriters' major function is to plagiarize the president's old speeches and give them back to him to say.[10]

As president, Reagan busily conveyed the message he believed the nation and the world needed to hear. In his first press conference after taking office, he made it clear the he believed Soviet leaders would do anything dishonest in order to advance their ideological interests. In 1983, he denounced the Soviet Union as an "evil empire." He described the Nicaraguan *contras,* an American-backed guerrilla force fighting the leftist government of that country and suspected of terrorist activities, as freedom fighters who were "the moral equivalent of the Founding Fathers." He described the Vietnam War as a "noble cause." True to his idea of revolution but most unconservative in spirit, he approvingly repeated Tom Paine's statement: "We have it in our power to begin the world over again."

Reagan's interest as president was in the "big picture," in promoting those core values with which he had been associated throughout his career. Whereas Richard Nixon's campaign manager had once told reporters, "Watch what we do, not what we say," Ronald Reagan wanted his audiences to watch both what he was saying and doing. For him, presidential words were as important as presidential deeds.

Despite the strength of his rhetoric, the second element of Ronald Reagan's style was his willingness to compromise on substance in order to advance his larger goals. Of course, this willingness was not unlimited, and on some issues he refused to compromise at all (for example, income tax increases). But Mr. Reagan did not consider it inconsistent or hypocritical to make a deal with his opponents while continuing to talk tough.

He was more willing to compromise in order to achieve partial success than his rhetoric suggested. For example, despite Reagan's alarmist claims about threats to democracy in El Salvador and charges about what the leftist Sandinista regime of Nicaragua was doing to abuse its citizens, and complaints about Soviet expansionism in the Western Hemisphere, he confined the American response to covert actions and aid to the government of El Salvador and the Nicaraguan contras. Despite the fact that the president's rhetoric frequently suggested that nothing short of armed intervention by the United States would be sufficient, no conventional military intervention was undertaken, and Reagan even accepted compromises with congressional Democrats that limited contra assistance to "non-lethal aid."[11] He wanted to oppose Marxist advances in the region but was unwilling to risk unpopular and politically costly actions to further his cause.

The third key element of President Reagan's leadership style enabled him to focus on the "big picture" and to maximize his personal resources: the extensive delegation of power to subordinates. So far as foreign affairs was concerned, power was allocated in two ways: First, the president delegated policy-making authority to the departments traditionally associated with foreign affairs. Preaching the virtues of "Cabinet government," as have most recent presidents, he selected two strong individuals for the relevant posts. He chose Alexander Haig, former Nixon chief of staff and former commander of NATO, to be his activist secretary of state. He was charged with bringing "toughness" to a department that Reaganites considered "soft." Caspar Weinberger, a Reagan aide in California and a Nixon Cabinet officer as well, was named secretary of defense. Within the Defense Department, responsibility for defense planning was to be devolved from the Office of the Secretary to the individual armed services.[12]

The president then delegated power in a second way. Within the White House, he placed a "troika" of senior aides in charge of the staff. In this way, Reagan used a sort of modified hierarchical system of management. White House operations were organized hierarchically, but the pyramid of power culminated in a chief of staff, James Baker, who handled matters of management and policy implementation; a deputy chief of staff, Michael Deaver, who was in charge of the president's schedule and public relations; and a counselor to the president, Edwin Meese, who was responsible for policy-making.[13] In a departure from nearly three decades of practice, but consistent with Reagan's philosophy of delegation, the national security adviser reported to the president's counselor and not to the president himself.

What President Reagan sought with this scheme was a foreign policy government that would be run by strong officials but kept as part of the president's overall team.[14] His system of dual delegation, creating a cadre of officials to manage foreign policy while he set the overall course and articulated important themes, did not work exactly as promised. The Reagan administration, especially in its first two years, was marked by instability and infighting among its foreign policy cadre. Secretary of State Haig tried to establish himself as the president's "vicar" for foreign affairs, which brought him into conflict with Counselor (and old Reagan friend) Meese. Policy coherence was not forthcoming, as had been promised. Rather, while the rhetoric was more strident than Jimmy Carter's had been, the disarray was similar. Then, in an unrelated matter, in January 1982 National Security Adviser Richard Allen was forced to resign because of an incident involving money received from a Japanese journalist.[15]

By the end of 1982, the president would have a new secretary of state, George Shultz, and a new national security adviser, William Clark, the second of six who would serve Mr. Reagan over the course of his presidency. The national security adviser was promoted within the White House hierarchy to the level of the troika (making it now the "quadriad") and relations between the State Department and the president's aides became smoother. Whatever the system's limitations, Ronald Reagan was able to put his stamp on American foreign policy and his cadre served him, after a fashion.

True to his core principles, the president was determined to move forward with his goal of restoring the United States to its position as world leader. In response to the challenge of Soviet military power and adventurism, growing instability in the Third World, and a sense that America had become a sort of "crippled giant,"[16] he undertook a campaign for American military superiority. That effort would last for four years and it represented the administration's main foreign policy initiative during Ronald Reagan's first term. The push to rearm sheds light on Reagan's leadership style, demonstrating what he was able to accomplish, as well as the costs incurred by his particular approach to the presidency.

NATIONAL LEADERSHIP: PRESENTING THE CASE AT HOME

Reagan came to office determined to proceed with a major buildup of national defenses after what he called a "decade of neglect."[17] He argued that declining defense spending since the time of the Vietnam War meant that the nation would soon face a "window of vulnerability." In other words, failure to maintain and improve American military strength during the 1970s had not only allowed the United States to slip from its leading position in the world, but would actually leave the nation vulnerable to a Soviet attack in the near future.[18] To combat this eventuality, the country needed a vigorous program to upgrade defense and provide a "margin of safety." In his Inaugural Address he emphasized that the United States must be in a position from which it could, if necessary, prevail over its adversaries.

In his first address to Congress on his economic program, on February 18, the president stated his rationale for rearmament. He argued that since 1970, "the Soviets have made a significant numerical advantage in strategic nuclear delivery systems, tactical aircraft, submarines, artillery, and anti-aircraft defense. To allow this imbalance to continue is a threat to our national security."[19] He indicated a willingness to discuss arms negotiations, but Reagan's emphasis was on the need for a "realistic defense program."

On March 4, 1981, the president began the process of converting rhetoric to policy. His themes implied large increases in the Pentagon budget for several years. His proposal to Congress substantially revised the last military spending program of the Carter administration (which called for an increase of 5 percent after inflation) and projected a five-year rise in the defense budget. Defense was the only budget category for which President Reagan proposed a spending rise in his preliminary request to Congress, and it was clear to most observers that he was likely to get much of what he wanted. As *Newsweek* summarized the situation:

> It will cost an unfathomable $1.5 trillion over the next five years, fundamentally alter the economy and radically change America's military posture in the world. Yet for all its revolutionary impact, the massive defense buildup planned by the Reagan Administration—the largest peacetime rearmament since World War II— has so far drawn little dissent.[20]

Ronald Reagan had the good fortune to preside over a domestic political environment that largely welcomed his proposals. The executive bureaucracy, editorial commentators, security specialists, the general public, and Congress were all ready to spend more money on defense. The new president, once regarded as an extremist, now spoke for a national consensus.

To no one's surprise, the executive branch greeted Reagan's plans with glee. The White House and National Security Council staff, filled with pro-defense "Reaganites," were solidly behind the president's proposal. Of course, so were the armed forces. As *Fortune* commented: "Broad smiles flash beneath every braided cap."[21] This was not a policy that had to be hidden from or sold to the bureaucracy. Defense secretary Weinberger, who became Reagan's point man on the buildup, could speak on behalf of a united military establishment.

But eagerness for more defense money was not unique to the Pentagon. The "security culture" of defense experts and editorialists on defense issues generally agreed with the need for more military spending. While there certainly was not unanimity among those outside government whose specialty was national security issues (hence the term "security culture"), the pro-buildup view was dominant among those discussing defense during that period.[22] Giving voice to the prevailing position, Carter's Defense secretary, James Schlesinger, concluded: "Increases in defense outlays are long overdue."[23]

There was some argument with the president's plan, but it had little effect on the fate of his program. Some analysts, such as Richard Barnet[24] and James Fallows,[25] maintained that the defense buildup was a misappropriation of resources. Other critics, while supporting the defense increases, faulted the president for a lack of strategy. In other words, they argued that Reagan was trying to increase American security merely by "throwing money at defense," rather than fulfilling his promise to develop a coherent program for reviving American power. Schlesinger noted that "there must be a vision and explicit strategy along with expenditures,"[26] while William Hoehn of the RAND Corporation said, "Our strategy is the best-kept secret we have."[27]

Ronald Reagan could easily withstand these barbs, however. He had delegated questions of defense planning to Weinberger, so criticisms in that area were directed at the secretary rather than the president. It was Weinberger who had to face reporters and congressional committees, while Reagan strode above the fray as commander in chief and defender of the West.

More to the point, the public supported his defense buildup. To be more accurate, the public favored more defense spending even before Reagan took office. In December 1980, a poll by the Roper Organization showed that 56 percent of the respondents thought that the United States was spending "too little" on defense.[28] Another poll by NBC/Associated Press put support for more military spending at 74 percent.[29] Therefore, President Reagan could plausibly argue that he was doing what was popular as well as what he believed was right. Attacks on particular weapons systems or the question of strategy were not significant to a public that wanted the United States to be respected around the world and believed the nation's military had been allowed to decline in the wake of the Vietnam War.

Broad support for defense increases meant that the president had little difficulty prevailing in Congress during the crucial budget votes in the first half of 1981. For example, the Senate voted in May to approve the FY 1982 (fiscal year ending September 1, 1982) defense authorization bill with only one dissenting vote. Even long-time critics of defense spending, such as Senators Edward Kennedy (D-Massachusetts) and Paul Sarbanes (D-Maryland), voted for Reagan's plans. In reporting on the vote, the *New York Times* noted the "widespread support in Congress for increased military spending."[30] Speaking a few days later at West Point, the president acknowledged this endorsement even as he continued to push for his program:

> Already the Congress has voted the greatest reduction in the budget ever attempted and, at the same time, has mightily increased the spending for the military. The argument, if there is any, will be over which weapons, not whether we should forsake weaponry for treaties and agreements.[31]

In September 1981, Reagan was forced to trim his defense plans slightly because reestimates of the budget revealed that the federal deficit would be higher than originally expected. But even as a number of Democrats and liberal Republicans urged him to cut further, the president drew the line at greater defense cuts and won the support of Congress in December. He even succeeded in winning acceptance of his plan to begin production of the controversial B-1 bomber. He had succeeded in reordering budget priorities to make his plan for a "margin of safety" national policy.

The B-1 presented a problem for Reagan. He had campaigned against Jimmy Carter's 1977 decision to cancel the weapon, claiming that it was needed to replace the aging B-52 bomber fleet. But critics of the new plane said that it was too expensive and would do little to enhance national security. Even Senator John Tower (R-Texas), the security-minded chairman of the Armed Services Committee, expressed a preference for developing the experimental B-2 Stealth bomber over the B-1. And Democrat Joseph Addabbo (New York), chairman of a House defense subcommittee, attacked the putative effectiveness of the B-1. The president was adamant, however, and dispatched Weinberger and top military officers to press the plane's case before Congress. Then, in November 1981, Reagan delivered a speech proposing the elimination of all medium-range U.S. and Soviet missiles from Europe. The speech came shortly before the House was to take up the defense bill and it changed the whole debate. Now, as the *Congressional Quarterly* put it: "House members stampeded to support Reagan's B-1 [proposal] as a symbol of backing for the arms cut initiative and to ensure that the president would enter U.S.-Soviet arms talks Nov. 30 with 'bargaining chips.' "[32]

By 1982, the president's plans were beginning to come into focus. During the 1980 campaign and in several statements defending his military-spending program, Reagan had spoken about the need to upgrade the readiness of American forces. This suggested a need for more fuel, ammunition, and spare parts. But the Reagan rearmament program tended instead to emphasize procurement of new weapons: the B-1 bomber, the MX missile, new tanks, attack helicopters, anti-aircraft guns, and similar (and very expensive) hardware. The goal of this "buying spree," as critics called it, was to enable the United States to "prevail" over the Soviet Union in the event of a nuclear war.

In contrast to its predecessor, the Reagan administration had begun to stress the possibility of a protracted nuclear war in its defense planning (all presidents have done some of this kind of planning, but the Reagan plans made it a higher priority). In October 1981, the president had even spoken of the possibility of a limited nuclear war in Europe.[33] In 1982, administration statements revealed the new policy. Thomas C. Reed, a consultant to the National Security Council, told an audience of the president's view that "prevailing with pride is the principal new ingredient of American security policy."[34] (He defined *prevailing* as reversing the geographic expansion of Soviet political influence and military presence in world politics.) The word *prevail* also ran through a strategic guidance statement by Defense secretary Weinberger released that year, applying the term to the administration's strategy for a protracted nuclear war.[35]

Statements such as these, combined with growing concern over mounting deficits (which were now skyrocketing to over $100 billion and would continue climbing through Reagan's first term), fueled opposition to the president's aggressive rearmament plans. Critics of the defense buildup would not be able to reverse or abort it, but they were able to affect Reagan's rhetoric and administration policy.

Anticipating trouble, the administration went on the offensive. Speaking before a conservative group in February, the president made it clear that the defense buildup took priority even over his cherished goal of a balanced budget:

> The protection of this nation's security is the most solemn duty of any President, and that is why I've asked for substantial increases in our defense budget—substantial, but not excessive. . . . During the campaign I was asked any number of times: If I were faced with a choice of balancing the budget or restoring our national defenses, what would I do? Every time I said, "Restore our defenses." And every time I was applauded.[36]

The Pentagon also got into the act, with a lobbying campaign that claimed that the defense budget had been purged of all waste and inefficiencies. Spokesmen such as Deputy Secretary of Defense Frank C. Carlucci further argued that the administration was buying weapons more efficiently by purchasing them before inflation raised costs further. Moreover, Defense also adopted another tactic that made budget cutting all the more difficult. No matter how hard he was pressed on where military spending might be trimmed, Secretary Weinberger refused to specify any areas for spending reductions. He argued that every dollar requested was essential; thus, any cuts would be dangerous.[37]

Through the first half of 1982, the White House and Congress were deadlocked over the budget, particularly the defense request. All the while, a grassroots nuclear-freeze lobbying campaign was acquiring momentum. This movement called on the superpowers to begin a freeze on the testing, production, and deployment of all nuclear weapons or nuclear delivery systems, such as bombers. Emboldened by the campaign, congressional critics put pressure on President Reagan to demonstrate his commitment to peace even as he called for greater military power.

In response, Reagan modified his rhetoric and his policies. In speeches and exchanges with reporters, the president identified himself with the goal of freeze advocates: peace. He argued that he, too, respected and shared their dream of world peace, but that a freeze could come only after the United States had eliminated the Soviet Union's advantage in nuclear weapons. Furthermore, on May 9 he unveiled a negotiating offer for the Strategic Arms

Reduction Talks (START) going on with Moscow that would sharply reduce land-based missiles held by the superpowers.[38]

As the summer wore on, however, the freeze movement continued to press its case.[39] It was powered by effective organizing and public concern about the possibilities of nuclear war. In August, the campaign reached its climax, with the House of Representatives scheduled to vote on a freeze resolution. The White House intensified its lobbying, offering moderate Republicans and conservative Democrats an alternative resolution to support that used the term *freeze* but defined it in a way that supported the president's "build, then freeze" logic.[40] Reagan then warned that a freeze would undermine American arms negotiators, while his arms-control ambassador (General Edward Rowny) phoned Capitol Hill from Geneva to emphasize the point.[41] The freeze resolution failed in the House by one vote.

Skillful lobbying helped the president, but so did public opinion. A CBS News/*New York Times* poll in May showed that 52 percent of the respondents trusted Reagan to make the right kind of decisions about control of nuclear weapons.[42] Other polls also indicated that a majority of the American people continued to believe that the United States should be stronger than the Soviet Union militarily (56 percent in January 1982 and 51 percent in November).[43]

After surviving the freeze fight, the president tried to shepherd his defense proposal through the remainder of the 1982 congressional budget process. Public opinion continued to support him. Polls indicated that a majority of the nation believed that spending for defense was too little/about right.[44] But this overall and general support was backed by powerful lobbying by the defense industry, which is influential in Congress because the vast majority of districts are home to military bases and/or defense-contracting businesses. While there was a feeling in Congress that defense had been underfunded during the Carter years, *National Journal* also noted the "happy coincidence between the Pentagon's emphasis on procurement and special-interest lobbying."[45] One congressional committee staff aide observed: "The most intense pressures are in the procurement and research and development accounts, where you have all the built-in special interests . . . when we cut operations and maintenance or military personnel, we hardly hear a murmur."[46]

After protracted negotiations between the White House and Capitol Hill, in December the president was forced to accept a cut of about 7 percent from his original request. The bill did, however, maintain an overall increase in defense spending. The cut was "the largest congressional swipe at a defense bill in years,"[47] but it was also much less significant than it appeared. As *Congressional Quarterly* concluded: "Despite the size of the congressional reduction, most of it came from the routine cheeseparing rather than dramatic changes in the shape of Reagan's program.[48] The bulk of the cuts came from items such as a smaller pay raise (which was also imposed on all federal employees) and less money for fuel (possible largely because of falling oil prices). The only major defeats that Reagan experienced were when the House refused to support his basing plan for the controversial MX missile and his plans to resume production of chemical weapons.

As he ended his second year in office, Ronald Reagan could claim success in that he had secured a sizable increase in defense spending. Assessing him at midterm, observers foresaw "a rosy future" for defense.[49] Both the B-1 bomber and the navy's plans for two additional nuclear-powered aircraft carriers had been approved. "Once started, these big-ticket procurement programs are all but unstoppable and will affect the shape of defense planning for years to come."[50]

Over the next two years, Ronald Reagan continued to press his case for rearmament. But his message contained new elements. Responding to his critics and to public unease about war, he would put greater stress in his rhetoric on his desire for peace and initiatives in the area of arms control. He was, however, for "peace through strength." He would also reveal to the nation his controversial "vision of the future" of American defense.

Reagan's critics had been hitting him effectively on the issue of peace. They charged that the president was risking war by his harsh talk and defense buildup. They faulted him for his opposition to a nuclear freeze and for not pursuing arms control vigorously enough. The prospects for Reagan's rearmament program remained good, but he could not ignore his critics or the pressure on him from factors such as the continuing nuclear-freeze campaign. Defeat in the House in 1982 had not slowed that movement, only stimulated it to continue trying.

In response, the president framed his appeals for greater defense spending with arguments about his interest in peace and the wisdom of a policy of peace through strength. In his 1983 State of the Union Address, for example, he reiterated his complaint about the "neglect of the last decade" for defense and boasted of his "realistic military strategy." But then he quickly turned to arms control, blaming the Soviet Union for the absence of an agreement.

> For our part, we're vigorously pursuing arms reduction negotiations with the Soviet Union. . . . With firmness and dedication, we'll continue to negotiate. Deep down, the Soviets must know it's in their interest as well as ours to prevent a wasteful arms race.[51]

In a February 1983 radio address to the nation on defense spending, he held to that approach, arguing: "If we continue our past pattern of only rebuilding our defenses in fits and starts, we will never convince the Soviets that it's in their interests to behave with restraint and negotiate genuine arms reductions."[52] The message had not changed, only the terms in which it was presented. But the old Reagan was still very much alive. It was in March, speaking to a group of evangelical Christians, that he made his controversial reference to the Soviet Union as an "evil empire."[53]

The controversy over that comment had barely subsided when the president introduced his "vision of the future" in a nationally televised speech on the defense budget. Along with appeals for money for defense and restatement of his desire for peace, Reagan unveiled his Strategic Defense Initiative (SDI), a program for research aimed at developing the technological capability to "intercept and destroy strategic ballistic missiles before they reached our own soil or that of our allies."[54] Such a development, he argued, would enable "free people [to] live secure in the knowledge that their security did not rest upon the threat of instant U.S. retaliation to deter a Soviet attack."[55] The idea of defense against nuclear attack was not new—each of the superpowers had experimented with antiballistic missile (ABM) systems and restricted their development through the SALT I agreement—

but what Reagan proposed was a space-based shield against all missile attacks.

The idea, soon called "star wars" by its critics, became the center of a raging controversy. The biggest issue was whether the president's "vision" was even technologically feasible, or whether such a system would really increase security. Another issue was cost: the 1983 budget proposal already included about $1 billion for research in this area, but Reagan's new emphasis on it suggested that much more would be needed to develop the technology.

The president's vision became part of his pitch on defense, but he continued to emphasize his other themes of peace and strength. Despite Reagan's efforts to appear as a man of peace, [56] the House, on May 4, 1983, voted in favor of a nuclear-freeze resolution. But the president stood his ground, counting on the Republican Senate to assist him. And on October 31 it did indeed defeat a freeze proposal.

Although he was concerned about the possibility of being embarrassed and repudiated by a congressional resolution in favor of a freeze, President Reagan never really had to worry about the fate of his defense buildup.[57] It continued to win support in Congress, even from the pro-freeze House.[58]

In the final year of Reagan's first term, Congress and the White House repeated the same negotiation process over again. Again, the president called for continued increases in his defense proposal for the FY 1985. Again, he established the same priorities. Again, he called for a "real" increase in military spending above what Congress would accept.[59] And again, after months of discussions and deals, Reagan would get most of what he wanted.[60]

Meanwhile, President Reagan's defense buildup became an issue in the 1984 presidential campaign. The Democrats, led by former vice president Walter Mondale, charged that Reagan's rearmament program was excessive, that it drove up deficits while ignoring social and economic problems on the domestic front, and that it threatened nuclear war.[61] In a debate with the president, Mondale asked voters to consider the results of the Reagan rearmament. "The President's question is: Are you better off? . . . Are we better off with this arms race? Will we be better off if we start this star wars escalation into the heavens?"[62] Mondale's answer, of course, was negative.

Responding to such charges, the president accused his critics of wanting to return to the "failed policies of the past" and argued that only through his policies would peace eventually come. In an address to the nation on the eve of the election, he reiterated the familiar theme: "We can keep this nation strong enough to protect freedom for us, for our children and our children's children. And one day, all nations can begin to reduce nuclear weapons and ultimately banish them. . . ."[63]

In the end, Ronald Reagan handily won reelection. Defense and foreign policy were certainly not the only issues of the campaign, but they did play a role in the president's victory. Although 28 percent of the nation, in April 1984, thought that military spending ought to be decreased, 73 percent thought it was about right or too little.[64] Two-thirds of the respondents to an October 1984 CBS News/*New York Times* poll believed that Republicans would do a better job of keeping America strong.[65] Overall, a majority of the nation was satisfied with President Reagan's performance in defense and foreign affairs.[66] Reviewing public opinion in 1984, Scott Keeter concluded:

After four years of relative peace, most of the public no longer feared that a reckless Reagan would provoke a war. Over 60 percent of those interviewed by CBS News/*New York Times* in October said they weren't worried that, if re-elected, the President might get us into war. While much of the public quarreled with specific elements of Reagan's foreign and military policy, it clearly liked the image of certitude and strength. Even if the United States couldn't control the world as it once did, many people liked a President who acted as if it could.[67]

WORLD LEADERSHIP: IMPLEMENTING THE POLICY ABROAD

The international environment was important to Ronald Reagan's defense program in two ways: First, there was the question of how the Soviet Union and America's allies would react to the president's program. Second, Reagan needed allied cooperation to implement a vital part of his defense buildup.

But President Reagan belied this importance by his behavior during his first year in office. Devoting most of his attention and energy to winning congressional approval of his economic policies and rearmament, the chief executive paid little attention to international events. When he did take note of world politics, it was primarily to reiterate the usual anticommunist themes: Soviet dominance of Eastern Europe (attacking Soviet intervention in the 1981 suppression of the solidarity movement by the Polish communist government); instability in the Third World (Central America and the Middle East); and the need for the West to stand firm against a common enemy (as in the Soviet gas-pipeline dispute).

But he did make two moves that were relevant to his defense buildup. The first was a decision to proceed with the deployment of Pershing II and ground-launched cruise missiles in Europe. In 1979, at the insistence of German chancellor Helmut Schmidt, NATO had decided to deploy these weapons in order to counteract new Soviet SS-20 intermediate missiles aimed at Western Europe.[68] President Reagan decided to proceed with this plan, even dispatching Secretary of State Haig to New York in November 1981 to meet with Soviet foreign minister Andrey Gromyko. At that meeting, Haig made clear to his counterpart that the United States would proceed with deployment because it countered the Soviet buildup. Meanwhile, a protest movement (against the missiles and in favor of a nuclear freeze) was gaining momentum in Germany and Britain. This resistance, as well as the the administration's opposition to European purchases of natural gas from a new Soviet gas pipeline, put strains in the NATO Alliance. Allied governments were committed to the missile plan and determined to resist their own protestors, but they nevertheless felt caught in the middle of a struggle between the superpowers.[69]

The alliance held together, but the incident affected President Reagan's approach to Europe. After George Shultz became secretary of state, American opposition to the pipeline was dropped. The president began to emphasize his desire for peace (this was also in response to domestic pressures) and in November 1981 undertook a second major initiative: he proposed to the

Soviets the *zero option* for European missiles—that is, a plan in which the United States would forego the deployment of Pershing II and cruise missiles for NATO (scheduled for 1984) if the Soviet Union would remove its SS-20s and other intermediate-range missiles.[70] The idea went nowhere with the Soviet Union, but it became the basis for negotiations and helped to partially convince America's allies of the president's commitment to peace.*

During 1982, Ronald Reagan settled into the pattern for dealing with the world that would characterize the rest of his first term in office. Not surprisingly, it resembled his behavior at home, combining rhetoric about the superiority of the West and the need for strength with talk about his desire for and determination to seek peace. At Eureka College (Reagan's alma mater) in May, he proposed that the United States and Soviet Union agree to drastically reduce their land-based missiles.[71]

Soviet leader Leonid Brezhnev immediately rejected Reagan's proposal. He argued that the president's plan would allow the United States to go on developing the weapons it wanted, such as the cruise missile (a robot missile capable of low-altitude flight and complex flight plans), while at the same time cutting the Soviet advantage in heavy land-based missiles.[72] Nevertheless, the two sides agreed to go on observing the force limits imposed by the unratified SALT II treaty (which had been put on hold by the Senate following the 1979 Soviet invasion of Afghanistan).

Indeed, despite the fact that Reagan had been an outspoken critic of Jimmy Carter's SALT II agreement, calling it "fatally flawed," he was now informally observing the treaty's limits and proposing to move beyond it with his strategic arms reduction (START) plan. This action put the president in an interesting position: he ensured that SALT II would have a longer life than even President Carter could have hoped for it. Although he refused to formally endorse it, Reagan was now obeying the treaty (and would even extend its life beyond the pact's own deadline in 1985) by means of Parallel Unilateral Policy Declarations (PUPD). These devices, essentially parallel statements issued by the two superpowers pledging adherence to the treaty, enabled Reagan to take firm control of American arms-control policy.[73] Thus, while the United States went along with an unratified agreement, the president was free to negotiate another one.

Reagan was not, however, in a hurry to conclude an arms accord. Indeed, the White House would soon announce that the United States would not renew negotiations with the Soviet Union for a ban on all nuclear testing, nor would the president ask for Senate approval of treaties (already concluded but unratified) to limit the size of underground nuclear tests.[74] Reagan's rearmament program would require tests of new weapons. As the president repeatedly made clear, he believed that his defense buildup had to precede any arms pact.

Meanwhile, the strains in NATO were healing and the president and gaining experience in the international arena. His efforts to patch up the Atlantic Alliance included a trip to Europe in June 1982, in part to attend a Western economic summit in France, but also to take his message directly to allied leaders. Speaking to the British Parliament in June 1982, President

---

*In 1988, an Intermediate Nuclear Forces Treaty between the superpowers was ratified. After extensive negotiation, it contained the zero option proposed seven years before.

Reagan contrasted democracy and communism, arguing that with resolve the West would ultimately defeat the Soviet Union. Ronald Reagan, the arch-conservative politician, was now attempting to transform himself into Ronald Reagan the statesman:

> Our military strength is a prerequisite to peace, but let it be clear we maintain this strength in the hope it will never be used, for the ultimate determinant in the struggle that's now going on in the world will not be bombs and rockets, but a test of wills and ideas, a trial of spiritual resolve, the values we hold, the beliefs we cherish, the ideals to which we are dedicated.[75]

A few days later, speaking to a United Nations General Assembly session devoted to disarmament, Reagan took his message to the international community beyond American allies. First, he explained that his accession to the presidency had affected his outlook on war: "Since coming to the Presidency, the enormity of the responsibility of this office has made my commitment [to peace] even deeper. I believe that responsibility is shared by all of us here today."[76] Then he proceeded to justify his skepticism about arms-limitation pacts:

> Agreements on arms control and disarmament can be useful in reinforcing peace; but they're not magic. We should not confuse the signing of agreements with the solving of problems. Simply collecting agreements will not bring peace. Agreements genuinely enforce peace only when they are kept. Otherwise we're building a paper castle that will be blown away by the winds of war.[77]

Finally, he recited the efforts of his administration to shape agreements that could lead to stability and peace.

Reagan's new message would be repeated in a number of international forums, from interviews with foreign journalists to the annual economic summit of the leaders of major industrial democracies to speeches before the legislatures of other nations.[78] In May of 1983, the president hosted the annual economic summit at Williamsburg, Virginia. This gathering, which brought together many of the nation's European allies and the Japanese prime minister, issued a statement on security issues that gave support to the "peace and strength" message of Reagan the statesman:

> ... it is our first duty to defend the freedom and justice on which our democracies are based. To this end, we shall maintain sufficient military strength to deter any attack, to counter any threat, and to ensure the peace. . . . We wish to achieve lower levels of arms through serious arms control negotiations. . . . The security of our countries is indivisible. . . . Attempts to avoid serious negotiation by seeking to influence public opinion in our countries will fail.[79]

Despite this endorsement, Reagan's policies continued to meet resistance both in Western Europe and the Soviet Union. Allied leaders stood behind the president, but there were continued protests in West Germany and Britain against the missiles. Toward the end of 1983, the Soviet government announced that it would not negotiate on intermediate nuclear forces while the United States proceeded with deployment in Europe of Pershing II missiles.[80] Reagan responded with an address "to the nation and other countries"[81] that expressed more sorrow than anger at the Soviet decision. When the NATO missiles were deployed in 1984, the Soviet defense minister responded by announcing that additional nuclear submarines would be stationed in waters off of the United States and that more missiles would be added to the East bloc's European arsenal.[82] Relations between the two nations appeared to be at a low point.

Nevertheless, the situation was much less clear than these actions suggested. Just as he was proceeding with his rearmament program and pushing ahead with missile deployment, Reagan the statesman was offering an olive branch to his adversaries. In his January 1984 address, the president asserted that his administration was interested in developing a better working relationship with the Soviet leaders:

> If the Soviet Government wants peace, then there will be peace. Together we can strengthen peace, reduce the level of arms, and know in doing so that we have helped fulfill the hopes and dreams of those we represent and, indeed, of people everywhere. Let us begin now.[83]

Because of such mixed signals, observers asked, "Who's the real Reagan behind U.S. Soviet policy?"[84]

The probable answer is that both were the "real Reagan." He believed in peace but also that military strength was the only means to bring his adversaries to a bargain. But the president did not have to resolve any differences between the two messages he was sending because his campaign for rearmament did not require agreement with the Soviet Union. Reagan needed only the compliance of the allies in deploying the Pershing II and cruise missiles. He got that, and NATO held together. He was less interested in an arms deal, so could resist both European protestors and Soviet leaders.

The "real Reagan" believed in both dimensions of "peace through strength," but found that international audiences were more interested in hearing about the former. Allied leaders essentially supported his defense buildup but because of their own domestic pressures wanted the president to emphasize responsible statesmanship. Nonaligned nations were concerned about growing tensions between the United States and Soviet Union. Therefore, Reagan's rhetoric came to stress peace while his actions emphasized strength. As long as he put his defense buildup first, which could be won at home, then he could focus on the role of statesman when he faced the world.

RONALD REAGAN AS WORLD LEADER

Ronald Reagan saw world politics as a contest between the "evil empire" of the Soviet Union and America's "shining city on a hill." He came to the presidency proclaiming that he would restore the might and the resolve of the United States, so it could stand up to Moscow and anyone else who might challenge American interests. His rearmament plan was not revolutionary, but it did represent a significant change in American policy.

As a percentage of the national budget, the military portion rose from 22.6 percent in 1981 to 26.8 percent in 1984, reflecting what one observer called a "substantial reallocation of resources from domestic programs to defense."[85] Although the president came to office without a specific outline for his defense buildup, he had long been associated with a set of broad policy goals that guided his campaign for military superiority over the next four years. He was for "peace through strength," an unparalleled military machine, and an end to actions that had "unilaterally disarmed" the nation while the Soviet Union achieved a "clear advantage" in weapons. He transformed this sweeping language into policy by committing to large increases in defense spending, concentrating on procurement of new weapons, and by employing rhetoric both to sell his plans and to assert American power.

How are we to account for Reagan's success? There was a tendency among many of the president's critics to attribute his achievements to his personality and skillful political bargaining at important junctures. But such facile explanations are inadequate. While Reagan's charm at times disarmed his opponents and smoothed over disagreements, it could not move mountains. It enabled him to establish and maintain congenial relations with congressional and allied leaders, but it alone could not reshape policy. Bargaining helped, but does not explain why the president's agenda was repeatedly adopted, even in the face of mounting deficits and Soviet resistance. In pushing for a military buildup, Reagan was not fighting an uphill battle for passage of a single bill. Rather, he managed to win support for rearmament over a four-year period. Therefore, we must see the larger picture around the president if we are to understand the fate of his program.

Timing played a key role in Reagan's success. Indeed, it is not too much of an exaggeration to say that he was riding a wave. As Samuel Huntington has noted, American defense spending has followed a cyclical pattern since the end of World War II.[86] Reagan's good fortune was to come to the White House just as the third cycle was cresting, when there was widespread support for a military buildup among security experts, Congress, and the general public. He was thus presented with a golden opportunity to push for rearmament. He had been calling for a stronger defense for years but was often out of step with the times. By 1981, however, Americans wanted to be reassured that their nation had not lost its power in the world. After the Vietnam War, the OPEC oil embargo, the Iranian hostage crisis, the Soviet invasion of Afghanistan, and other incidents that suggested the decline of national might, Americans were ready for Ronald Reagan's message. They agreed with him that national defense had been neglected for nearly a decade. Indeed, support for military spending reached its peak even before Reagan took office. He gave voice to the consensus and helped to keep it alive.

Furthermore, Reagan's first term coincided with a leadership crisis in the Soviet Union. From 1981 to 1984, the "evil empire" was headed by three old and sick leaders in succession—Leonid Brezhnev, Yuri Andropov, and Konstantin Chernenko. The upshot of this development was to contribute to a general sense of instability in world politics and to rule out a strong challenge to American assertiveness during Reagan's first term.

Reagan was careful to create the right image. Throughout his tenure in office, he engaged in a variety of activities meant to convey the picture of a popular, confident, and skillful president at work: photo opportunities, effective staging and backdrops for speeches, and careful control of press coverage to prevent the media from showing him in a bad light.

More importantly, he spoke regularly on behalf of his rearmament program, employing his capacity for strong, direct language and on his polished style of delivery. He used television, radio, and a succession of public appearances to express his goals and sell his plans. In 1981, his proposal of the zero option in Europe turned the tide for the B-1 bomber, making it a "bargaining chip." When in 1982 it became apparent that the public was concerned about nuclear weapons and the possibility of war, Reagan was careful to begin emphasizing his desire for peace even while making his pitch for strength. In 1983, he used the Williamsburg summit to paint a self-portrait as leader of the West. And in 1984, he combined governing with campaigning to sell his policies along with himself.

Reagan's rhetoric was important to his success in several respects.[87] First, it gave his policies momentum. With an emotional, take-charge, optimistic approach, the president spoke of what he wanted to achieve in broad and comprehensible terms. He was trying to sustain the pro-defense climate that made possible his early victories. Second, the president's rhetoric was simple. Ronald Reagan did not achieve popularity as a public speaker for ringing Churchillian phrases, but for plain speech. As Roderick Hart has observed: "His words never force his listeners to imagine things they are incapable of imagining or require that they make a taxing intellectual association. . . . His language is drawn from life as it is lived most simply."[88] For example, Reagan's 1983 star wars speech made that technology, which was in reality no more than a combination of theory and some experimental evidence, seem obvious and within easy grasp of American science. Finally, Reagan's rhetoric evoked national traditions. For example, in his 1984 speech at the scene of the D-day invasion, Reagan identified his goals and programs with powerful symbols of freedom.

Not surprisingly, the president's message was well received in the bureaucracy. The Defense Department certainly supported the president in his quest for greater military power, although by 1984 there were complaints surfacing that the emphasis on procurement had not been sufficiently directed toward improving the readiness of American forces. An internal Defense Department memorandum by Lawrence Korb, assistant secretary for manpower and reserve affairs, questioned assertions by Secretary Weinberger that readiness had been restored after years of neglect.[89] Interestingly, however, Korb's criticisms, and similar complaints, were directed at the president's subordinate and not at the chief executive himself.

There were also objections from defense experts, but they were powerless to stop or change Reagan's rearmament program. Despite suggestions that the administration lacked an overall strategy or that its priorities were wrong, the buildup proceeded. In fact, the experts generally supported the broad outlines of the president's program, even if they faulted the administration for too much emphasis on procurement or for being too friendly with defense contractors.

Reagan's critics on Capitol Hill were also unable to get the administration to change course. Of course, the Republican Senate was an important asset. Even when they disagreed, the president could count on most of his fellow partisans to stand with him. This support enabled Reagan to put pressure on the House and win significant victories in 1981. But Democrats in Congress also supported the president's program, whether because they agreed with it, because it coincided with constituent interests, or because the public endorsed the buildup.

Obviously Reagan's primary reliance on rhetoric and compromise was further enhanced by the administration's employment of traditional political tactics and by the president's own popular public image. In addition, Ronald Reagan drew on the usual deference given presidents by Congress and the public in foreign policy matters. In sum, this was a president who knew where he wanted to go and who was willing to do what was politically necessary in order to get there.

This included campaigning abroad, for if the administration's agenda appeared to alienate America's allies, then Reagan's rearmament plans would be that much more difficult to usher through the domestic policy—making process. The chief target of the president's policies and rhetoric was the Soviet Union. But there was little the Soviets could do to interfere with his plans. Part of the problem was that the president did not really need much from them. He needed to show that he was negotiating over arms reductions, but a central tenet of his policy was to build first and then discuss cuts. Had Reagan been eager for an arms treaty, Moscow might have had more leverage over his behavior. Had the Kremlin been led by someone more skillful (such as Gorbachev), the Soviet Union might have been more intransigent (for example, by not talking at all) or more effective at separating Europe from the United States in the first half of Reagan's term. But as the situation presented itself, President Reagan could press on with his program even in the face of resistance from Moscow.

In contrast, Reagan more clearly needed America's allies to demonstrate his leadership capacity outside of the United States and to carry out the planned deployment of NATO missiles. After initial strains in allied relations, Reagan was able to keep the nation's friends in line by balancing his rhetoric on strength with his rhetoric on peace. In addition, both he and Secretary of State Shultz endeavored to promote allied unity through personal contacts at summits and other meetings between American and foreign leaders. Using this approach, the president won at least a partial vindication in 1983 when the heads of the seven industrial democracies pledged support to Western solidarity on security issues.

Reagan's style of leadership was clearly effective, but it also entailed a number of significant costs. For example, as we have seen, his emphasis on rhetoric was very important throughout the period 1981 to 1984. As Roderick Hart has put it, the president used rhetoric to communicate his goals, justify his buildup, undercut opposition, qualify his tough talk with the soothing rhetoric of peace, and keep himself popular and in the public eye. Overall, Reagan used it to put his critics, whether at home or abroad, on the defensive. Of course, it was rhetoric that also engendered opposition to the president as a warmonger and an ideologue. Talk about limited nuclear war contributed to this image among some observers and could have threatened his plans. Only by modifying his language could statesman Reagan salvage what the old Ronald Reagan might lose.

The president's engaging personality made his rhetoric all the more effective but did not work magic in his cause. Opponents took to referring to Reagan as "the Teflon president" because problems and failures seemed not to "stick" to him. But he was not made of Teflon. Rather, he was able to deflect criticism by several tactics: appearing to ignore it while modifying his rhetoric, using delegation to allow subordinates such as Weinberger to absorb attacks, and spreading both credit and blame for his policies by compromising with Congress.

The president's willingness to compromise also illustrates how his style helped him, but at a cost. His overall goal was rearmament, so he was willing to accept some trimming in his annual budget requests so long as total military spending continued to grow steadily. Thus, Reagan got the increase he desired, while Congress was able to reduce those aspects of defense that were politically easiest to cut. But the cost was in letting domestic politics drive the defense buildup.

Problems such as these seldom touched the president, however, because he deflected criticism to subordinates. But his use of delegation also meant that the president did not always control what his subordinates were doing (as became more apparent during the Iran-Contra affair).

In the end, Reagan got most of what he wanted, although a final cost was involved. His campaign for rearmament came at the price of huge deficits in the federal budget, the consequences of which have not yet been realized or fully understood. Moreover, because the buildup invested heavily in procurement, it committed the nation to a series of multiyear contracts for new weapons purchases. Such a commitment meant that Reagan's program increased the "uncontrollability" of the federal budget, because a larger share of future appropriations were, in effect, already spent. Therefore, Congress and Reagan's successors would be paying for his defense buildup for many years.

By the end of his first term, however, Ronald Reagan had reordered national priorities in accordance with his own vision and won at least general support of his policies from America's allies. Whether Reagan made the United States more secure is an open question. In any case, what is clear is that after four years in the Oval Office, Ronald Reagan's impact on world politics was considerable.

Notes

1. On Reagan's prepolitical career, see Anne Edwards, *Early Reagan* (New York: William Morrow and Co. 1987); Lou Cannon, *Reagan* (New York: G.P. Putnam's Sons, 1982); Garry Wills, *Reagan's America* (Garden City, N.Y.: Doubleday, 1987); and Ronald Reagan and Richard G. Hubler, *Where's the Rest of Me?* (New York: Dell, 1965). Edwards has the most thorough treatment of Reagan's acting career, including a list of all of his films.

2. Cannon, pp. 157–65.

3. Ibid., p. 13.

4. Quoted in Hedrick Smith, "Reagan's World," in *Reagan: The Man, the President,* ed. Hedrick Smith et al. (New York: Macmillan, 1980), p. 100.

5. Ibid.

6. Cannon, p. 298. On the "Reagan Revolution," see Martin Anderson, *Revolution* (San Diego: Harcourt Brace Jovanovich, 1988), pp. xvii–xviii.

7. Wilson Carey McWilliams, "The Meaning of the Election," in *The Election of 1984,* ed. Gerald Pomper (Chatham, N.J.: Chatham House, 1985), pp. 157–83.

8. William K. Muir, Jr., "Ronald Reagan: The Primacy of Rhetoric," in *Leadership and the Modern Presidency*, ed. Fred I. Greenstein (Cambridge, Mass.: Harvard Univ. Press, 1988), pp. 260–95. On the importance of rhetoric to Reagan's foreign policy, see Mary Stuckey, *Playing the Game: The Presidential Rhetoric of Ronald Reagan* (New York: Praeger, 1990).

9. Roderick Hart, *The Sound of Leadership: Presidential Communication in the Modern Age* (Chicago: Univ. of Chicago Press, 1987), p. 14.

10. Quoted in Muir, p. 278.

11. Also referred to as "humanitarian" aid. For an overview, see *U.S. Foreign Policy: The Reagan Imprint* (Washington: Congressional Quarterly, Inc., 1986), chapter 3, especially pp. 68–73. For a discussion of rhetoric versus compromise in Reagan foreign policy, see Coral Bell, "From Carter to Reagan," in *The Reagan Foreign Policy*, ed. William G. Hyland, (New York: Meridian, 1987), pp. 57–77.

12. See Samuel P. Huntington, "The Defense Policy of the Reagan Administration," in *The Reagan Presidency: An Early Assessment*, ed. Fred I. Greenstein, (Baltimore: Johns Hopkins Univ. Press, 1983), pp. 82–116. See also *National Journal* (February 4, 1984): pp. 208–9. The best description of the internal politics of the Reagan foreign policy government during the first two years is in I. M. Destler, "The Evolution of Reagan Foreign Policy," in *The Reagan Presidency*, pp. 117–58.

13. Much has been written about the Reagan White House "troika." For a description of its creation, see Laurence I. Barrett, *Gambling with History: Reagan in the White House* (New York: Penguin, 1984), chapter 4. See also Colin Campbell, S.J., *Managing the Presidency* (Pittsburgh: Univ. of Pittsburgh Press, 1986), pp. 93–105; Cannon, chapter 22; and John H. Kessel, "The Structures of the Reagan White House," *American Journal of Political Science* 28 (May 1984): pp. 231–58.

14. Quoted in Destler, p. 118.

15. Haig's side of the story is told in detail in Alexander Haig, *Caveat* (New York: Macmillan, 1984). See also Destler, especially pp. 118–24; and Barrett, p. 232.

16. Smith, p. 98.

17. The phrase was repeated in several of Reagan's speeches. See William G. Hyland, "Introduction," in *The Reagan Foreign Policy*, p. ix.

18. *Congressional Quarterly Almanac 1981* (Washington: 1982), p. 191. For further discussion of Reagan's approach to defense, see Huntington, *op. cit.*; Richard Burt, "Arms and the Man," in *Reagan the Man, the President*, pp. 83–94; and Barry R. Posen and Stephen W. Van Evera, "Reagan Administration Defense Policy: Departure from Containment," in *Eagle Resurgent?*, ed. Kenneth Oye et al. (Boston: Little, Brown, 1983), pp. 75–114.

19. *Public Papers of the President* (February 18, 1981), p. 112.

20. *Newsweek*, 8 June 1981, p. 28.

21. Donald D. Holt, "A Defense Budget for the 1980s," *Fortune*, 26 January 1981, p. 52.

22. *National Journal*, 24 January 1981, pp. 128–32.

23. Quoted in *Newsweek*, 8 June 1981, p. 28.

24. Quoted in *Newsweek*, 18 May 1981, p. 41.

25. Ibid. See also James Fallows, *National Defense* (New York: Random House, 1981).

26. Quoted in *Newsweek*, 8 June 1981, p. 28. For a similar view, see Destler, p. 88.

27. Ibid., p. 29.

28. *Public Opinion* (April/May 1983), p. 28. See also Daniel Yankelovich and Larry Kaagan, "Assertive America," in *The Reagan Foreign Policy*, pp. 1–18.

29. Cited in Huntington, p. 105.

30. *New York Times*, 15 May 1981, p. 15.

31. *Public Papers* (May 27, 1981), p. 462.

32. *CQ Almanac 1981*, p. 201.

33. See Barrett, p. 308.

34. *New York Times*, 17 June 1981, p. A23.

35. Ibid. See also Huntington, pp. 101–4.

36. *Public Papers* (February 26, 1982), p. 228.

37. *CQ Almanac 1982* (Washington: 1983), pp. 73–74.

38. *Public Papers* (May 9, 1982), pp. 580–86.

39. *CQ Almanac 1982*, p. 74.

40. Ibid., p. 75.

41. Ibid., p. 75.

42. *Public Opinion* (August/September 1982), p. 40.

43. *Public Opinion* (August/September 1983), p. 30.

44. Ibid.

45. *National Journal*, 16 October 1982, p. 1761.

46. Ibid.

47. *CQ Almanac 1982*, p. 74.

48. Ibid., p. 74.

49. *National Journal*, 1 January 1983, p. 11.

50. Ibid.

51. *Public Papers* (January 25, 1983), p. 108.

52. Ibid.

53. *Public Papers* (March 8, 1983), p. 364.

54. Reprinted in *Congressional Quarterly Weekly Report* (March 26, 1983): pp. 632–33. For an inside view, see Anderson, pp. 75–79.

55. Ibid. For a discussion of the debate over star wars, see *National Journal*, 7 January 1984, pp. 12–17.

56. *Public Papers* (March 31, 1983), p. 483.

57. For an extended discussion of this point, see Anderson, p. 241.

58. *CQ Almanac 1984* (Washington: 1985), p. 33.

59. Ibid.

60. Ibid., p. 33.

61. See Henry A. Plotkin, "Issues in the Campaign," in *The Election of 1984*, (Chatham, NJ: Chatham House, 1985) pp. 35–59.

62. *Public Papers* (October 7, 1984), p. 1461.

63. *Public Papers* (November 5, 1984), p. 1796.

64. *Public Opinion* (April/May 1984), p. 36.

65. Cited in Scott Keeter, "Public Opinion in 1984," in *The Election of 1984*, p. 100.

66. Ibid., pp. 100–101.

67. Ibid., p. 100.

68. Haig, p. 226. See also Miles Kahler, "The United States and Western Europe," in *Eagle Resurgent?*, pp. 306–10.

69. On European reactions to Reagan, see Kahler, *op. cit.*, and Robert Osgood, "The Revitalization of Containment," in *The Reagan Foreign Policy*, pp. 32–36.

70. Destler, pp. 144–45.

71. *Public Papers* (May 9, 1982), pp. 580–86.

72. Amos Yoder, *The Conduct of American Foreign Policy Since World War II* (New York: Pergamon, 1988), p. 170.

73. Ryan J. Barilleaux, "Executive Non-Agreements and the Presidential Congressional Struggle in Foreign Affairs," *World Affairs* 148 (Spring 1986): pp. 217–27.

74. Yoder, p. 169. See also Osgood, *loc. cit.*

75. *Public Papers* (June 8, 1982), p. 747.

76. *Public Papers* (June 17, 1982), p. 785.

77. Ibid.

78. For examples, see *Public Papers* (May 10, 1983), pp. 674–75; (November 11, 1983), pp. 1574–579; and (December 22, 1983), pp. 12–17.

79. *Public Papers* (May 30, 1983), p. 795.

80. Yoder, p. 170.

81. *Public Papers* (January 16, 1984), p. 40–44.

82. Yoder, p. 171.

83. *Public Papers* (January 16, 1984), p. 44.

84. *National Journal,* 15 September 1984, p. 1705.

85. Plotkin, p. 54.

86. Huntington, pp. 82–88.

87. Discussed in Roderick Hart, *Verbal Style and the Presidency* (Orlando, Fla.: Academic Press, 1984); Robert E. Denton, Jr., *The Primetime Presidency of Ronald Reagan* (New York: Praeger, 1988); and Hart, *The Sound of Leadership,* esp. pp. 14–15.

88. Hart, *Verbal Style,* p. 224.

89. *National Journal,* 25 February 1984, pp. 356–60.

10

Comments, Comparisons, and Conclusions

I find that throughout our own history the greatest strides occur when courageous and gifted leaders either seize the opportunity or create it.
—Harry S Truman

The linchpin of this book is leadership. The questions to which we particularly address ourselves center on the presidents' capacities for initiating change at the international level. The three areas of inquiry that are threaded through the analysis include the leader, his followers, and the domestic and foreign contexts within which leadership—or the attempt at leadership—took place. Moreover, we have been especially interested in process. By what means did presidents try to shape and implement foreign policy? And which leadership tactics were the most likely to succeed?

Without stopping at this point to wrestle once more with the distinctions among power, authority, and influence, we offer instead a simple taxonomy of leadership tactics employed by each of the presidents discussed in this book:

1. *Politics* refers to leadership attempts relying primarily on interpersonal exchange.
2. *Propaganda* refers to leadership attempts relying primarily on the manipulation of verbal communications.
3. *Diplomacy* refers to leadership attempts relying primarily on negotiation.
4. *Economics* refers to leadership attempts relying primarily on resources that have a monetary value.
5. *Military* refers to leadership attempts relying primarily on violence, weapons, or force.[1]

Our main point in this regard is that the president who would first shape foreign policy (a domestic activity) and then implement it (an international activity) is engaged in purposive behavior. That is, he is interested in reaching a particular goal, objective, or aim. But generally the executive cannot act alone. In order to get to where he wants to go he is compelled to bring others on board. And since he lacks the authority simply to order these other actors to do his bidding, he must in some way provide incentives—either positive or negative—for followership.

The nature of these incentives, that is, the choice of leadership tactics, depends on who is president, whom he must mobilize at a given moment, the nature of the task at hand, and the context within which the leadership activity is taking place. Some executives prefer to rely on politics, propaganda, and diplomacy, while others move more quickly to offer carrots (such as economic aid) or brandish sticks (such as the threat of military force). Similarly, some would-be followers (allies), and some tasks (when interests are shared) are amenable to gentle forms of persuasion. Still others require (or appear to require) the blatant use of power.

Clearly, then, each situation is so complex as to make it virtually impossible to draw exact parallels between one case and the next. At the same time, as we indicate in Part I, "The Big Picture," there are constants that pertain to the issue of the president as world leader. In fact, the international environment, which is changing rapidly even as we write, is characterized by a basic structure that has remained essentially intact for hundreds of years. Now, as before, the key unit in global politics is the national state. Now, as before, this unit operates in a setting devoid of an overarching authority. And now, as before, the most valuable coins in the international realm are economic and military power.

Similarly, the considerable tradition of American foreign policy provides an anchor for those moments in history when the wind takes a sudden shift. The American experience has been forged out of a common history and ideology, and the American national character is the product of that experience. Thus presidents who would take the lead in foreign affairs can call on the past to legitimate the present. To this day executives invoke the sense of the United States as special that has characterized America's perception of itself since the beginning of the Republic. To this day U.S. government officials justify foreign policy decisions on the basis of moral imperatives. To this day faith is put in the power of economics and open markets. And to this day Americans are generally persuaded that their particular mission is to spread freedom and justice around the world.

Even major turning points in American foreign policy, such as the war in Vietnam, do not have the power to undermine the basic assumptions on which American foreign policy is based or to radically alter the processes that ultimately give it shape. Thus, countless differences notwithstanding, presidents who would take the lead in international relations are operating within contexts, both foreign and domestic, that are, in important ways, familiar.

Perhaps the best example of how powerfully the situation facing late–twentieth century presidents resembles that of their predecessors is the executive's role in the foreign policy process. In particular, the issue of what constitutes the proper balance between the president and the Congress in the conduct of foreign policy exercised by the Founding Fathers, just as it does the denizens of present-day Washington. The pendulum of power has always shifted between the White House and Capitol Hill, and no president can completely avoid the struggle to control the foreign policy agenda.

To be sure, other characteristics of the executive's role in the foreign policy process are of more recent vintage. For example, it has been only during the second half of this century that the American president has been called "leader of the free world." As the title suggests, the United States' deep involvement in international relations has been taken for granted only for about fifty years. Similarly, it is only in the postwar period that the foreign policy bureaucracy has expanded to the point where the executive's managerial skills have become of paramount importance. And it is only in the last three decades or so that technology, particularly television, has become a key instrument in foreign policy–making. Since the first televised presidential debate between Kennedy and Nixon in 1960, and in any case since the first television war (Vietnam), the tube has, by dint of its capacity to bring foreign affairs into the living room, made the people into participants in the policy-making process—even if only on those few issues they deem especially important.

While the details of every case of attempted leadership at the international level necessarily make each one unique, it is clear that there are nevertheless constants, patterns and regularities that persist. In other words, presidents who would be world leaders have something to learn from the experiences of those who came before. More particularly, the five presidents scrutinized in this book operated under circumstances both at home and abroad that, for all the changes that had taken place over four decades, were nevertheless far more similar than they were different. Moreover, while the presidents' own personalities and proclivities led them to adopt one or another leadership style, the repertoire of leadership tactics available to them remained much the same. Consequently, Kennedy, Johnson, Nixon, Carter, and Reagan all faced essentially the same task: *to exercise power, authority, and influence in the contexts of U.S. and world politics in order to reach a foreign policy goal in which they were heavily invested.*

The fact that the five presidents were in situations that had much in common makes it possible for us to compare their relative capacities as world leaders with some conviction. To be sure, since the specifics of each case are so complex and the cases, therefore, not ultimately analogous, such comparisons are more art than science, more impressionistic than definitive. Nevertheless, to group the five and then ask which ones were able to articulate their goals clearly and consistently; to employ power, authority, and influence energetically and effectively; to motivate domestic and foreign constituencies to follow in their paths; and, finally, to oversee implementation; is to get at least some indication of how relatively effective they were as world leaders.

For the comparisons among the five to have meaning we need to look at both the international and domestic environments during the time the attempt at leadership was initiated. We must also consider the nature of the man, those whom he had to bring along as followers, and the task he chose to undertake.

International Environment.   John Kennedy was the last president whose entire experience in the White House was in the context of a cold war during which the face of the enemy seemed etched with complete clarity. It was a bipolar universe in which the U.S. was on the side of the angels, and communists, particularly Soviet communists, were a clear and present danger to everything Americans held dear. The executive's charge was therefore clear: to make the world safe for the American brand of democracy while at the same time keeping the Russians at bay.

It might be argued that the death of Kennedy, which brought to a close a more innocent time, when the world was seen in black and white rather than in the more subtle hue of gray, signaled a sea change in international relations. Thus President Johnson was trapped in a transition. For a constellation of reasons, in which the Vietnam War played the paramount role, by the time he left office the rules of the game had changed. Images of a guerrilla war in Southeast Asia flickering in millions of American homes, faces of dead North Vietnamese soldiers who on television looked no different from the faces of dead South Vietnamese soldiers, thousands of American casualties to an end that was, at best, ill defined—all called into question the very nature of the enemy. In short, it was during Johnson's presidency that the distinctions between "us" and "them" became blurred.

Richard Nixon ultimately capitalized on changes in the international environment that had been set in motion in the mid-1960s. Drawing on what was, by then, a slightly more moderate approach to communism among Americans and also on the general anxiety over the threat of a nuclear holocaust, he was able to undertake bold overtures toward both the Soviet Union and China without risking his political neck. In other words, Nixon's foreign policy initiatives were made possible by changes in world politics that had taken place only in the recent past.

By the time Jimmy Carter took office, the international environment, and America's role in it, was again undergoing significant change. A multipolar, rather than bipolar, universe was clearly beginning to emerge. The Soviet Union, while still a formidable military power, was being slowed by a stagnant economy and an aging and enfeebled leadership cadre; and other countries, particularly Japan, were coming to the fore on the strength of their formidable prowess in the economic sector. In fact, it was in the 1970s that American attention shifted from Europe to Asia. This is not to say that our allies and adversaries in West and East Europe were ignored, but merely to point out that by the time of the Carter administration our foreign policy agenda had necessarily become more inclusive. Indeed, President Carter's preoccupation with the Middle East was made possible by a world in which the Soviet-American relationship was no longer all-important.

But Americans were manifestly not ready to accept a diminished role in world affairs, and in 1980 they elected a man of whom it could be said that his world view befitted the days when the cold war was at its most intense. At least early on, Ronald Reagan's universe was one in which the two military superpowers were the only national actors who really mattered. Reality, however, was at odds with the president's vision. By the early 1980s, the serious weaknesses of the Soviet system had become glaringly apparent: China was beginning to experiment with a relaxation of economic controls; and several countries of the Pacific rim, such as South Korea, had gained considerable economic clout, while Japan surged forward to become no less than a world-class economic power. Thus, in the mere two decades that elapsed between when John Kennedy and Ronald Reagan moved into the Oval Office, the international environment had undergone a significant change. Indeed, by the time George Bush became president, it was difficult to imagine that the world would ever again be viewed as bipolar.

Domestic Environment. John Kennedy was also the last president to enjoy the broad consensus that had characterized the conduct of American foreign policy since the mid 1940s. What this meant in practice was that while there were arguments between the administration and Congress with regard to specifics, the overarching goals of America's policy abroad were scarcely called into question. Above all, there was general agreement that the U.S. had to be actively involved in creating a just and stable world order and, more particularly, in preventing the Soviets from threatening this order.

Again, Lyndon Johnson was victimized by changing times. Although he came into office a master of Washington politics, he was poorly equipped to cope with a situation in which people took to the streets. Now that lives were at stake, Johnson was in a brand-new game in which the political skills that had served him so well for so long were simply inadequate. Once Vietnam became the central issue in domestic as well as foreign politics, the old pro was lost. Unable to address or contain the antiwar protests that swelled as U.S. involvement in Southeast Asia dragged on, LBJ was ultimately forced out of office by popular disapproval of what had come to be known as his war.

It took President Nixon several years to persuade the American people that he would end the conflict in Southeast Asia. But when it became clear that in fact he was prepared to do so, he was given a relatively free hand in international relations. By the early 1970s, Americans had had their fill of foreign adventure; thus Nixon's overtures to the communist superpowers were made in a domestic environment in which there was considerable support for finally breaking bread with our adversaries.

Although it was Gerald Ford who carried the main burden of helping the nation recover from the trauma of Watergate, in fact Jimmy Carter was the first man elected to the presidency since the scandal first broke. As such, he had an opportunity to break with the past—which included charting a foreign policy course different from that of his immediate predecessors. And, indeed, foreign affairs during the Carter administration did deviate from what came before. It can fairly be said that Carter's priorities in this area—the Panama Canal, human rights, the Middle East—represented a departure from America's past preoccupation with Soviet-American relations.

Ronald Reagan benefitted from the fit between his personal proclivities in foreign policy and the national mood of the moment. He came into office hard on the heels of the Iranian hostage crisis, a singularly humiliating collective experience. Thus, at the outset at least, the American people welcomed Reagan's militant first-term rhetoric, which promised to restore the U.S. to a position of strength in the world; and the Congress was willing to back the president's crusade with dollars. In fact, Reagan's experience was quite typical. Like him, Kennedy, Nixon, and Carter all enjoyed a confluence between what they were inclined to do in the foreign policy realm and what the public was ready to support. Only Johnson was caught heading in one direction, while the American people went in another.

The Nature of the Leader. John Kennedy had long had a particular interest in Latin America. His world view had been shaped by the anticommunist mentality of the cold war. And his political style befitted that of a young man in a hurry. Thus the Alliance for Progress had several virtues: it was targeted at an area of the world toward which the president was particularly disposed; it encouraged both economic development and political democracy (thereby keeping the Western Hemisphere safe from further incursion by the

Soviets, who had already established a beachhead in Cuba); and by catapulting the nations of Latin America from the backward past into the prosperous present, it represented a suitable vehicle for the president's vaulting ambition.

Lyndon Johnson's element was domestic, not foreign, politics. His political skills were spawned and sharpened in the hills of Texas and corridors of Congress. His view of the world was shaped by the Franklin Roosevelt who had beaten the Depression rather than the Nazis. And his personal style was more suited to down-home domestic politics than international diplomacy. In short, the past master of "politics as usual" was relatively ill equipped to cope with a land war in Southeast Asia. So far as international relations were concerned, LBJ was a fish out of water.

Richard Nixon was just the opposite. Never comfortable in the role of chin-chucking, hand-grabbing, back-slapping politician, he welcomed the opportunity to retreat to his study with his yellow lined pad to plan in secret his overtures to the communist superpowers. Moreover, he found the perfect, if unlikely, partner in Henry Kissinger who, while a member of the Eastern establishment from which Nixon had always stood apart, nevertheless was clever and well educated in both America and Europe; ambitious, energetic, and thoroughly pragmatic; and ready, willing, and able to carry out the details of what was, in effect, a new U.S. global strategy. Moreover, Nixon and Kissinger had a similar worldview and a mutual penchant for cloak-and-dagger diplomacy.

As president, Jimmy Carter—born-again Christian, one-term governor of Georgia, brand new to the Washington scene, and virtually devoid of experience in foreign affairs—followed the course that made him most comfortable: one on which the way was pointed by moral guideposts. Abroad as well as at home, Carter's policies were draped in the language and logic of what was right. Hence, what some considered an excessive preoccupation with the apparently intractable problems of the Middle East. Hence, the success at Camp David, which owed much to the president's dogged—one might even say quixotic—quest for peace in a region in which the only political investment was the kind that entailed high risk.

In many ways Ronald Reagan is a simple man and when he came into office he had a few basic goals he wanted to reach. High on the Cold Warrior's list was a defense buildup so as to achieve "peace through strength." Reagan's personal and political successes had always depended on his capacity to ingratiate, and his victories in foreign policy followed suit. To get to where he wanted to go he charmed and cajoled his way into the hearts and minds of Congress, the foreign policy bureaucracies, and the American people. In short, the communications and interpersonal skills that had stood him in good stead all his life also greased the wheels of his presidency.

The Nature of the Followers.   As Kennedy learned to his chagrin, in order to realize the dream of the Alliance for Progress, bringing Congress and the American public on board would not suffice. The governing elite of Latin America, and indeed Latin Americans at the grass roots as well, would also have to embrace the arrangement. Johnson was similarly compelled by experience to appreciate what might seem obvious: that leadership abroad requires followers who are foreign as well as those who are domestic. Of course,

Johnson's task was made infinitely more difficult by the fact that even at home he was increasingly alone. Caught in a middle ground between the hawks and the doves, he was ultimately deserted by many in Congress, by the media, and by too high a proportion of the American people. When push came to shove over Vietnam, no one followed where Johnson led.

On the other hand, Nixon and Carter had the luxury of needing to engage only a few other actors. In order for Nixon's overtures to the communist superpowers to reach fruition, and in order for Carter's involvement in the Middle East to reap rewards, only a handful of players had to sit at the table. To a considerable degree domestic constituencies could be, and in fact were, ignored; and as to foreign constituents, they were generally confined to the top leaders of the nations directly involved. In other words, simply in terms of the numbers of those who would have to become followers in order for their leadership tasks to be successfully accomplished, Nixon and Carter had less to contend with than did Kennedy and Johnson.

Reagan had a knack for making leadership seem easy, but in fact his initial foreign policy success depended on getting large numbers of people to follow where he led. He was able to generate public support, the foreign policy bureaucracy by and large followed suit, and Congress soon signed on as well. Moreover, by emphasizing his desire for peace, Reagan eventually overcame resistance in the Western Alliance. Despite strong reservations, particularly in Western Europe, our friends ultimately pledged their commitment to the American quest for security.

The Nature of the Task. Above all, what makes comparisons among presidents risky business are the differences in the nature of the leadership task. Clearly a chief executive who undertakes a major initiative is more likely to run into resistance than one who undertakes only a minor initiative. In fact, we have already seen that the leader who needs only a few followers in tow is generally better off than one whose success depends on the cooperation of large and variegated constituencies.

Yet if our interest is in judging the capacity for leadership, the nature of the task the president seeks to accomplish is of some significance. This first step—defining the goal, determining the direction—is in fact an integral, critical part of the leadership process. It might even be argued that unless the initial job is well done, unless the course is wisely chosen, everything that follows is wasted effort. Thus the foreign policy tasks the five presidents chose to undertake are themselves indicators of their skills as world leaders.

The Alliance for Progress was a vast undertaking—so vast, in fact, that President Kennedy himself seems not to have understood at the outset that what would be required for the dream to be realized was no less than massive social, political, and economic change. The Alliance was, to be sure, just that: a dream in which American largesse would transform an entire continent. For it to become reality, the U.S. would have to provide aid on a massive scale for many years; a cadre of American bureaucrats would have to sign on in strong support; and, above all, a key leadership role would have to be played by one or another group within Latin America itself. But domestic obstacles notwithstanding, no Latin American constituency was qualified for, or even willing to accept, the challenge. Thus President Kennedy's initiative was probably doomed from the outset. While the ideals of the Alliance were worthy, and while some good came of it, the magnitude of the task it embodied ultimately sank the enterprise.

One of the problems with President Johnson's involvement in Vietnam was that the task he set was never really clear. Did he send men and machines to Southeast Asia merely to hold the North Vietnamese at bay? Did he intend to win a war? Or was he just buying time for the Great Society, hoping that some day peace would break out and this nagging foreign policy problem would go away? LBJ's lack of a distinct vision and the administration's consequent equivocation were evidence that throughout his time in the White House America's task in Vietnam had never been well defined. The middle course to which the president held manifestly satisfied no one and so both at home and abroad he ran into trouble.

Moreover, the issues involved in this case were of a different magnitude than those in which the four other presidents became embroiled. Johnson's effort to lead at the international level resulted in the death and injury of hundreds of thousands of men. In other words, this president was eventually trapped in a situation in which what was clear above all was that American lives were being jeopardized on behalf of a cause his administration had failed to justify adequately.

Life had taught Richard Nixon that pragmatism and persistence pay. Having himself returned more than once from the ashes of political defeat, he had learned the hard way that the wheel turns. And so this president, who in his salad days was one of the nation's more outspoken and virulent anticommunists, was able to reach out to the Soviet Union and communist China with scarcely a backward glance. The task, as Nixon saw it, was clear: to update two major international relationships that had remained mired for decades in the grip of the cold war. Almost twenty years after the death of Stalin, the Soviets had begun to take on a human face; similarly, the Chinese were no longer in the throes of the Cultural Revolution or under the iron first of Moscow. Thus Nixon had an opportunity to engage the Soviets in an agreement that would enhance American security and to explore with China an arrangement that would similarly further America's geopolitical interests. Throughout the process his goals were well defined. His timing was right. And the steps that had to be taken were relatively clear. In sum, the task of getting from point A to point B was manageable and ultimately accomplished.

Jimmy Carter's mission in the Middle East was nothing if not daunting. To make peace between Israel and an Arab state was a goal that had eluded diplomats since the state of Israel was established in 1948, and there was no particular reason to assume that this time around would be any different. Moreover, while Carter determined at the outset of his administration that conflict resolution in the Middle East was a priority, he had no clear idea of how precisely to proceed. In fact, the record shows that a variety of negotiating strategies were tried before the proposal for a Camp David summit was even put forth. Thus Jimmy Carter's success at Camp David was against all odds. Had history been his teacher, the president would never even have tried to hammer out an agreement between Israel and Egypt. But Carter's drive to reach an accord and his deep personal commitment to the peace process carried the day. To be sure, Carter's achievement depended on the cooperation of Anwar Sadat and Menachem Begin. In fact, his task could never have been accomplished without the change in climate wrought by Sadat's visit to Jerusalem in 1977. Still, the president's contribution to the final accord was testimony to his capacity for world leadership.

Again, Ronald Reagan makes it all look easy. And, indeed, the scope of the task he set for himself was relatively narrow. Most of his work could be done at home; from abroad he required not much more than a general show of support from friends. Still, if the domain to be mastered was comparatively small and familiar—however arcane the American bureaucracy and however elusive the support of Congress, they scarcely compare to foreign terrains such as those in Southeast Asia and the Middle East, about which most Americans remain profoundly ignorant—the task itself was considerable. For President Reagan wanted to do no less than substantially reallocate resources from domestic programs to defense. His goal was to strengthen America's position in the world by reordering its national priorities.

In time it became clear that to accomplish the task major costs, including a mounting national deficit, would accrue. Still, the president remained undeterred, and by the end of his first term the die was cast: the U.S. was on a new and different course that would, at the least, make it militarily more robust than it had been in the recent past.

Are we then comparing apples and oranges? Is it fair or even useful to make comparisons among leaders who are operating in international and domestic contexts that are so different, who themselves bear faint resemblance to each other, and who chose to undertake such diverse tasks? We would argue that the answer is yes, that to be an effective leader requires taking into account the settings in which your activity will take place, the ways in which your particular persona is suited to the task at hand, the malleability of various constituencies, and whether or not the goal that has been established is realistic.

One of John Kennedy's strengths as a leader was his abilty to communicate a sense of purpose, a vision of a New Frontier. Hard on the heels of Dwight Eisenhower, who had been in office eight years and belonged to an older generation, the new young president—handsome, witty, bright, and ambitious—seemed to embody a future full of promise. And at the start, at least, he persuaded his listeners with convincing rhetoric that the Alliance for Progress could and would change the face of the Latin American continent. The crunch came with implementation. It was apparent rather quickly that dollars alone could not solve the enormous problems the Alliance was supposed to address and that Kennedy did not have, either at home or abroad, cadres available to do the requisite trenchwork. Thus while this president demonstrated some of the skills associated with effective leadership at the international level, his overarching conception was flawed from the start. The gap between the ideal and the reality would never be closed and so, ultimately, the Alliance was a major disappointment.

It has been said of Lyndon Johnson that his particular tragedy was that his great accomplishments at home would forever be obscured by his abject failure abroad. As chief architect of America's increased involvement in Vietnam, Johnson made mistakes at every point. He did not establish a clear goal. He did not persuade people to follow in his path. He did not engage in rational decision making. He did not implement his decisions with adequate intelligence and care. And he did not understand until it was too late how deep were the wounds the Vietnam War had inflicted on the American body politic. Thus, while the early years of Johnson's tenure in the White House will endure as testimony to his great accomplishments as a domestic leader, his conduct of the war in Southeast Asia will, at the same time, bear witness to his disastrous performance in foreign affairs.

In many ways Presidents Nixon and Carter's accomplishments as world leaders were comparable. Both men were of an introverted nature and, as a consequence, both gravitated toward foreign policy issues that could be addressed in small circles. Both had a clear idea of what they wanted and doggedly kept their eyes on the prize through years of uncertainty. Both tended to steer clear of the American people generally and the foreign affairs bureaucracy particularly, relying instead on a few key foreign policy advisors. Both enjoyed negotiating on a personal level with other world leaders. And both preferred to work slowly and secretly toward an end that would, in a dramatic moment befitting the occasion, surprise and gratify constituents around the world who vastly preferred presidents who made peace to those who made war.

It should not surprise us that history treats both Nixon and Carter more kindly as world leaders than as domestic leaders. Neither was particularly good at using the media to forge ties to the American people. Neither was enamored of the wheeling and dealing of which the Washington establishment is so fond. And neither was comfortable on either an emotional or intellectual level with the idea that in the American political culture leadership and politicking are one and the same. Ultimately, of course, Nixon was forced to resign, and Carter was turned away at the polls after only one term. In other words, as leaders at home they manifestly fell short. But as leaders abroad they had their day in the sun, and, indeed, the fruits of their labors are in evidence to this day.

Of Ronald Reagan's capacity to bring about change—of his capacity, in other words, to exercise leadership—there is no doubt. The evidence that he led America in new directions is all around us, and the legacies of his initiatives in foreign affairs endure as well. Reagan's quest to rebuild America's military strength and, thereby, restore (as he saw it) its position in the world demonstrates just how he did it. In fact, future presidents intent on engaging followers might do well to turn to Reagan and pick up a few pointers.

To begin with, he let it be known, clearly and consistently, that he was interested in reaching a particular goal. This goal was embedded in language that was easy to understand and designed to trigger both nationalistic (primarily for domestic consumption) and humanistic (primarily for foreign consumption) impulses. Moreover, the message was conveyed by a man who was a past master at selling himself and his wares, in person and on television (and radio for that matter), and who had a remarkable capacity to be ingratiating. Reagan further surrounded himself by a team that by and large worked well together (although there were a few turf battles in the first few years and some organizational reshuffling) and that was unfailingly devoted to the cause. There were no weak links in the chain of command, which meant, among other things, that the president, who liked to delegate, could trust those who were in charge of daily business. Moreover, in so far as it was necessary, President Reagan was good at, and indeed enjoyed, the interpersonal politicking that was required to get Washington insiders—whether members of the bureaucracy or Congress—on board. He knew when to be hard-nosed and when to compromise. In other words, unlike his predecessor, this was a man with whom professional politicians could do business.

Reagan's foreign constituencies were treated no differently; and by and large, after much initial skepticism about the "grade B actor" in the White House, America's allies lent support and its adversaries took due note of the changes he was able to effect. To be sure, the president was fortunate in that a range of objective circumstances suited him especially well. These included a Republican Senate, a national mood that was more than ready for America to "stand tall," and a Soviet leadership cadre that for a variety of reasons was almost completely ineffectual. But these do not diminish Reagan's accomplishments. His capacity to get to where he wanted to go, demonstrated again in this particular case, is proof that in both domestic and foreign affairs—the glaring exception of the Iran-Contra scandal notwithstanding—this president was a leader to be reckoned with. While the consequences of Reagan's policies are a matter of legitimate debate, of the fact that he had the leadership skills to make an impact there can be no doubt.

Perhaps the main lesson to be learned from the five case studies of leadership at the international level is that the margin for error is unusually small—while the chances of making one, given contexts and constituents that are foreign as well as domestic, are unusually big. We are talking about process here, a process that begins at the moment the task is conceived and ends only when the task has been implemented. As we have seen, it is quite possible for a president to do well at one stage of the leadership sequence and fall down at another, in which case, since failure then is likely, energies and resources will have been expended for nothing. Thus presidents who would be world leaders would be well advised to chart their course in advance. This does not mean that they should, or even could, fill in the details before starting out. As Camp David made clear, no one can tell before the fact exactly how a story will unfold. It does suggest, however, that before leaving the gate presidents should have a reasonably clear idea of what constitutes the finish line, of how the track must be run in order to reach it, and of whether in fact they have the will and skill to run a good race.

Hardly a day goes by without a news story that in one way or another confirms that the United States is becoming merely a leading member of a community of nations rather than a giant looming over all.[2] Not only has America lost some of its pride of place, Japan is an economic superpower and other countries of the Pacific rim are hard on its heels, the countries of West Europe are joining to form what by the mid-1990s will be a new and powerful collective dominated by Germany, and the Soviet Union and the nations of East Europe are struggling to overcome the legacy of communism and revive their stagnant economies. In short, while certain fundamentals of international relations remain intact, the hallmark of the last decade of the twentieth century is change rather than stasis.

What is particularly provocative for us to contemplate in the context of this book is the notion of the global village. "The planet has become an intricate convergence," Lance Morrow has written, "of acid rains and rain forests burning, of ideas and Reeboks and stock markets that ripple through time zones, of satellite signals and worldwide television, of advance-purchase airfares, fax machines, the miniaturization of the universe by computer, of T-shirts and mutual destinies. The planetary circuits are wired: an integrated system, a microchip floating in space."[3]

The role of technology in all this—specifically the marriage of computers with telecommunications—can scarcely be overestimated. Television in particular has the capacity to make familiar events unfolding in faraway places and to make known information that would heretofore have been concealed. Even the most isolated and repressive regimes are now vulnerable to the intrusions of facsimile machines, computers, and telephones. When in mid-1989 the Chinese police cracked down on dissident Buddhist monks in "remote" Tibet, a group of Australian tourists used their hotel phone to relay the news that at least thirty Tibetans had been killed.[4] And in that same year, when Chinese students were protesting against the government, their colleagues in the U.S. were able to communicate directly with Beijing by faxing the very latest news.

So far only one national leader has either intuitively or by design capitalized on this "intricate convergence," on what is inevitably a blurring of the margin between leadership at home and leadership abroad. Whatever the future of Soviet leader Mikhail Gorbachev, his name will forever be remembered not only as a man who brought about dramatic change in the Soviet Union but also as one who transformed the nature of international relations. Described by experts as a magician of much élan who has wrought changes that "are nothing short of miraculous,"[5] at the global level Gorbachev's most significant achievement was to make cold war attitudes seem hopelessly outdated. (His progress in this regard depended, of course, on the active cooperation of President Reagan. Reagan proved remarkably flexible in his attitude toward the Soviet Union; after two terms in office he was a far cry from the Cold Warrior he had been at the outset of his presidency.) Tellingly, Gorbachev's inventive diplomacy—which may be described as an unusually fortuitous mix of style and substance that has further profited from comparisons to the rigid, aggressive, and parochial presentations of earlier generations of Soviet leaders—so transformed the U.S. view of the Soviet Union that two out of three Americans now say that Moscow no longer poses an immediate military threat to the United States, and nearly three out of four consider nuclear war unlikely. Moreover, Gorbachev the man has scored impressively with Americans. By 1990 almost 80 percent considered him significantly different from, and vastly superior to, his Kremlin predecessors.[6]

What is clear, in any case, is that as the planet shrinks, and as the importance of military power wanes while that of economic power waxes, distinctions between leadership in domestic and foreign affairs will diminish. In fact, American presidents will discover that those communications and interpersonal skills that serve them well at home will be increasingly applicable abroad. Politicking will be the order of the day, on the tube and in person, which suggests that a premium will be put on executives who have the capacity to engage foreign followers at both the elite and grass roots levels. This is not to deny that there will continue to be a place for the more secretive, narrowly defined leadership initiatives that Nixon and Carter preferred. Rather, it is to declare that the shrinking planet will inevitably impact on how world leaders engage followers, and that under these new and different circumstances cross-national mobilization represents the wave of the future.

Because this book has focused on the president's capacity to bring about change at the international level, the picture has necessarily been skewed. To train our eye on only a few men is to shortchange the multiplicity of other variables that necessarily influence outcomes in world politics. Some of the variables are confined to the domestic environment, others to the international environment, and still others—an oil price shock, for example—intrude on both domestic and foreign affairs. The point, in any case, is this: The greater the number of variables in a given case, the less important any single one, such as the American president, is likely to be.[7]

At the same time, the supposed demise of the "American century" notwithstanding, the U.S. president who is so disposed remains in a relatively strong position to be a world leader. In fact, a powerful American presence is indicated even for global integration and growth to proceed in an orderly fashion. Thus the "courageous and gifted leader" of whom Harry Truman spoke so admiringly is hardly passé. As we ourselves have witnessed, the president who has the internal resources to "seize an opportunity or create it" has the external resources to make a big difference.[8]

Notes

1. This taxonomy is based in part on David A. Baldwin, *Economic Statecraft* (Princeton: Princeton University Press 1985), p. 14. See Baldwin's chapter 1 for an excellent discussion of how the analysis of power applies to international politics.

2. "The Talk of the Town," *The New Yorker,* 8 May 1989, p. 31.

3. *Time,* 29 May 1989, p. 96. For some interesting insights on the impact of global convergence on American power, see Joseph S. Nye, "The Transformation of American Power," *AQ* 2, no. 1 (Winter 1990): pp. 9–35.

4. Edwin Diamond, "Playing the China Card" in *New York,* 5 June 1989.

5. Timothy Garton Ash, "Refolution: The Springtime of Two Nations," *The New York Review,* 15 June 1989, p. 17.

6. *New York Times*/CBS News Poll reported in the *New York Times,* 16 May 1989.

7. Richard Rose, *The Postmodern President: The White House Meets the World* (Chatham, N.J.: Chatham House, 1988), pp. 53, 54.

8. For a good discussion of why the study of statecraft is important, see Baldwin, pp. 26–28. (Where Baldwin uses "statecraft," we use "leadership at the international level.") For a thorough analysis of how the lessons of history can actually be used by leaders, see Richard E. Neustadt and Ernest R. May, *Thinking in Time: The Uses of History for Decision Makers* (New York: Free Press, 1986), especially chapters 13 and 14.

Epilogue: George Bush as World Leader

Some see leadership as high drama and the sound of trumpets calling. And sometimes it is that. But I see history as a book with many pages—and each day we fill a page with acts of hopefulness and meaning.
—Inaugural Address, January 20, 1989

New presidents generally take considerable pains to proclaim their own approach to American foreign policy. This was not the case, however, with George Bush, who sought the White House as vice president and political heir to Ronald Reagan. During the 1988 presidential campaign, Bush affirmed the legacy: "The most important work of my life is to complete the mission we started in 1980."[1] He planned to maintain Reagan's program of peace through strength, employ hope and "prudent skepticism" in his approach to U.S.-Soviet relations, and modernize America's strategic defenses.

Bush, however, faced an image problem. Whereas Ronald Reagan appeared strong, decisive, and eloquent, George Bush seemed weak and awkward—a "wimp." He thus had to sell himself to voters as a candidate who possessed both the will to carry on with Reagan's agenda and the skill necessary to get the job done. He ultimately won the White House by highlighting his own foreign policy credentials—which included service as United States ambassador to the United Nations (1971–1973), America's representative to the People's Republic of China (1974–1975), and director of the CIA (1976–1977)—and portraying his opponent, Governor Michael Dukakis (D-Massachusetts), as a man who would not adequately defend American interests.

Upon taking office, Bush undertook to transform his apparent weaknesses into virtues. In contrast to the larger-than-life image of his predecessor, this president reveled in a more modest approach to the presidency. Five key features characterized his leadership style: (1) caution—with an occasional dash of boldness; (2) the search for consensus; (3) heavy reliance on personal contacts; (4) a proclivity for secrecy and surprise; and (5) a hands-on approach to policy-making.

CAUTION—WITH AN OCCASIONAL DASH OF BOLDNESS

President Bush is known for his instinctive wariness. His primary concern is to avoid making a serious mistake because of haste or imprudence.

210

This caution has led to charges that Bush is drifting along on the tide of great events—particularly the stunning decline of communism—rather than exercising strong leadership. For example, on the important question of what the United States can or should do to assist Mikhail Gorbachev's program of reform in the Soviet Union, some analysts have called for an assertive American response (e.g., technology transfers, economic assistance) in support of Soviet change. But Bush has by and large resisted such moves. As *The New Republic* observed, his reaction to *perestroika* has been "confined to moral support and trying not to get in the way."[2]

Bush's critics have charged repeatedly that he is too passive in his conduct of the presidency. Fred Barnes, also of *The New Republic,* labeled him a "caretaker" president.[3] Conservative columnist George Will attacked the chief executive for the administration's "intellectual and oral flaccidity."[4] And Charles Maynes, editor of *Foreign Policy,* complained that Bush and his advisers were ill-prepared to "seize opportunities" in changing East-West relations.[5]

In contrast, Bush's defenders (in and out of the White House) believe that the president's instinct for caution is particularly well-suited to a time of upheaval in world politics. But even Bush's supporters take note of the thin line between prudence and passivity. The *New York Times,* reflecting on the president's first year in office, concluded: "Most of the time, he has let the dramatic saga of Eastern Europe run its course, and because the stream of history has been flowing in his direction, that policy has proved successful."[6]

While "prudence" is generally the watchword of the Bush administration, the president has on occasion exhibited flashes of boldness in his conduct of foreign affairs. The most dramatic moment of Bush's first year in the White House was the American military intervention in Panama and the subsequent capture of longtime Panamanian dictator General Manuel Noriega. By deciding to invade, the president exhibited a willingness to use force—even in the face of strong criticism from other Latin American countries. But Bush has also taken diplomatic risks. For example, in February 1990 he unveiled a proposal for cuts in Soviet and American conventional forces in Europe that would eventually result in an imbalance favoring the U.S. To the astonishment of the diplomatic community, after a brief stab at resistance, Gorbachev gave in to Bush's demand with alacrity.

THE SEARCH FOR CONSENSUS

Bush prefers to formulate and conduct foreign policy by achieving consensus among the key players. He wants a foreign policy that has widespread support, is politically feasible, and will not be undercut by bureaucratic resistance.

From the time he took office, Bush worked—through phone calls, frequent meetings, friendly visits, and private notes—to build a cooperative relationship with Congress. As the *National Journal* put it: "He invited members of Congress, who were used to presidential standoffishness, to bounce on beds upstairs in the White House."[7] He also tried to build consensus by excising the more controversial elements of Ronald Reagan's policies from his agenda. For example, he negotiated a deal with Congress on providing humanitarian aid to the Contra rebels fighting Nicaragua's Sandinista (communist) government, thus eliminating what had been a major source of executive-legislative animosity during the preceding eight years. Because of congressional objections and because a range of defense experts, including his own adviser Brent Scowcroft, had doubts about its utility, Bush also deemphasized Reagan's strategic defense initiative. And in February 1989, he reopened an internal administration debate over the sale of advanced weapons technology to Japan because the decision to allow such a sale, made under Ronald Reagan, had ignored Commerce Department doubts about the deal.

This search for consensus extends to Bush's style abroad. In dealing with America's NATO allies, Bush "builds consensus rather than dictates it."[8] A good example of the president's approach is his handling of the issue of NATO short-range nuclear weapons. Because many of his constituents had responded enthusiastically to Gorbachev's calls for a lessening of East-West tensions, West German chancellor Helmut Kohl felt the need to identify himself with efforts to reduce the risk of nuclear conflict in Europe. Thus, in April 1989 Kohl publicly called for early negotiations with the Soviet Union on reductions of short-range nuclear weapons.

The chancellor's pronouncement caused a rife in the Western Alliance. The United States and Great Britain quickly and openly opposed the idea of such negotiations, believing that early talks might lead to an overall ban on battlefield nuclear weapons and ultimately leave NATO countries vulnerable to the Warsaw Pact's overwhelming superiority in conventional forces. Disagreement among the allies thus threatened to dominate and possibly disrupt the NATO summit scheduled at the end of May.

Faced with this unhappy prospect, and under growing pressure anyway to respond to Gorbachev's peace overtures, Bush undertook a search for a conventional arms-reduction proposal that he could offer in place of Kohl's proposal. He wanted something of impact that was, however, not too risky. As the president often told his staff, "I don't want to do anything militarily dumb." By mid-May, an administration task force had outlined a plan for a 20 percent cut in manpower and a 15 percent cut in aircraft. President Bush then invited French president François Mitterrand to his home in Maine for consultations on the issue. Finally, after rejecting a State Department suggestion of 25 percent cuts, Bush went with the task force plan. Still, he felt a need to confirm his decision with the secretary of defense. "Now, is 20 percent all right? You can live with that?" When Secretary Richard Cheney responded affirmatively, Bush concluded, "O.K., that's consensus. Let's go."[9] Once the decision was made, presidential envoys were dispatched to present an outline of the proposal to NATO leaders.

Bush's plan transformed the NATO meeting from an expected row to an expression of allied unity. It was Bush's first major foreign policy victory. After twelve hours of intense negotiations, allied leaders agreed to offer the Soviet Union a three-part initiative: (1) NATO and the Warsaw Pact would both reduce their military hardware in Europe; (2) troop strength would be reduced by about 20 percent; and (3) the two sides would agree to further force cuts by May 1990. Satisfied that his needs had been met, Chancellor

Kohl affirmed Bush's role: "Here we go on the offensive, with a proposal that is bold, [and that] once more impressively affirms the United States' leadership."[10]

HEAVY RELIANCE ON PERSONAL CONTACTS

Every president looks to friends and former associates when confronting the task of building a new administration. But George Bush transformed standard practice into a third element of his leadership style. He demonstrated an unusual reliance on personal contacts to assemble his foreign policy team. Coming to the White House after being a longtime player in the Washington power game, Bush possessed an elaborate network of colleagues on whom he could draw when forming a government. As the *National Journal* noted: "This administration's policy makers have ties not only to the President but to one another. This tangle of past political and personal relationships . . . has created an Administration of colleagues."[11] Indeed, all of the top members of the administration were drawn from the seven interlocking circles that reflected the president's political career: the Texas Republican party, Congress, the Ford administration, the 1980 Bush presidential campaign, Bush's Office of the Vice President, the Reagan White House, and the 1988 Bush presidential campaign.

The president's three senior foreign policy appointments demonstrate the Bush style in action. On the morning after his election, Bush nominated James A. Baker III to be his secretary of state. Baker is not only the president's best friend, but he worked with Bush in the Ford administration, managed his 1980 presidential campaign, served in the Reagan White House as chief of staff and Treasury secretary, and again managed Bush's 1988 campaign. Baker is known as a political pragmatist and deal maker. Secretary of Defense Richard Cheney (nominated after the Senate defeated Bush's first choice, former Texas senator John Tower), was chief of staff in the Ford administration while Bush served as U.S. representative to China and as director of the CIA. A five-term member of the House of Representatives from Wyoming, he is known as a conservative Republican who will compromise in order to govern. For the post of assistant for national security affairs, Bush called upon Brent Scowcroft, who held the same job under President Ford. Scowcroft also served as foreign policy consultant to the Reagan administration.

President Bush also employs interpersonal exchange as a tactic of governance. In foreign policy, this approach is most apparent in his extensive "telephone diplomacy." As the *Wall Street Journal* observed: "He develops personal friendships with world leaders, talks with them with great frequency as he weighs his options, and finally makes decisions."[12] He frequently calls British prime minister Margaret Thatcher, Chancellor Kohl, and President Mitterrand, and by the spring of 1990, he had on three occasions telephoned Mikhail Gorbachev. Bush commented that these relatively unstructured conversations were "very constructive." Because they are "forthright," he maintained, "where we differ we can spell out the differences without rancor."[13]

PROCLIVITY FOR SECRECY AND SURPRISE

Whether it is to unveil new arms-control initiatives or send the marines to capture Manuel Noriega, President Bush believes strongly in concealing his plans and actions until, from his vantage point, it is time to reveal them. As a consequence, because his subordinates are often not privy to policy planning or to telephone conversations or personal notes, they are sometimes caught off guard. For example, although the president had been planning the December 1989 Malta summit for four months, his secretary of defense was unaware of the meeting until it was publicly announced.

HANDS-ON APPROACH TO POLICY-MAKING

Because it draws heavily on personal relationships, the president's decision-making style tends to be informal. Bush uses his staff to explore problems and identify options, which are then debated before him at Cabinet sessions called "scheduled train wrecks." He participates in these meetings by asking questions and taking notes. Then he retires to the Oval Office to "shop around" for further advice from associates in Congress, foreign leaders, and friends whose counsel he values. Ultimately, the president decides on which course to take, usually by selecting one of the options prepared at an earlier point by his staff.

Bush is interested in the details of government. According to his chief of staff, this interest keeps him involved in matters that in other administrations would have been considered too trivial for Oval Office attention. Chief of Staff John Sununu has said that President Bush will learn of an emerging problem and deal with it immediately. "It might mean a call to [Costa Rican president Oscar] Arias if it's a Central American problem . . . or maybe getting Baker on the phone to [Soviet foreign minister Eduard] Shevardnadze to deal with a little rough-edged development. It's a lot of daily activity that never makes headlines."[14]

Although Bush came to office to build on Ronald Reagan's legacy, history intervened. In the first thirteen months after he took office, the president witnessed the surprisingly swift fall of communist regimes in Eastern Europe, the dismantling of the Berlin Wall, and the acceptance by the Soviet Union's leadership cadre of a multiparty system. Indeed, some observers went so far as to proclaim 1989 as the "end of the Cold War."

Over the course of his first year and a half in office, President Bush tried to promote stability in a rapidly changing Europe. On his own, and in concert with other nations, he offered aid to Poland and Hungary, undertook modest economic and political initiatives to improve relations with Moscow, proposed cuts in Soviet and American troops on the European continent, and helped construct an international arrangement to facilitate the peaceful transition toward German reunification. These actions have helped dispel Bush's "wimp" image and sharpened the distinction between prudence and passivity.

But where exactly is President Bush headed? The answer is not clear.

Despite talk of moving "beyond containment," he has articulated no specific policy goals. To be sure, he has stood for orderly change. In February 1990, he reiterated: "The enemy is unpredictability, the enemy is instability."[15] Critics contend, however, that stability is a means, not an end.

As his conduct of diplomacy during his first year in office suggests, Bush's strength is in fact process rather than promise: a formula for negotiating German reunification, a solution to the NATO force-reduction rift, a decision on who should coordinate aid to Poland and Hungary. It remains for him to provide a picture of what American foreign policy will look like beyond the Cold War.

Does a grand design matter as much as critics suggest? Charles Maynes has insisted that to change East-West relations requires "somebody almost like [George F.] Kennan,"[16] the chief theorist of America's containment policy. Maynes believes that without the clear direction that guided foreign policy during the Cold War, the U.S. will drift into trouble. However, presidential scholar Richard Neustadt argues that overarching policy designs may be overrated. He speculates that President Bush may be proceeding "inch by inch toward vision" as he develops policy initiatives for the evolving European political order.[17] Furthermore, White House officials have revealed that the National Security Council staff is constructing four or five scenarios for superpower relations and continental politics, which Bush plans to use as a framework for policy planning.[18]

Bush's exercise of national and world leadership has thus far been uneven. On the one hand, his foreign policy has had the approval of the American public and most of Congress, he has enjoyed warm relations with foreign leaders, and he can point to a record of some achievement in his conduct of foreign affairs. If he can keep up his performance in these respects, Bush might yet be considered a major architect of post–Cold War Europe. On the other hand, his lack of a clear vision may leave him vulnerable. Given the swift pace of global change, President Bush may ultimately be relegated to a minor role, merely reacting to other world leaders who articulate ambitious plans. Obviously, only time will tell whether, in the end, George Bush will make a significant difference.

Notes

1. Quoted in *Congressional Quarterly Weekly Report*, 20 August 1988, p. 2353.
2. "Annual Check-Up," *The New Republic*, 29 Jan. 1990, p. 7.
3. Fred Barnes, "Four Bore Years," *The New Republic*, 27 March 1989, p. 12.
4. Quoted in *New York Times*, 18 February 1990, p. 6.
5. Quoted in *National Journal*, 6 January 1990, p. 10.
6. *New York Times*, loc. cit.
7. *National Journal*, 6 January 1990, p. 7.
8. Quoted in *Facts on File*, 21 July 1989, p. 530.
9. This paragraph drawn from *Time*, 21 August 1989, pp. 16–17.
10. Quoted in *Facts on File*, 2 June 1989, p. 393.
11. *National Journal*, 30 September 1989, p. 2418.

12. *Wall Street Journal,* 30 November 1989, p. 1.
13. Quoted in *Cincinnati Enquirer,* 1 March 1990, p. 1.
14. Quoted in *National Journal,* January 6, 1990, p. 7.
15. Quoted in *New York Times,* 26 February 1990, p. 7.
16. Quoted in *National Journal,* 6 January 1990, p. 10.
17. Loc. cit.
18. Loc. cit.

Index